Proud to Be:
Writing by American Warriors
Volume 3

Southeast Missouri State University Press • 2014

Proud to Be:
Writing by
American Warriors
Volume 3

Edited by Susan Swartwout

Partners in the Military-Service Literature Series

Proud to Be: Writing by American Warriors, Volume 3
Copyright by Southeast Missouri State University Press

ISBN: 978-0-9903530-4-1

First Published in the United States of America, 2014
Southeast Missouri State University Press
One University Plaza, MS 2650
Cape Girardeau, MO 63701
http://www6.semo.edu/universitypress

Southeast Missouri State University Press, founded in 2001, serves as a
first-rate publisher in the region and produces books, *Big Muddy: Journal of
the Mississippi River Valley*, *The Cape Rock* poetry journal, and the Faulkner
Conference series.

The Missouri Humanities Council is a 501(c)3 non-profit organization that
was created in 1971 under authorizing legislation from the U.S. Congress to
serve as one of the 56 state and territorial humanities councils that are affiliated with the National Endowment for the Humanities.

The Warriors Arts Alliance is composed of organizations and individuals
dedicated to building communication and understanding between veterans,
families, and communities through creative writing and visual arts.

Table of Contents

Fiction

Poetry

Essays

Introduction

On behalf of the Board of Directors and the staff of the Missouri Humanities Council, we are pleased and honored to have been a part of the *Proud to Be: Writing by American Warriors* anthologies from their inception two years ago. That this is the introduction to Volume 3 is a testament to the importance of this project to the writers and readers alike.

There were a record number of works submitted for consideration as a part of Volume 3. I congratulate the winners of the Warriors Anthology Writing Competition in each of the five categories. As important, I applaud each veteran who took the major step forward to put his or her thoughts on paper. Writing is an incredible tool for self-expression. And as evidenced in this book, it is often the best—if only—way for veterans to share their experience with loved ones, other veterans, and a civilian population so acutely in need of learning what it means to have served.

Many individuals and organizations make the production of this anthology possible. For the third year, Editor Susan Swartwout and the Southeast Missouri State University Press have done yeoman work to bring this anthology to fruition. A special acknowledgement goes to Deborah Marshall, who had the foresight to see the need for this project. And as Deb retires, we welcome Lisa Ann Miller as the new Director of the Warriors Arts Alliance.

Lisa is a Lieutenant Colonel with 30 years of military service in the army, both active and reserve. In addition, she is President of the Missouri Writers Guild and Managing Editor of Walrus Publishing, Inc. One of Lisa's first tasks will be to implement *Standing Together: The Humanities and the Experience of War*—a grant just received by the Missouri Humanities Council from the National Endowment for the Humanities. This grant will allow us to reach many more veterans throughout the State of Missouri as we push forward with our mission.

And though there are many others to thank, this anthology, as well as the two that came before, is dedicated to the writing veterans, military-service personnel, and their family members.

Jim Weidman
Interim Executive Director
Missouri Humanities Council

Winners of the Warriors Anthology Writing Competition

Essay judged by Daniel Simon, editor-in-chief of *World Literature Today*

Winner: Lisa Miller for "Still Falling Snow"
From Daniel Simon:
"Still Falling Snow" does what the best writing about war can do, which is to convey the unspeakable loss symbolized by the Fallen Comrade service in a way that moves the reader not only to remember the sacrifices of the fallen but also to empathize with the emotional toll such losses inflict on their fellow soldiers. "Questions without answers are hateful things," Miller writes, but the profound silence of the fallen, who no longer respond when their names are called, is the most dreadful answer of all.

Honorable mentions: Diane Cameron for "Iambic Pentameter and the Meter of War" and Jay Harden for "My Mother of All Letters"

Fiction judged by John Mort, author of *Soldier in Paradise* and *The Illegal*

Winner: Jay Harden for "Bramble Fire"
From John Mort:
"Bramble Fire" is about a gathering of Vietnam War veterans, Americans and Vietnamese, on Vietnamese soil. Seeking forgiveness and peace, they tell their somewhat fantastical stories. The narrator was a B-52 pilot, always above it all, though on the night of the Bramble Fire, he finds out where those bombs went. The story is full of extraordinary phrases, such as, "One of the great cruelties in war is that you never know anything for certain" and "the silent ear of empathy." In its sense of history, its encapsulation of more than one war story, and its vivid though objective accounts of agony, "Bramble Fire" recalls Joseph Conrad.

Honorable mentions: Katherine Bell for "The Sulphur Sink" and Frederick W. Cutter for "Something's Wrong"

Interviews judged by Geoff Giglierano, historical consultant

Winner: S. Lorraine Norwood for "D-Day, Korea, Vietnam: An Old Warrior Lives to Tell the Tale," an interview of Earl W. Norwood

From Geoff Giglierano:

This is a remarkable story told in a conversational manner that worked very well. The presence of the interviewer (and her relationship to Mr. Norwood) was understated, almost to the point of invisibility, so that I felt like Earl was talking directly to me without an intermediary. The story itself is intriguing: not only that Earl served in three wars but that in one of those conflicts he had an extremely interesting role, serving as a coxswain on a Higgins boat during the D-Day invasion of Normandy. Looking at this interview as an historian, I felt that the details Earl shares are of considerable historical value, but it is also the fact that he compares situations and attitudes across three very different wars that makes this a special document.

Honorable mentions: Casey Titus for "Interview of Vietnam Veteran Jim Lewis" and Gloria Pape Caviglia for "Epiphany of Maturity"

Photography judged by Bradley Phillips, professor of photography, Southeast Missouri State University

Winner: Sheree K. Nielsen for "jimmie (pier)"

From Bradley Phillips:

As I pored over each of the submitted images, the photograph "jimmie (pier)" struck the loudest chord. From a technical perspective, I found the smooth light well complimented the large depth of field that runs the length of the pier, giving viewers many details to digest. The shadows from the railing cast wonderfully unique shapes onto the boardwalk, giving this image strong lines and composition. However, it was the straightforward perspective and subtle emotion that kept me searching it over again. I found myself wanting to know more of the story, yet as a viewer I am trapped at the edge of the pier, unable to enter and learn the details of the narrative within. It is then we as viewers are forced to look and extract the photograph's subtleties and let our imaginations answer the unexplained. After searching over the image, it seems our subject is ill content with his surroundings and sees something beyond which we are unable to turn and see ourselves. His posture is alert, yet the confine of his chair does not hinder his powerful gaze. It seems only natural for our subject to look head-on, unwavering into the oncoming light. What he sees we will never know, but we definitely have taken notice.

Honorable mentions: Jay Harden for "For the Arc Light Fallen" and "War's Shiny Things"

Poetry judged by Colin Halloran, poet, veteran, teacher

Winner: Dominika Wrozynski for "Retrieval"
From Colin Halloran:

"Retrieval" was the clear-cut winner of this year's contest. A strong sense of storytelling and flawless poetic technique combine to weave a powerful, multi-perspective narrative in a mere 15 lines. The poet delivers both the tale of the soldier and the tale of the spouse, through the voice of the latter, without taking anything away from either. The imagery of the homefront (tarot cards and guitar strings) merge with the tales of the combat zone (limbs, nomads, shifting sand) as the worlds of these two characters have merged. Each carefully chosen word does its part to carry the weight of the subject matter, but the reader is not left wanting. We are reminded that the title word not only represents the act of regaining but the chance of recovery and restoration. There is a quiet hope here. This is an important perspective of the deployment experience to explore, and I look forward to reading more from this talented writer in the future.

Honorable mentions: D.A. Gray for "Whistling Past the Graveyard" and Paul Hellweg for "Ghosts"

Winning Writing

Still Falling Snow

Snow. Snow was falling, soft flakes mixed with tiny nuggets of ice. The air was cold, but it felt warm as it so often is when snow comes down. You know it's cold, but somehow it feels warmer when that white stuff blankets the ground and fills the world around you.

It had snowed since early morning, so I when I stepped out of my metal container, late as usual, the brown world I'm used to seeing was a sweet white. It made me smile. I smiled even more as my feet crunched and sloshed down the road to work. Snow was making me think of home, and I liked the memories. Then I looked up from my thoughts

Damn. A formation. A big formation. Why in the hell? Oh shit. I remembered then. The "Fallen Comrade" ceremony. How in the fuck did I forget that? I walked around to the back of the formation, thanking God I wasn't completely late and could slip into line without much disturbance. It hadn't started yet.

The Command Sergeant Major was directing the late comers to places at the back behind the other soldiers. I took my place. It was getting cold. The snowflakes were getting bigger and wetter. I could feel my cotton coat getting damp. The commander put us at Parade Rest, in unison, 400 pairs of hands slapped hard behind our backs as our feet stomped on the ground into a wider stance.

We waited. I watched the snow build up in the crook of the soldier's arm in front of me. One second it was just a few flakes, quickly melting, then more, until there was a small mound built up.

"Commanders, bring your units to attention."

The snow fell from his arm as we snapped our hands to our sides. The ceremony had begun.

The Master of Ceremonies started by describing the Fallen Comrade service and introducing the dignitaries. The Major General was attending. That meant it was going to be a long ceremony. The snow was now melting down from the soldiers' hats and coats, dripping off ears and fingers. One poor fool didn't even have a coat. He must have been freezing.

Our chaplain came up first to say the prayer. It was a good prayer. He didn't ask God for clarity of purpose. He didn't ask God to explain it. He asked God for strength for the friends and family of the fallen men. It was a good prayer.

"Commanders, bring your units to Parade Rest."

Our brigade commander stood next. I don't remember the details. He said their names. He told the story of their deaths. He said they were the best kind of leaders—the ones who lead from the front. They had gone forward first to make sure their soldiers were safe. He said they were sons and brothers, husbands and fathers. He said that their deaths had made them "sons of Afghanistan." The statement caught my attention. "Sons of Afghanistan?" Who in the hell would really want to belong to this place forever? I want to understand why that statement is true and right. I really do, but I just can't. I had to let it go. Whether I believe or not or like it or not, they are forever linked to this place. Perhaps that's what makes the statement true.

After the brigade commander came our two generals. They said proud words, good words about the sacrifice made, the lives given. I watched the snow and bent my knees to keep from getting dizzy. My toes were numb. It was hard to concentrate. The commander's words were swirling in my mind like the snow was swirling around my head. I couldn't grab on to any one idea. I could just feel the words as they drifted through our ranks.

Music played and then their friends came up and spoke. I listened as they shared both good and bad about the men who had died. They weren't saints. They were men: men with hopes and dreams and families, men with faults and goodness. I looked to my left and to my right. I was standing beside the same people. Everyone in the formation could have been the men we were honoring. I almost asked why them, not this one or that one or me? I almost asked this question, but I left it alone. Questions without answers are hateful things. I went back to watching the snow fall and the water drop from the ear of the man in front of me to his shoulder and down his arm.

Again, we were brought to attention and again our hands slapped down as one.

"Call the Roll."

I heard the words. I knew what they meant, but I had no idea how they applied. A name was called and answered. Then another name was called and answered. Then a third. That was the one. The Commander of Troops called out "SSG Jason E. Burkholder." They called his name. They called it again and again. No answer. There was no answer. We waited. Then we heard the next name. "LT Jared Southworth . . . LT Jared W. Southworth . . . LT Southworth!" Again and again and again no answer. The silence was profound. Each named called invited the expected response. We anticipated the answer. We waited for it. The silence marked the absence and called the dead to draw near.

The music began to play again—"Amazing Grace" with its melody filled with equal measures of pain and joy, with the simple tone threaded beneath the notes, so much like life. To my right, there was a stir, someone had fallen. It was the cold, and time spent standing in that cold was taking its toll, but it was coming to an end. As the last note faded, we were invited to pay honor to the dead and then dismissed from the formation.

I watched as some soldiers moved to the memorial and others left the square, still others held each other, tears flowing freely, giving voice to their grief. I walked to the memorial at a distance and watched as friends of the dead stood before the empty boots and turned-down rifle. With slow salute, they honored this memorial; they honored the dead, these members of our family, now resting in the arms of eternity as we, the living, were held in the cold embrace of the still falling snow.

Lisa Miller is the President of the Missouri Writers Guild, a member of the St. Louis Writers Guild, and a founding member of the St. Louis Literary Consortium. Lisa has a B.A. in English from the University of Baltimore and an M.A. in English from the University of Missouri–St. Louis. Lisa has served in the military for more than 30 years. She was deployed to Afghanistan in 2008, part of Joint Task Force Phoenix as a member of the Illinois National Guard.

Diane Cameron

Iambic Pentameter and the Meter of War

In the 1940s, a young Marine returns from China to a small Pennsylvania town. He enrolls in graduate school and begins to work as a high school teacher. He marries the young woman who had waited for him through the war. They buy a house and invite her widowed mother to live with them.

One year later finds the body of the mother-in-law sprawled on the kitchen floor, the body of the wife in the living room, both perforated by bullets. The former Marine is handcuffed and taken away by the sheriff. The local newspapers are filled with testimony from the man's former employers, neighbors, and students. Each interview is a tribute to the good worker, teacher, and neighbor they knew Donald Watkins to be.

After more than 30 years of hospitalization, Donald Watkins married my mother. He was 84; she was a younger woman of 70. For a decade, Donald was part of my life. He was a gentle and reserved man, whose past always seemed like it must belong to someone else. My mother had told me Donald's story, and, though he rarely spoke of it, over time his story had begun to haunt me.

In September 2000, four years after Donald's death, I placed ads in *The Marine Gazette* and *Leatherneck*, seeking Marines who served in China between 1937 and 1940. I gave my address, phone number, and email address, expecting one or two responses at best.

The first day the ads appeared, my answering machine flashed with seven messages. "This is Staff Sergeant Clifford Wells," the first one announced in a no-nonsense voice. "I served in China 1938 and departed Shanghai on the USS Truman, 23 March 1940. I usually bowl on Monday and Wednesday, so it's best to call me on Friday." The messages were all delivered in similarly clipped tones. The callers recited rank, name, duty assignment, and location in China, including exact date of arrival and departure. I received letters and e-mails from engineers, corpsmen, a chef for enlisted men, even a chauffeur to the commander.

The former Marines who contacted me were in their late 80s and suffering from diminished capabilities. "I am happy to help you," one wrote, "but please don't call. I am extremely deaf." Another said, "I will write back to you again but only when my son comes on Thursday to help me with the mail."

These men had saved crucial documents from their service: scrapbooks, Shanghai phone books, box-scores of Chinese ball games with the rosters of players, the 1938 Thanksgiving dinner menu, copies of the *Walla Walla*, the weekly Marine newspaper in Shanghai. And they wanted to send it all to me.

These men became my teachers. They told me what it was like to be young and far from home, to see death all around them, and then to have to kill. Many had never discussed these events with anyone. My most regular correspondent and phone pal was Frenchy Dupont from Louisiana.

Frenchy and I corresponded for more than three years. As we got to know each other, I told him why I was writing about Donald, that I wanted to understand how this nice elderly man could have had such a scary past. That I wanted to know why my mother could marry a man who had killed his first wife and mother-in-law, and yes, that I thought that being a Marine in war might have something to do with what had gone wrong with Donald.

Under Donald's reserved and always polite demeanor was a hum of tension. There was his obsession with a TV show called *Combat* that was in re-runs. He had to watch it no matter where we were: at the mall, eating dinner, at a baby's birthday party. Then too there were his infrequent but almost exquisite moments of paranoia that came and went in seconds, always occurring in restaurants. He'd turn on a waiter or other diner and scream, "I see you," and then just as quickly return to his quiet dinner.

Frenchy's letters arrived every two weeks. I would manage to send at least a short note in response to each of his six-page letters. I told myself that because Frenchy needed a magnifier to read word by word, it was good to be brief.

In one letter, which I go back to often, he answered the question I'd kept asking him: why hadn't he suffered shell shock following the torture he endured in the Palawan prison camp? He'd been starved, beaten, set on fire, and nearly blinded before he'd even turned 25. "I was so happy to be rescued," he wrote, "that this was never a problem." That's a glass half-full, I thought.

"Our conflicts weren't the glorious battles," he went on. "There weren't any cameras where we were, and the current history books never mention our piece of World War II."

Temperament and upbringing—crucial determinants of resilience in the face of trauma—must have been key factors in Frenchy's emotional survival. At 85, he remained an outgoing optimist, no cynicism, always kind, and the perfect barkeep in the Hospitality Suite at the China Marines reunion.

There was one moment though, he told me, when he had a taste of what the other China Marines live with. Here is what Frenchy wrote:

About three months after I came home, I had one flashback. It was a dream that several Jap guards had come to my home. I saw them coming up the front walk. As I ran down the hall to go out the back door, I saw one of them standing with his back to the porch wall by the door, and as I ran by I heard his rifle fire and I was hit in the back with the bullet. My feet flew out from under me and I fell between two rows of roses in our back yard.

"One taste and never another," Frenchy's letter continued, "You are the first one, except my wife, to hear of this incident." So much for therapy, I think. "Some fellows do have problems though," he said. "A few still attend weekly group therapy at VA hospitals." That is, he means, 57 years later.

It's mid-January and Vermont is sunny and snow-covered. I have taken a break from Donald and the Marines to visit Bennington College to hear the poet Robert Bly speak to the MFA students. It's bright and cold when I walk the short path to the lecture hall.

Bly has just begun his lecture as I slip into the back of the darkened hall. I peel off my parka while my eyes adjust. He is talking about how structure is part of the message in any writing. He focuses on the early 1940s, his younger days, when he learned the formal shapes of poems and the rules of poetry. Strictness of form and careful structure were critical to the work they were all doing then.

"Prescribed forms were important because we were, at that time, writing about social madness. It was World War II," he says, and I lean forward in my seat. "We were writing about the war, bombing. America was at war on two sides of the world—it was a crazy time filled with chaos." Volatile content required strict form to contain it.

I lean back in my seat and put my feet up on the rail in front of me. As I listen to Robert Bly describe the war and the turmoil of that time, I think of Donald and Frenchy and my other Marines. They were part of this social madness. They were young, away from home for the first time. They had been at sea for weeks on the USS Chaumont. When they finally neared their exotic destination, ready for the promised worldly adventures, the ship pulled into a harbor full of floating dead bodies. Once on Chinese soil, their job was to go out each day, after the Japanese bombs struck, and collect the dead bodies.

I think about that fact many times. For most of us, our picture of a dead body comes from a relative we've seen in a funeral home, or maybe a visit to a deathbed in hospital or hospice. But these young Marines faced the dead in parts and pieces—heads, arms, and torsos separated and tossed about. Their job was to pick up the body parts and load them on trucks. Every day. How could they not go mad?

Robert Bly asks this audience of aspiring writers if they can let go of form or "at least the overused iambic pentameter." He explains that we learned this rhythmic pattern from the Greeks who used it to express irony. The Greek poets had a repertoire of rhyme schemes, and each one was used for a specific purpose.

This is news. Did Shakespeare know that? Did he also use iambic pentameter to express irony? What do we miss when we don't know small pieces of literary or historic context? What do we miss when we don't know, for example, that these young Marines were not allowed to engage the Japanese until 1945, that for eight years all they could do was watch people get torn apart? And then pick up the pieces.

A woman across the room is waving her hand excitedly. Before Bly can call on her, she blurts out, "But we can see form as a cage which is outside of us and therefore limiting us, or we can see it as a support, as something internal, like a skeleton that provides structure, that allows us to hang things on it."

I think of Frenchy. What allowed him to survive in the Palawan prison, to structure his chaos? On what did he hang his experience so that he could come home more or less intact? Was it simply youth? Faith? The Marine esprit de corps?

I think of another Marine, Cliff, who told me how he came to be a China Marine. "It was the Depression, no one could get a job." So he and two friends went off to join the Marines. He was excited but nervous when he was selected. He would go to China: foreign, exotic. I learn that there were Mama-San houses which provided rice and meat and well, a little piece too. Of course Cliff didn't use that kind of language. He said, "The Marines made sure we had all the things a young soldier needed to keep him happy, girls of course, providing pleasure."

I think about what part pleasure and sex might have played in counter-balancing the chaos, in facing down the madness. Picking up shredded body parts by day, going to the Mama-San house for sex and dinner at night.

I wonder now how aware these young men were of the greater geopoliti-cal picture? The war was coming to the Pacific. Picking up body parts was a prelude, preparation for what was to come. Very soon they would do their own killing.

Cliff told me about the medals he received for hand-to-hand combat. Hand-to-hand sounds so innocuous. Like they were shaking hands or arm-wrestling. Cliff asked if I knew what "hand-to-hand" meant. "Sort of," I said, "but I'm not really sure."

"Well," he said slowly, "you look at a man who is about to kill you, and you kill him first. You look a man in the eyes and then stab him over and over with your bayonet."

How could we have expected our soldiers to survive that? Even our words look the other way. Bly reads to the college audience from Robert Frost. "Listen to the form" he says. We can hear the despair, madness, and emotional chaos of Frost's life in the poems. "Frost chose to convey his life's words in iambic pentameter because it just barely contains the chaos."

Perhaps this is the key, how well a person can contain the chaos of their life, the chaos of heartbreak or war or murder or mental illness. If there is a form—linguistic, emotional, or spiritual—they survive. Maybe some Marines like Frenchy possess a form, an iambic pentameter that courses through their lives, keeping their chaos in check. But for others, like Donald, their meter is more fragile, more unmanageable, and the chaos spills over in unruly and violent waves. These waves crash into other lives—Donald's wife's, her mother's, my mother's—and then into mine.

This then may be Donald's gift to me—a unexpected one certainly from a man whose measure I am still taking—to look at the meter of my own life, valuing those things that keep me from chaos and, as much as I can, counting on the good.

Diane Cameron has written about the history and politics of addiction and of mental illness. She currently writes about popular culture, and she is the author of the new book, *Out of the Woods—A Guide to Long-term Recovery*, which describes life in recovery—from any addiction—after ten or twenty or even thirty years. Diane's other book is *Looking for Signs*—a collection of essays. Diane is a frequent speaker and presenter. She has a long career in human services and is an advocate for people in poverty at Unity House in Troy.

Jay Harden

My Mother of All Letters

Among other things, war brought to me the intensest of emotions.

I left her one overcast and late September day in 1968 as I mounted the blue flight crew bus taking my bomb wing to the tarmac and a flight over The Pond to combat in Vietnam. It was an unceremonious farewell, so clumsy casual, hiding the deep and wonderful love that was our shared secret. I was gruffly brave and she never more shining, bright in the eyes, with that trademark embracing smile and a glowing beauty that still blinded me, the luckiest man in the universe. We tried to say our intimate goodbye the night before, but I was already withdrawing into my protective warrior shell, knowing well, as she did not, what I was about to do half a world away, although I had no idea how severely my actions would affect me—and us—for the rest of our too-short life together.

I lived many lifetimes in my months away, each one its own story worth telling. But one constant that bound those days together in one sane and blessed whole for me was her letters. She wrote me faithfully, constantly, and vitally, each her small gift of grace across the sea. Along with the audio-tapes we exchanged, I heard from her, on average, every single day, although the military mail system in those days and my unpredictable movements to Guam, Thailand, and Okinawa made mailcall feast or famine for me.

Some days I got nothing, and other days I got bundles of letters, pastel and faint of perfume. I must have told her the depth of joy those physical papers gave me, for certainly I told my crew. In fact, I gloated and soon learned the indiscriminate power that letters from home possess.

My bombardier, who sat to my left in the belly of the B-52, outranked me. I was the lowest of the low, a first lieutenant, even lower in status than the gunner, a grandfather sergeant with eight stripes, who had more wisdom than we five officers put together. After seven weeks or more, the bombardier had not received a single letter from his wife, no communication at all, no word of their young son. They were our neighbors back on Westover Air Force Base, Massachusetts, where we lived in housing so substandard and infested with termites that it would be condemned outside the base, but we felt fortunate anyway because we lived across from the 8th Air Force commanding general, and that meant we got our shared street plowed first when the snows came, snows that made two Georgia peaches shrivel and gasp.

Lacking any letters, the bombardier tried to phone his wife long-distance. Then he tried MARS, the Military Affiliate Radio System, a 20-year-old amateur shortwave network of phone patches operated by volunteer ham radio operators primarily for morale and personal emergencies. He still could not reach her. Slowly he became absolutely frantic within. I watched his emotional balance deteriorate. Every possible night, he would leave our Bachelor Officer Quarters to go drinking, then stumble back, turn on the shower, and curl up under his personal waterfall in the corner. By morning, and by miracle to me, he appeared sober and took to the sky with the rest of us, adding to my increasing secret anxiety about the constant grim work with him I was bound by duty and promise to do.

But every plump letter I received from Carolyn—a beautiful rolling sound in my mind that I still hear—soothed my accumulating stress and erased every grimy line on my face. Her letters meant more joy to me than any quantity of gold. They, innocent and without intention, preserved my emotional heart. Her unconditional love, her acceptance, and her non-judgment of me, a young killer in the making, to this day still feeds my soul though she is gone. No one else can know the depth of that gift, not even she, and that is why I need to record this story of her treasured writing.

One night, my bombardier returned to quarters with his right hand immobilized, the same hand needed to aim the crosshairs on our bomb runs. The flight surgeon had inserted a stainless steel pin through his pinky fingernail and bone. The pin was under tension with rubber bands to somehow align a fracture, I suppose. That evening, the painkillers wore off and he was in unremitting agony.

I did not see him again until morning. The scary contraption was gone, replaced by a conventional plaster cast. To my amazement, he was not grounded, and we flew another combat mission the next day. I learned later that he had been in a fight with some guy in civilian clothes who ducked his punch, causing him to crack a concrete urn of flowers behind. Even later, I learned that the other guy was an enlisted man, but I never heard if the captain was court-martialed.

Eventually, after about one-third of our combat tour, the bombardier heard from his wife. All I learned secondhand was that she and her girlfriend had taken off for fun in Cape Cod, whatever that implied. And every day that I picked up my letter or bundle of letters, my ecstasy must have wounded him again and again.

I remember exactly when I got my mother of all letters. The date was October 20, 1968. Five days earlier I had hopped a ride on a bombing mission from Andersen Air Force Base, Guam, and landed at Kadena Air Base, Okinawa, where I joined a new B-52 crew. We flew our first mission together the next day on my 25th birthday and landed on Guam. (Only four weeks later, that very aircraft aborted takeoff with a full bomb load and blew up off the end of the Kadena runway, killing two. Against all logic, I felt spared.)

Those longer sorties from one base to another were particularly draining, but all of them repeated the same emotional sequence for me: growing anxiety while roaring inbound to Vietnam with eight lungs breathing righteous fire and 60,000 pounds of bombs; next, the sensational adrenaline rush for seven minutes on the bomb run when time melts with your mind in a thrilling, private taffy flow; then the temporary liberation of tension after bombs away and steep breakaway turn realizing we beat the enemy yet again. These extreme emotions were followed by the intolerable stupor and exhaustion of flying across thousands of miles of Pacific Ocean, only to be compounded by my deep navigation doubt of finding a sneaky island only 40 miles long, and finally ending with the safe landing of our massive beast on 10,000 feet of undulating runway, while in the back of my mind was the Marianas Trench below the 600-foot cliff at the end of the runway, an abyss that had already swallowed a completely loaded combat B-52 and crew without a trace.

That day's bombing mission left me worn-out and impatient beyond my usual self. I was trapped in a body screaming with every step for rest and relief after over 12 hours of relentless demands by a dominating metal mistress.

After the tedious, irritating, but necessary, debriefings, I stumbled to the mailroom and clutched a single, unusually thin, and lumpy letter, and another later dated one, my prizes for surviving yet another ever darker dance with death, seven miles above a deceptive lush green jungle.

This time on Guam, we were randomly assigned to two-man rooms in the Visiting Officer Quarters. I sat cross-legged on my bunk at the front of the room, back to the door, anticipating the comfort I held in my hand, my heavy, salt-encrusted flying boots still zipped to my feet, in my stinky, greasy, sweat-stained, olive flight suit, bulging with the hanging weight of war tools: pens, pencils, checklists, plotter, dividers, orange survival switchblade, gloves, keys, wallet, and my life-saving E-6B dead-reckoning computer (really a simply ingenious circular slide rule on steroids). Somewhere beside the bed, I had dumped my brain bucket and flight bag of maps, star tables, and other navigation stuff I have since forgotten.

The first treasure in my hand felt uniquely odd. In an anxious, fumbling caress I opened it, pulling out a single sheet of pastel with smaller blue paper attached in the upper left corner and pink in the opposite. My heart cranked up to racing. Could it be? Could our future be coming true?

Each corner was a folded piece of construction paper, familiar visual fare to any man in love with an enthusiastic elementary-school teacher. Each color had been cut into a triangle and the corners folded in, overlapping each other into a suggestive shape. In each center was a shiny, petite brass safety pin.

Now I was in a daze, softly trembling with anticipation, breathing rapidly and happily, and well seasoned by fatigue from the subsiding vibrations of aeronautical intimacy with my 400,000-pound metal mama.

There in the middle of the page, in her confident, generous, and open swirls, she had simply handwritten these exquisite, echoing words:

We are going to have a baby.
I'm so happy & I love you so much.

These were the only words of hers in my mother of all letters, and no more were needed.

That moment, the entire universe stopped for me, in our honor. The rest of you did not notice that fleeting beat, but I can recall it at will even now. And when I do, I smile into the wind.

There I sat on a small tropic island, breezy in the setting sun, a place coconuts and coral call home, where it rains a little every day. There I sat on a drab and itchy G.I. blanket and just wept the first, best joy I ever knew. There I sat alone with her presence in paper, lonely not at all.

In that superb and shining moment, I was innocent of destruction and killing, whole, perfect, and unstained.

In that moment, hope conquered death.

In that moment, I knew I would survive my war for my woman and my child.

In that moment, my passion for living outshined the darkest deeds of mine against my fellow human beings.

In that moment, I fell in love with a little girl I had yet to meet and with my grownup girl yet again.

In that moment, thanks to the mother of all my letters and the mother I had made, I became a father and a man reborn.

Suddenly the door opened and an unknown officer entered, my roommate for the night. I put my head down, arms around my knees. He walked past and threw his flight gear on his bed, then sat down. After a pause, he asked me if anything was wrong. I simply turned my back to him and kept crying, unable to explain or share my ineffable happiness with another stranger.

Soon enough, I tore through the letter that followed, finding more of her lovely words:

Oh how I wish we could rejoice together.
We are lucky to have been given the opportunity to raise a child.
I will try to be brave and good so our baby will have a happy time inside me.
I feel like a little bird with a huge wonderful song to sing.
Please take care of yourself, for the daddy must be in top shape to play, read,
love, and help the baby.

The following morning, I rushed to the Officers' Club and called Carolyn long distance at her parents' house, 12 hours past my time. She picked up the phone. And the beauty of her hello silenced me so I could not speak. Feelings as grand and pure as chocolate flooded me, triggered by her soothing Southern lilt and words of tender admiration for her man, her private hero. Life flowed back and forth through those wires, now embracing a third one: the most beautiful telephone conversation I ever had.

She was fine. The baby was fine. And in her voice was something new:

a richness, a beginning of the wisdom we needed to guide a fresh baby into a beautiful world. That woman and that child in that moment gave me a zest and strength I had never known and helped me through my war.

There were other letters from my war days, of course, and audiotapes. I did not write her in return nearly as many times, for reasons she did not understand and never could. But she forgave me anyway for my omissions and the accumulating wounds of war to my soul.

I kept all her letters in the basement, in a box plainly labeled. Over the years before her unexpected death at 42, she often asked me to throw her letters away. One day in anger I told her I would, but I destroyed only the box, and secretly repackaged and moved the letters elsewhere, put them out of my mind along with my worst memories of Vietnam, and eventually forgot they existed.

Some years after she died and we moved away, a friend got me interested in genealogy, and I started family research at the Library of Congress and the National Archives. In time I stumbled across the Civil War letters of my great-grandfather in a Georgia library.

Then I remembered Carolyn's letters to me in Vietnam. In my search for them, I also found my letters to her she had hidden away that I thought lost, and my mother of all letters, the one so short, so simple, and so treasured from the mother of my children to me.

I insisted we name our baby after her, and when that little girl grew up, she did the same with her daughters.

Mr. Harden retired from government science after combat in Vietnam. He has lived in Georgia, California, Massachusetts, Missouri, Virginia, Guam, Thailand, and Okinawa; wandered to Japan, Sri Lanka, Bhutan, England, Mexico, Panama, France, and Italy; and studied yoga in India extensively. He still travels and writes mostly of love, war, childhood, and personal growth, favoring poetry, essay, children's books, family history, and lyrics. You can see some of his early photography and writing at http://www.jayharden.com.

Earl W. Norwood/
by S. Lorraine Norwood

D-Day, Korea, Vietnam:
An Old Warrior Lives to Tell the Tale

When I look back on my life, I don't know how I survived. I fought in three wars—World War II, Korea, and Vietnam—and escaped death more times than I can count. I saw things in combat that are hard to imagine. I went into my first war as a wet-behind-the-ears kid. When I mustered out of my last war, I was bitter, lonely, and lost. For a long time I didn't talk about any of it. I drank instead.

Today I'm a recovered alcoholic. I'm a survivor of colon and lung cancer. I have COPD and require oxygen twenty-four hours a day. I recently broke both hips, but thanks to hip replacements, I can get around. I live in a very nice retirement facility in Asheville, North Carolina, where I try not to talk politics with the old farts in the dining room. I have no intention of getting married again, but my lunch table consists of me and three very intelligent women. The other seniors, mostly the jealous ones, call them my "harem." Truth is, we just talk. I'm way too old for shenanigans. I've had enough adventure for one life.

* * *

When the U.S. entered World War II, I was in high school. I was sick of school and ready to fight Hitler. I had always had trouble with academics and thought of myself as the family dummy. I flunked third grade, and then, when I flunked seventh grade, my little brother passed me in school. I felt really stupid. My father harped at me for not being as smart as my brother. He always called me a dummy. So when war broke out, I decided to join the military. The day after I turned 17, I enlisted in the U.S. Navy, but because I was underage, my father had to give his written permission.

I went to basic training in Bainbridge, Maryland. Near the end of my training I was asked whether I had experience operating small boats. I answered "yes" and explained that my brother and I spent summers helping my maternal grandfather, a lighthouse keeper, pilot his 37-foot workboat as he tended beacon lights along the coast of North Carolina. My grandfather taught us how to handle a boat in rough seas, how to read the tides and pull up to a buoy, keeping the boat in neutral until he changed the beacon light. I expected to be sent to Norfolk, Virginia, with the other seamen, but two days later my chief called and said, "You've got a special assignment. You won't be going to Norfolk. You're going to Little Creek to be an LCVP operator."

Little Creek, Virginia, was the site of the major operating base for amphibious forces in the Navy's Atlantic Fleet. Ship's crews were trained there, including boat crews for the LCVP or Landing Craft Vehicle, Personnel, commonly known as the Higgins boat. I was to be a coxswain.

I didn't know it then, but the Navy had big plans for the Higgins boat. All our training was geared toward one moment—a beach assault somewhere in Europe. I knew we were going to invade. I just didn't know when or where.

After we finished our training in the U.S., we were shipped to England. I was a 17-year-old sailor turned loose in London for three days of shore leave. Since I had never been in a huge city, I went to the Red Cross in Piccadilly Circle to make sure I had a bunk. While there, I saw a poster advertising a New Year's Eve dance with Glenn Miller and Marlene Dietrich, and I said to myself, man, I've got to see that, so I looked at London for the next couple of days and then came back for the dance. I danced with English girls and then saw a woman sitting all by herself, so I got brave and asked her to dance. When she found out my age, she said, "My God, you're going to war to fight the German army?" She asked me where I was from, and we talked about home. Then she asked me what I wanted to do when the clock struck midnight. The English government hadn't let Big Ben strike since 1939, but I told her I'd love to be looking at Big Ben to welcome in the New Year. That's how I found myself on New Year's Eve 1943, sitting on Waterloo Bridge watching Big Ben with my arm around Marlene Dietrich.

On the morning of June 5, 1944, General Eisenhower gave the go-ahead for an invasion of Europe by sea. The Allies were now committed; there was no turning back. At 4:30 a.m. on June 6, I stepped out of the hatch of our mothership, LST 357, and looked around. The sun was just coming up on the English Channel and there were ships everywhere—I've never seen so many ships in my life.

The amphibious invasions began at 6:30 a.m. The English Channel was very rough, with waves running about two feet. There was no wind and the visibility was good, but it was hazy. Omaha Beach was the most heavily fortified of the five beaches on the Normandy coast. We faced intense resistance there, which made the landings worse than expected.

We hit the beach at low tide. The Allied high command had determined that high tide would be too risky due to the structure of the beach. However, invading at mean low tide meant that there would be a quarter-mile of open beach which soldiers would have to cross. All kinds of obstacles would be in front of us—artillery mortar rounds, machine guns, and rifle fire.

My Higgins boat was in the third row of landing craft. In my hands were the wheel and the lives of 36 soldiers. I had just turned 18 years old. I ran aground on Omaha Beach at full throttle, sliding the boat as far onto the beach as I could, so the soldiers could wade ashore. All of us were targets from the waist up. On the right side of the boat was the motor; on the left side, there was nothing but plywood. I yelled, "Drop the ramp!" The first four soldiers started running down the ramp when a German artillery shell tore through the hull and exploded, instantly decapitating two men and wounding the other two. The rest of the men didn't hesitate. They stepped over the two men who had been cut in half and went over the ramp toward the beach. Talk about bravery—those men knew they were running into the gates of hell.

I had made a mark on the steering wheel indicating dead center for the rudder, so I could hold the boat steady. I lined the wheel up with the mark, and when the last man was off the boat, I threw the boat into reverse full speed and got the hell out. Once in deep water, I spun the boat around and headed to sea. The hole from the artillery shell was leaking with every big wave on the five-mile trip back to the LST. I got the bow up and started planing, but water was still coming in. I looked down and the bilge pump wasn't working. I grabbed one of the crew, opened the bilge door, and saw that it was clogged with intestines from the two men who had been killed. We scooped the bilge out with our bare hands, then got the two wounded men back to the hospital ship before heading for LST 357.

At the LST, I was assigned another Higgins boat and started back to the beach again. I think I made four trips. I would pilot the boat, drop the ramp, and the soldiers would go ashore. Then I would feather the throttle to hold the boat straight, and we would wait to pick up the wounded. Around us there was intense, incoming fire. That was the worst part of each trip to the beach—waiting for the medics to load the wounded.

By our third trip, the machine gun fire had stopped. Instead, German artillery was firing from maybe five miles back. Artillery rounds were coming in as we unloaded the troops and waited for the wounded. An 88 artillery shell exploded, and I remember seeing a stretcher cartwheeling through the air in slow motion.

After the battle, we were assigned to collect the dead from the water. The Higgins boat was perfect for the job because we could roll the body onto the ramp and then pull the ramp up and bring the body on board. After three days, the bodies were bloated and the faces were busting open. The smell was horrible. We asked a senior noncom officer if we could stop. He reminded us that every dead GI we found meant that one more family would know what happened, that they would get a telegram that their son was no longer missing. So we picked up bodies for two more days until a storm blew the rest offshore. Less than a week later, the beaches were fully secured.

After the invasion, we transported material to the beach for the supply depots, then for two months we hauled supplies from England to France. Finally we came home on leave, temporarily stationed in Florida. Our next assignment was going to be the invasion of Japan, but on May 5, 1945, the Allies formally accepted the unconditional surrender of Nazi Germany and the war in Europe was over. Everybody was talking about buying a steak dinner to celebrate the end of the war, so we headed for a restaurant. After dinner, the rest of the guys took off for the bars. I had something else in mind. I went to a bakery and bought a whole apple pie for dessert. I asked the baker for a spoon and then I went to the movies. I sat up in the balcony and ate the whole pie.

After the war, I volunteered to go to Germany. I was sent to Bremer-haven, where I stayed until my grandmother died in December 1946. The Navy wanted me to come back and go on a battleship, but I didn't want to do that, so in 1948, I enlisted in the Army, going in as a buck sergeant MP. I was sent to Salzburg, Austria, to work in a displaced persons' camp. I took my GED in Vienna when I was 22 years old.

After Germany, I was stationed at Fort Bragg, North Carolina, and then got sent to Kokura, Japan. Two days later the Korean War broke out. I was sitting in a restaurant in Kokura having frog legs and a Singapore sling when they called me out and told me I was heading for Korea.

* * *

Truce is a loss. That's my opinion of Korea. It was a political war from the beginning.

We went over there as a show of force, but we were short of men by about half. The only readily available troops were in Japan, and we weren't really ready for combat, but there was no one else around. We were on our feet with no tanks, just Jeeps and ¾-ton trucks.

The first military group to arrive in Korea was commanded by Colonel Charles Bradford Smith. I was a sergeant first class in recon with Smith's Task Force, a group of 540 soldiers. We were ordered to delay the enemy advance. Our first significant engagement with the North Koreans was the Battle of Osan on July 5, 1950. We attacked but didn't have the weapons to destroy the North Korean tanks.

Smith ordered a withdrawal, but the North Koreans surrounded us at Tae-jon, and we had to fight our way through. We rode out in Jeeps, battling for two hours with machine guns and fighting through a tunnel to the Americans on the other side. Only 127 of us were left alive.

We fell back to the Pusan Perimeter, a 140-mile defensive line around the southeastern tip of Korea. Then we chased them to Seoul and pushed them north back to their side of the 38th parallel. We moved toward the border of North Korea and China on the Yalu River. The Chinese leader, Mao Tse-tung, warned the U.S. to keep away from the Yalu boundary unless we wanted a full-scale war with China.

In November 1950, I was in an intelligence recon platoon sent to the Yalu River to watch for enemy activity and report back. It was one of the worst winters Korea had ever seen. The Yalu River was frozen solid. I was sitting in a Jeep five miles from the river, scanning the Chinese side through binocu-lars, when all of a sudden a formation of Chinese soldiers marched across the ice toward us. I radioed back to the Intel officer that the Chinese were com-ing. I told him, "There are so many I can't count them," but the officer didn't believe me. He said aerial recon showed no Chinese in the vicinity. I told him I was looking at them. I said, "I'm telling you, Recon Sergeant, that they're here and there are thousands of them." I told him to call for air support and he said, "The colonel says we can't bomb because half the river is on Chinese territory." I said, "There are at least 15,000 Chinese here." He said, "The colonel says there are no Chinese in your area because Intel says there are no Chinese there." And yet there I was looking at the Chinese army marching into the Korean peninsula.

The North Koreans and Chinese drove us back into South Korea. They recaptured Seoul, and after months of heavy fighting, we were back at the 38th Parallel.

When my tour of duty in Korea ended in 1951, I came back to the States for four years. Then the Army sent me to Nuremburg, Germany. I was first sergeant of an MP company. After four years there, I came back to the U.S. where I was stationed at Fort Ord for one year. I got a job as a ROTC instructor at Seattle University in Washington. In 1964, and again in 1965, I was stationed in Korea.

Finally, I came back to Fort Ord in 1965 to retire from the Army. But I was shocked one day to get orders from the Army calling me out of retirement. I was 42 years old. Like everybody who leaves the Army, I was in the active reserves for a year, so legally they could order me to duty during that time. I told them I was retired and didn't want to go back. They said if I wanted my pension and all the other perks that came with being a military retiree, I would have to go or lose everything. When I got to Fort Ord, I was told I'd be training troops headed for Vietnam. They promised I would remain stateside. I should have known better.

* * *

In Korea, everybody seemed to pull together and try to emulate the way we fought in World War II. We had that experience to draw on. But Vietnam was different. It was a phony war from the beginning. The only thing real about it was the casualties.

In October 1965, I was on my way to Vietnam as a first sergeant in the infantry. I stayed in Vietnam for two years and three months.

I was no hero. For the first six months in Vietnam I was trying to kill myself. I felt really screwed over by being called back to the Army and sent to war. When I got shot at the first time, I just didn't give a shit. I started to drink pretty heavily. I hadn't been drunk more than a half dozen times in my whole life, but Vietnam tipped me over the edge. After about six months, I began to see what was happening around me—the stupidity of the officers, the lack of common sense, the craziness of the war—and I woke up to where I was and what I was doing.

I got five battle stars for Vietnam: An Loc, Loc Ninh, Parrot's Beak, Saigon Delta, and Suoi Tre. In between these battles were all kinds of ambushes and patrols that didn't have a name. It was very difficult to know who we were fighting because, unlike Korea or World War II, this was a guerrilla war.

On my first patrol, we got ambushed and lost eight men. I had to write letters of condolence to the parents. All the letters went to the same little town. The Army thought if one kid from a town got drafted and others from the same town wanted to join him, it would be good to keep them together. Unfortunately the town's entire high school basketball team was wiped out in that ambush.

In July 1967, we came to the aid of South Vietnamese troops who were being attacked by the North Vietnamese Army (NVA) near the village of An Loc, about 60 miles north of Saigon. We came in with troops and artillery, and defeated the North Vietnamese. Once we secured the area, we set up a base camp. We dug in, expecting to be there for the long haul. Instead, a week later we got orders to leave. I was on the last chopper out. As the chopper lifted off and flew away, I could see Vietcong slipping out of the jungle and occupying the camp that we had just left. I saw this same scenario happen over and over in Vietnam. We'd take a site in a battle, men would be killed and wounded, then we'd get orders to abandon the location, and the VC would sneak back as soon as we left. It pisses me off to this day that we would fight for a piece of ground and win the battle, only to get orders to abandon the site. All those young men who fought so valiantly died in vain.

One of the fiercest fights we were in was the Battle of Loc Ninh, about 80 miles north of Saigon. But it's not the fighting that I remember so vividly—rather, it's the stupidity of one officer, a lieutenant colonel who had never been to infantry school. He had always been a finance officer. In order to be promoted to a full or "bird" colonel, he had to have combat time in a combat unit, so he got his duty changed to infantry for six months. Before the Battle of Loc Ninh, we were out on a big patrol setting up a landing zone. The lieutenant colonel ordered us to bivouac near there for the night. My company commander pointed to a map and said, "Here's where we're supposed to be." He even radioed to get verification, but the lieutenant colonel wouldn't back down. He said he knew how to read a map and that's where we would stay.

It turned out we were sitting in our own predesignated fire zone. A radioman, medic, and dog handler, along with the dog, were killed by an incoming round of artillery fire. It took us two and a half hours to pick them up. I never knew if I put the right heads with the right bodies. Thankfully the bags and the coffins were sealed. I had to write letters home informing relatives that the men had been killed. I was told not to mention friendly fire.

One of the places in Vietnam that really sticks in my head is the Michelin Rubber Plantation. The rubber plantation, the largest in Vietnam, was about 31,000 acres and was located near Dau Tieng in the Binh Duong Province, 45 miles northwest of Saigon. It was also an important base for the Vietcong. The Michelin plant generated a lot of money for the South Vietnamese, but there were rumors that the plant also paid off the Vietcong so Michelin could continue operations during the war.

One day we were patrolling the rubber fields when we came upon a village where the women were boiling their clothes in washpots. We got outside the village and the radioman tapped me on the shoulder. He said, "Sarge,

there are six pots back there. Five have a fire under them and one doesn't."
I gave the order to turn around. We kicked at the washpot without a fire and turned it over. Underneath it was a hole. We sent our tunnel man down and he found a fullscale hospital under the village. The operating room included four beds, a table, and medical supplies, much of it still in crates. It took three trucks just to haul the stuff out of there.

Four weeks later, I was sitting in the mess hall at Dau Tieng having a cup of coffee when a man in fatigues and no markings started talking to me. He told me he was from CID and had seen the documents that came out of the tunnel. Every piece of medical equipment shipped to Dau Tieng came from the Michelin supervisor in Paris, France.

When we first bivouacked on the plantation, we tied our tents to the rubber trees, but there were so many trees close together that our tents sagged, which made them damp on the inside. When our colonel found out about the underground hospital, he was furious. He got back at Michelin by ordering us to make every tent airtight. To comply we had to knock down rows of rubber trees, which we were more than happy to do. The superintendent of the plantation went crazy.

After being stationed in Vietnam for 18 months, I vomited blood. The field hospital couldn't help me, so I was sent to the hospital at Vung Tau, where I was diagnosed with a bleeding ulcer. The Army doctor at the hospital got my bleeding stopped, but he said he didn't want me going back to the front lines until I healed. He sent me to headquarters to the support company for twelve weeks, where I could rest. I ended up running a bakery and ice cream parlor. I operated four soft-serve ice cream machines and froze the ice cream. Every day a helicopter from Saigon HQ flew down to pick up the ice cream and fresh bread. It broke my heart because I knew the poor guys on the front lines were eating C-rations. It made me so mad I thought about putting castor oil in the ice cream.

When I came back from Vietnam, I went off the deep end. I know now that I had PTSD. I understand that the war will hang in my mind for the rest of my life. Sometimes it comes out mean and rotten and then I say to myself, ok, guy, just put it into the box and don't think about it. You learn to live with it.

* * *

I retired from the Army after Vietnam. When I came back home to North Carolina, nobody could understand what I was going through. I was at the VA Hospital once for four days, and the colonel said, "Go home. You're taking up bed space." I was drinking heavily and having blackouts. I felt that if I could just get to Fort Ord and Monterey, I'd be okay. I had always loved that area. I left North Carolina and arrived in California, but my memory of the trip was blank. I woke up in San Jose. I had on a tie, clean shirt, and pants that were pressed. I put my hand in my pocket and pulled out a boarding pass from New Orleans to Chicago and Chicago to San Jose.

I didn't remember the trip at all; I had been in a total blackout.

I had been in the Fort Ord unit for five days when they sent me over to Beacon House, a private rehab facility overlooking Monterey Bay. My therapist was named Joanne. If it hadn't been for her and Beacon House, I don't know what would have become of me.

Joanne and I got married 60 days later. We broke every rule in the book. But she saved my life. And it was a great marriage. She was a trained counselor who practiced tough love. Don't take crap from nobody. Get up and get going. Most alcoholics never grasp that you cannot ever cure alcoholism. I've been in remission since 1971 when I met Joanne, but it hangs there all the time.

I wanted to go to school, maybe major in psychology or journalism, but I didn't know if I could do it. When the military handed me a responsibility, I rose to the occasion, but inside I always felt like a dummy. One day I called myself dumb and Joanne chewed me out. She ordered me never to say the word again.

Joanne had a friend at Northern Arizona University so we hooked up the travel trailer and headed for Flagstaff. We pulled into campus about 10 a.m. and I went to the registrar. I didn't know my head from a hole in the ground, but I told the registrar that I wanted to go to college. I was 47 years old. At first I was thinking of majoring in journalism, but when the registrar heard my life story, he convinced me to change majors. He said, "Man, you're living history. That's your major—history." I came back to the trailer and told Joanne that I was registered and had my class schedule. She says, "You mean you're enrolled?" I said, "Yeah, I'm a history major." We had a cup of coffee in our trailer to celebrate.

I carried 15 hours a semester and took summer classes. I loved every minute of it. I couldn't wait to open a book. I finished my undergrad degree in two years and my master's in one year. I was 50 years old when I finished.

I was hired by the military to be a wandering professor, teaching American history as needed at various bases. I spent twenty years traveling and teaching in the U.S.

Joanne was diagnosed with cancer of the bladder while I was at Fort Gordon, Georgia. We decided to stay put so she could get good care, so I taught at the University of South Carolina annex in Beaufort, South Carolina, and the Technical College of the Low Country.

When Joanne's cancer became terminal, I promised her I would take her to her favorite place to die. She loved Brookings, Oregon, where she could sit on top of the cliffs and look over the Pacific. Brookings was a small town with one stoplight and a huge store that sold everything from baby food to canoes. An old motel on top of a cliff overlooking the Pacific had been renovated into a hospice. Joanne's room faced the ocean, and every night we watched the sunset. She got a big kick out of a plaque on the wall that said Clark Gable and Carol Lombard used to meet in the room when they were lovers.

The day before Joanne died, she told me that she wanted me to go back to Morehead City, North Carolina, after her death. I called my brother and asked him to help me move across the country. We piled all my belongings and Joanne's ashes in the travel trailer and hit the road. We headed east and had almost made it home when we had an accident. I was driving along Interstate 40 through the mountains of Tennessee when the travel trailer started fishtailing and we flipped over. Luckily we weren't hurt. A state trooper offered to take us into a nearby small town where we could make arrangements for the rest of the trip. I was just about to get into the patrol car when I yelled to my brother, "Oh my God, Joanne is in the trailer!" I thought the patrolman was going to have a heart attack. He ran to the trailer thinking that somebody was dead inside. I opened the door. Clothes, food, and kitchen items were everywhere, but there was Joanne, urn intact, sitting upright on the bed just as I had left her. The trooper didn't think it was so funny, but Joanne would have had a big belly laugh over the whole incident.

* * *

Four years ago I discovered that the Navy League had designed a monument to commemorate the sailors who had participated in D-Day and was planning a memorial service. I decided to go. I flew to Paris and traveled by train to Bayeux where I was presented with the Legion of Honor for Valor in Normandy. The seventieth anniversary of D-Day will be held in June 2014. My health won't permit me to go, but I'll be there in spirit.

When I look back on my military life, I don't know how I survived. But Normandy started it all. I got courage and insight on D-Day that lasted me for the rest of my life. I still have dreams about D-Day, but not bad ones anymore. When times are stressful or my health takes a turn for the worse, I have nightmares about Vietnam, but I've learned to keep the bad stuff locked in a box and go on about my life. I've seen things that no man should ever see. I've survived things that are hard to even imagine. But here I am today, sitting on my deck overlooking the woods, watching wild turkey peck through the leaves. Occasionally a bear will lumber by.

I sit here in silence, surrounded by my memories, aware as few men are, that life can indeed be very fragile. Finally, I am at peace.

S. Lorraine Norwood is a North Carolina native who lives in Hendersonville, North Carolina. She has been a professional journalist for over 20 years, working in print and television journalism. She also writes fiction and is working on a historical novel and a collection of short stories, one of which won a Western North Carolina Emerging Artist Award. Ms. Norwood is the author of *Duluth*, Images of America series, Arcadia Publishing 2011. Ms. Norwood is a member of the North Carolina Writers Network, the Atlanta Writers Collective (a critique group), and the Historical Novel Society.

Casey Titus

Interview of Vietnam Veteran Jim Lewis

Today, I will be interviewing a Vietnam Veteran named Jim Lewis. He is sixty-five years old and has fulfilled his life with a variety of careers: A sargeant in a sheriff's department, a helicopter pilot, a scuba diver, and an actor, stuntman, and cameraman in the film industry.

I visited Mr. Lewis at his home and had a direct interview with him. These are his exact words in quotations.

1. How old were you when you entered the service, and what branch were you in?

"I was nineteen years old when I joined the United States Marine Corps (USMC) in '67. Specifically, I was with the GOLF Company in the 2nd Battalion, 5th Marine Regiment, and 1st Marine Division and was honorably discharged under medical conditions in July of 1969."

2. Did you fight in any wars? If so, what was your job?

"Yes, I was a participant in the Southeast Asian conflict, also known as the Vietnam War. I had the rank of corporal and was squad leader. I was also a Grunt, which is known as the ground forces. We look for trouble and usually find it. Search and destroy the enemy; eliminate them. Operations have specific goals in mind. As Grunts, we went on military operations, and we fully expected to accomplish the mission.

"If someone tells me they are a Vietnam Veteran, Casey, there are three questions I would ask to know if they're 'the real deal':

When were you there?
Who were you with?
What did you do? (What was your job?)

3. What persuaded you to join the service?

"I wanted to be the best, and the Marine Corps was just that—the best in the world. Marines and Marine units are known all over the world for their fighting skills. World War I even referred to us as 'devil dogs.' In previous encounters, such as the Shores of Tripoli, we were given the nickname 'leather neck.' The reason we were called that is because leather was worn around the neck to protect against the slashing of a sword or saber. Being called a 'leatherneck' is an honor for a Marine."

4. Why did the Vietnam War take place, and what happened in the aftermath of the war?

"North Vietnam's leader Ho Chi Mein wanted the country to be ruled by communism. The southern half of Vietnam wanted a democratic form of government. When the two halves clashed, China and Russia joined forces with North Vietnam. America, Britain, Australia, and New Zealand opposed the north and joined forces with South Vietnam.

The United States was South Vietnam's largest force. Because of this, North Vietnam would agree to end the war based on one condition—the United States would withdraw their troops. The United States withdrew their troops from Vietnam in March of 1973. As American helicopters lifted off the U.S. Embassy in Saigon, the city was being overrun by the North Vietnamese army. Saigon and South Vietnam officially fell in April of 1975."

5. What did you enjoy most during your years of service?

"The Marine Corps was very structured. I'm a very structured and organized person. Gradually, I rose in my rank. I loved the commitment, and I'm very proud to be a part of that and the Marine Corps. I'm proud to be a veteran and I'm very proud to be a Vietnam veteran."

6. What did you dislike most during your years of service?

"I had two years of service and I spent nine months out of those two years in a military hospital, wounded by an exploding device, specifically, a grenade in September of '68. I was staring at it, watching it go off, Casey. I consider myself the luckiest man in the world to be able to sit here and talk to you. I was wounded from head to toe from a large piece of shrapnel that went through my flak jacket and into my chest cavity. I suffered thirty-seven holes in my legs, a severe wound to my left hip, lost sight in my left eye, had the end of my nose cut off, and a severely damaged left hand and fingers."

7. What did you learn from the war?

"War is bad, really, really bad. But some wars are necessary. For example, Hitler needed to be stopped and the only way for him to be stopped was to be defeated. But wars are fought for political and economical reasons, Casey. I do not want to see that happen. When you lose someone, Casey, you don't just lose that person. You lose a part of yourself, and the worst part is the ripple effect of watching families suffer along with you. I do fully support defending ourselves from any terrorist threat, without a doubt in my mind."

8. Based on your experience, what advice would you give to young men and women joining the service?

"I support them 100 percent. Not everybody has to be a Grunt like I was. In my service, Casey, it took nine people to support that person—doctors, cooks, etc. But to serve this country is one of the greatest honors there is, and you carry that for the rest of your life, anywhere you go.

"I'd tell them, 'Be quiet and listen. It will probably save your life.'"

9. Are you involved in any charities?

"Yes, mostly nonprofit. I do give to organizations, but I am very involved in one non-profit and it is Vietnam-related. I am involved as a volunteer with a non-profit, NGO (Non-governmental organization) named PeaceTrees Vietnam, located in Seattle, Washington. Their goal and mission is to bring healing, whether emotionally or physically, prosperity where there is poverty, and to help a war-ravaged country recover. PeaceTrees Vietnam (PTVN) was the first humanitarian organization to be allowed into the country for projects to help children and citizens after the 'American War.'

"Here's the history behind it, Casey. A woman named Ray Cheney had two children, Dan and Jerilyn. Dan was a helicopter pilot in Vietnam. Jerilyn is a world-known baker. Well, Dan was shot down and killed in '71. Jerilyn went to live in Vietnam for two years trying to find peace for herself, her brother, and her family. She wanted to understand what took place in a country so far away that took her brother's life. Jerilyn then came home to Seattle, Washington, and started PeaceTrees Vietnam with her mother.

"They build kindergartens and libraries, but most of all, building community in Quang Tri province, located in the central highlands of Vietnam. PTVN also funds full-time ordnance disposal teams to locate and destroy unexploded ordnance, which continue to maim and kill children and citizens of Vietnam. We lose a child a month to these unexploded munitions left over from several nations and the wars they fought there.

"You can visit their website at www.peacetreesvietnam.org."

10. What are your thoughts on the VA scandal?

"First of all, it makes me very, very sad. I don't feel that I know enough about it, Casey, to make any in-depth comment. But it makes me sad if what is being said is in fact true, then it has to be fixed immediately. It is just unacceptable, Casey, it's just unacceptable."

11. What did you do upon leaving the service?

"After being honorably discharged from the Marines in July of 1969, I enrolled in a two-year college, and in January of 1970, I was appointed as a deputy sheriff for the Scott County Sheriff's Office in Davenport, Iowa. I achieved the rank of sargeant and resigned in good standing in 1977, and then moved to Florida, where once again I entered college: Palm Beach Junior College. I have an AA in Theater, and in 1980, I was chosen from an audition process to receive a one-year acting apprenticeship at the Burt Reynolds Dinner Theater in Jupiter, Florida. It was also in '80 that I made my film debut in *Cannonball Run*. I graduated in January of 1981 and moved to Los Angeles to continue my film and theater career. I retired from the film industry in 2004.

"In 1981, I co-founded the Palm Beach County Chapter #25, of Vietnam Veterans of America, a national organization that serves the needs of all Veterans.

"I am currently a volunteer, donor/sponsor for an N.G.O., non-profit, located in Seattle, Washington. PeaceTreesVietnam's mission is to help heal the wounds of war to all. PTVN builds libraries, kindergartens, and housing for victims of exploding ordnance, left over from previous wars and by several nations. My goal in sponsoring a kindergarten and a library dedicated to Jesse Griego and Pat Lucero, respectively, who both died in 1968, was to try and turn something very bad into something very good. It has brought peace to many, and the children, who would not otherwise have a chance at an education, now have the building blocks to do just that and a place to continue their learning skills. I was able to find my peace. I am currently a sponsor for another library to be built in Mo O Village, Vietnam. Fundraising is going well and can be monitored at: www.peacetreesvietnam.org.

"Just look for the Joe Rowe Campaign/Mo O library."

Casey Titus is a fifteen-year-old eighth grader at Florida Virtual School (FLVS) and lives in Jupiter, Florida.

Lou Caviglia/
by Gloria Pape Caviglia

Epiphany of Maturity

Graduation Day, 1965. I'm on top of the world. A full-time job, second shift at the IBM Corporation awaits me. It doesn't matter that it's on the assembly line; the pay and benefits will help support my widowed mom and two younger brothers. The company may even offer to train me in computer technology.

As I try out my best mature face in the mirror, my reverie is broken when my family beckons. The four of us walk the five blocks from our apartment to the high school.

One thousand days will pass before a town called Phu Lam changes my life. Forever.

My first year anniversary at IBM was fast approaching, as was my draft status. Rather than wait for the inevitable, I enlisted. My theory was that, although enlisting meant three years instead of two, at least I could choose where I wanted to be. I chose Army Hawk Missile System Maintenance and began basic training at Fort Dix in August 1966.

My assignment after basic was at Fort Bliss missile training. I was one of the top three students in my class and was assigned to be an instructor. I stayed there in that position for thirteen months before I decided to aim for additional skills relevant for IBM—namely, data processing. I had high hopes that when I returned from the service, I would qualify for a better position at a higher salary. After all, I had my family to support.

After graduation at the two-month school at Fort Ben Harrison, I received orders to report for duty in Vietnam. Before my journey began, I was given leave to visit with family and friends.

It was all too short, with many words left unsaid. What if I didn't return? How would my mom support herself and my younger brothers? They had always relied on me, and now here I was going into the unknown across the world. My heart was heavy, but I had no choice. Even now, it is a pain-filled memory.

Two weeks later I arrived in Phu Lam, assigned to the Phu Lam Signal Battalion of the 1st Signal Brigade.

Phu Lam was a large village with schools, churches, stores, and the like. Because of the Phu Lam Canal, it was also the hub for the movement of rice from the southeast to Saigon.

My job at Battalion HQ was to take care of the electronics parts for American military communications. I settled in with the rest of the guys—working our shifts, dealing with the occasional attacks, and going off-base into Saigon ten kilometers away on free days. It was risky, but base "cabin fever" was the less favorable alternative.

The village was also dangerous at times, more so during evening hours. When we couldn't take the green school bus into Saigon, we'd walk around Phu Lam during daylight, checking it out and taking pictures.

It was on one such excursion that some friends and I stumbled upon a makeshift "children's home." This brick house was "home" to approximately twelve children and a few volunteer "mama-sans" who took turns feeding and caring for these children orphaned by the calamities of war. The mama-sans saw it as their duty to volunteer their time. Clothing and food was provided by donations from the local Church of St. Jude's parishioners. Offerings consisted of shirts with no buttons, pants without zippers, and small handkerchiefs of rice. Poor giving to the poorer.

I knew poverty, but this was beyond even my experience. We walked back to the base in silence, wiping our eyes and blaming the heat and the dust.

No one spoke about our discovery until that evening when my buddy Pat, a professional photographer from California before being drafted, spoke up.

"Hey guys, pay days are charity days, so why not ask the men for some money to help support those kids? Lou, you're the great convincer, so why don't you try getting permission from the colonel?"

A week later, the colonel, his Vietnamese interpreter, and myself climbed into his jeep so that he could see for himself what we were up to.

We proposed that the American soldiers would set up a charity fund to pay the mama-sans with a Vietnamese teacher's salary to care for and educate the children. This would insure that the little ones would have some continuity in their disrupted lives. The American soldiers' charity fund would also pay for food for the mama-sans to cook healthy meals for them as well. I was elected the operations manager for this endeavor.

A teacher's salary in Vietnam was good money by Vietnamese standards, so the mama-sans were enthusiastic, to say the least.

We soldiers, especially the ones with kids back home, took it upon ourselves to visit the children on our free time. We played games with them, fed them, rocked them to sleep, and loved them. We were the closest thing to a dad or big brother that they had and, in some way, we felt that we *belonged* with them. They filled a void in our not-so-certain lives, as much as we partially filled the void left by war in theirs.

One child in particular whom the mama-sans named **hoa của tôi** (little flower) stole my heart immediately. None of the children had names, or if they did, they had long forgotten or blocked them out. The mama-sans gave her this name because she was so delicate. Little Flower couldn't have been more than two and a half to three years old with shiny, straight, black hair cut into a pageboy and the largest, darkest almond-shaped eyes one had ever seen. She was always smiling, belying whatever tragedy she may have experienced.

Little Flower loved to be cuddled by me, and I loved cuddling her as well. She would be dressed in the standard Vietnamese child's clothing—pajama-like tops and bottoms, cloth with mat-soled little shoes. Every time I arrived, she would run with her arms out to greet me, as if begging me to pick her up. Without hesitation I would scoop her up and hug her.

She loved cherry-flavored lollipops, and I would bring them whenever I could. Of course, she loved chocolate as well, and whatever care packages I received from home that had chocolate in them went directly to Little Flower and the other kids.

Like most toddlers, she would enjoy playing with blocks and putting together simple puzzles. The American soldiers saw to it that the children had games and toys to play with.

I bought Little Flower a small, brown teddy bear with a white belly which she immediately named "Chu-Chu." She loved sleeping with it.

I know now that I had needed Little Flower as much as she had needed me. She helped me to grow and to experience a love that I, too, had been missing. I realized that I loved children very much.

Word spread quickly and soon the orphanage of twelve grew to forty-two. Soldiers would find children alone in rice fields, by a dead parent, by the side of a road, or near a ravaged home.

The orphanage of Phu Lam was more successful than we could ever have imagined.

The Pacific Stars and Stripes, an American military newspaper in Vietnam, ran an article about the orphanage and the role that the American soldiers had played in making it a success. As the operations manager, I felt a pride in myself, my comrades, and my country.

However, my time in Vietnam was coming to a close. My journey home would be the reverse of my arrival here, and Long Binh was one of the last stops in Vietnam before setting foot in the USA. Although I had many emotions coursing through me, I longed to be home and to see my family after almost a year overseas. I didn't need to try on my mature face; it was already there.

Army command had instructed MPs operating as customs officers to confiscate any and all photographs from us before we left for the USA.

As the MP opened my bag, he saw my photo album and took it out. He did say that he was sorry, but that all photos had to be taken and not returned.

I watched as a piece of my heart was taken from me, and then I walked to my plane, bound for Oakland Air Force Base, USA.

It was evening when we arrived in California. An Army clerk came out to take us to our processing stations. There was no formation, no officer, and no one to salute us back in country. Where was our welcome home salute? Exhaustion and frustration hit me simultaneously. Had I really been away? It seemed so surreal. Everything that had been so-life changing for me 72 hours ago now seemed like a haunting memory. I felt a tremendous loss. All of my pictures of the children, my friends, and Vietnam were gone, but my memories will survive for the rest of my life.

It took me some five years to reconcile my experience of that chapter in my life. The mature me understands war much more clearly than the naïve me of long ago. I understand, but it doesn't erase the pain. I just learned to endure it by remembering all of the wonderful times with the children who taught me that they are the future, and we are responsible.

Lou Caviglia

Gloria Pape Caviglia is a teacher in New York State married to a Vietnam veteran. She writes poetry and stories, some of which have or will be published. Interviewing her husband Lou has been a healing journey for him. Before this, he had never spoken to her about his service time in Vietnam. Thank you for helping him work through his memories.

Jay Harden

Bramble Fire

The villagers started that bonfire with dried brambles—you know, the local jungle litter about those tiny huts of nipa palm somewhere in what used to be called Three (III) Corps half a world away from today's heartland of America where I started my return journey to Vietnam, finally ready to complete the story of my war, not knowing how it would end, only knowing I had to go and had to find out.

Some of the guys in our therapy group of veterans wanted to go back there, and in a moment of sympathy I agreed to join my friends. I was going for them, you see. Well, that is what I told myself then; I really had no other reason to go. I thought I was one of the lucky ones: an aviator. I never was actually in Vietnam, my black humor reminded me. I just flew over, let loose, and waved. Only I let loose about 60,000 pounds of iron vomit and never saw or heard a thing below, well above and serenaded by the numbing thrum of eight righteous, belching torches that gave the mighty B-52 its powerful reach. I did this 63 times, my log says. And that makes over 3 million pounds of shrapnel I left in the ground of Vietnam and surely many unknown pounds into the human flesh of Vietnam, too.To be completely truthful, I had no definite proof whatsoever that any person was ever hurt by my hand, but in the 45 years since, that dog just doesn't hunt anymore.

It is so easy to be young and to be motivated and to be challenged to do something that seems impossible, like directing a 450,000-pound bomber from a tiny Pacific island and climbing 5 miles high to find a tanker and a target box 3 miles wide and 6 long at a precise unchangeable time and then return all of us back safely over a 5,000-mile rumble of destruction and death. When I thought then about doing that, and even when I think of it now, that accomplishment I sought and repeated over and over again seems an impossible imagining of fantasy suitable only for video games and comic books.

But now is now, not then, and with every passing year, I think on what I did and what it meant to my country, but mostly of what it meant and did to me.

I did what I did and I did it deliberately and consciously, despite my young lack of awareness and wisdom disconnected from the created events below. So I can't claim I was mistaken or dumb or simply following the orders given by people I trusted, even though destiny may disagree.

Over the years, it has been a heavier and heavier burden to bear, which only tells me I can no longer successfully ignore my past. There is no place to run and hide, no sport or drug or bottle or relationship or job. For a time, I followed the well-meant conventional wisdom: stop dwelling on the past;

what's done is done; forget about it; get over it; get back to work; and for God's sake stop talking about it, etc., *ad nauseam*. That strategy leaves no room for either conversation or understanding or even the silent ear of empathy, and that didn't work for me anymore, and maybe not for anyone seeking their own freedom from then.

Maybe, that is why I am now on the ground in Vietnam, supporting my searching combat brothers, uncertain about what is to happen, supposing that simply my presence as their witness is enough. I am happy to do that for them, for I know they would do it for me, though my long flight over was not easy. I have little tolerance for travelers who share their cell conversations with the world and no sympathy either for loud teenagers snapping gum. Some uneasy things I just cannot abide as I age from once vibrant youth. I run from these kinds of people I judge, and their upsetting stresses I don't understand.

The brambles make a bright fire and crackle and spit for attention, drawing your mind into contemplative flames, but those flames could not be fed to fruition without some serious logs that somehow arced by muscle into that glowering glow. The fire became a gradual brilliant inferno illuminating every dark shadow as night quickly swallowed the village. I got the gradual feeling that whoever planned this has a serious agenda in mind. Once again, so many years later, I have walked into something unexpected and misdirected, the very emotion that B-52 navigators fear most: being temporarily disoriented, then finally lost. The holy grail of navigation is to always know precisely where you are, where you are going, and all that will happen in between. The unholy catastrophe to a navigator is to be deceived long enough to never find your way back home.

I sat on the periphery of the fire circle upon a makeshift bamboo stool dented into the hardpan of walked earth made smooth by decades, perhaps generations, of villagers. Scattered among the hundred or so Vietnamese were the combat brothers I traveled with and others I did not.

The villagers served food and drink and danced a greeting with simple, screechy music and drums, and seemed genuinely nice to their American guests, even gentle, as though they had forgiven us and forgotten, the very same things I had tried and failed to do for decades alone in our amnesiac nation.

Across the fire and through the flames appeared a big American who must have organized the whole thing. His booming voice, framed by a full shock of silver hair, matched a rugged frame, and he spoke with authority and hinted wisdom in English and also in Vietnamese. His words make clear what was about to happen. My blood slowed and my body trembled beneath the skin as I came to understand what my combat brothers were about to do.

The big American spoke out in Vietnamese, and soon an old man about my age rose, stepped forward, and talked to the fire in a cracking, rising, and descending voice between long pauses. According to the translation, he accused one of the Americans of attacking his village during the war, killing two Viet Cong suspects, and burning his home. He told how he screamed that his invalid father was bedridden inside and could not be moved, but, of course, the fog of war does not provide instant translators on site in the midst of battle, so his aged father was burned alive by the American now standing before him—both held in my view by the flames.

The pathos of the villager and the anguish of my veteran buddy were fully exposed to all of us by the fire and their words. And the big American, clearly an experienced and non-judgmental facilitator, guided these two fragile humans through a communication that seemed like mystical theater to me, for in those horrible, beautiful moments, two foes looked with locked gazes and, by some miracle of translation, came to exchange their stories and understand each other completely. And then, in a slow and sacred *denoue-ment* of rewarded tears and fears and hate and regret and action and inaction, they forgave and released each other, and clasped hands. There, in the light of that bramble-fed fire, the failure and forgiveness of two human beings found an end and created a free, innocent beginning.

I felt privileged to witness the end of their private, intimate war by the unconditional surrender of both sides to unvarnished truth, not at all realizing this scene was merely my preparation.

In that mental interlude before the bramble fire, my seeking mind (per-haps my heart) seemed to bend time and sense the back story of the American facilitator and his process of compassion that I later confirmed from him.

He had been down his own very lonely road to understand and then to forgive himself, and only then to find a way back to his enemy, tell his story, and offer to make amends. He discovered, quite by surprise, the actuality of forgiveness by his enemy and the unexpected release both gained that can only be understood—to the extent it can be understood at all—within the experience. This new power compelled him to refine his process into a cer-emony and offer it to others wounded like him beneath appearance, beneath the skin.

For the big American had done an unconscionable thing in the war, unacceptable to all American honor. In a fuel of rage at the explosion of his best friend's head standing beside him, in the drenching taste of his blood and brains, the big American had sprayed automatic fire into the village and killed a defenseless Vietnamese child, a little girl with open, innocent eyes, only four years old, her face an eternal companion in his dreams.

As the village night grew long, more ceremonies of testimony followed between native accusers and foreign accused: a massacre; a summary execu-tion; a flawed tactical plan; and other examples of the classic regretted mis-takes of war, universally unintended and unable to be undone.

Still I sat there on the edge of the fire, still feeling apart from their first-hand stories on the ground still unrelated to my own war experience high and untouchable above them all.

Soon a Vietnamese woman stood up and told a very different story, a story of her own people and her family. She told of the North Vietnamese Army coming one night with a few Viet Cong, demanding that the village actively fight Americans. One NVA officer told the village elder, her father, at gunpoint, to order his village to comply, but the old man refused. The major said every woman would be raped, then killed, one by one, until the village complied. Still, her father disagreed. So the officer dragged his 12-year-old daughter into the nearby jungle and raped her as she screamed in terror and pleaded with him and her father. The elder submitted to the NVA and the village complied, so the daughter was spared death.

Then the woman softly said: "I am that girl." In her pained silence, the American facilitator asked gently, "What did that act do to you?" And she told them all for the first time in eloquent intimacy of her lost worth and trust in others and of her present understanding that forgetting is different from forgiving.

Then she pointed and said, "I see that man here. There is the major who raped me and gave my father the reason to kill himself." She screamed out, "Stand in the light before me and tell what you did. Explain yourself! Tell us all of it here, and tell all of it true."

That man stepped confidently from the shadow and stood across from the woman. I could see the black coil around his forearm that looked like the habu I once found in our wheelwell, removing the gear locking pins. "Yes, I did what you said and I will tell you why. This is my story. I do not need your forgiveness. I did nothing wrong, the same as any man here would do in my situation. I did what you described for the same reason as all my other acts back then. I was at war with the running dog Americans and would do anything to drive them out of my country—and we did, didn't we? I never felt more powerful, never more alive than then. I have no regrets and would do it all again. And this, your accusation, is merely a trifle. Only the strong survive in this world."

The big American facilitator said nothing more in the growing tension, then gradual quiet, that followed the major's words. Soon, the two returned again to their previous places around the fire as the collective silent understanding of mothers and wives, daughters and sons, uncles and grandfathers made permanent the major's incurable public wound, but, by heard community, healed her shame and pain with a forgiveness earned by the telling.

And then the big American said to the gathering, "Are there any others who wish to speak?" For a time, the only sound was popping from the occasional freshly tossed bramble, tiny reminders of awareness and the ephemeral importance of rare opportunity.

Finally another villager said, "I have nowhere else to speak this and no

American to say it to, but I will talk of my village not far from here in the evening of September 22, 1968, just before dusk. The bombs fell in one great stunning, stitching string outside our village, creeping up toward us. It lasted only a few seconds. As I was running from the field toward home, I watched the last one explode on the house I built. My wife was bringing water from the river and I was supposed to be tending our new son inside…." Then, as the translator caught up with his words, his voice faded to a murmur, and the man fell to his knees, head on the ground, weeping his decades of unspoken, unresolved loss, guilt, and aimless rage.

Then, in a burst of remarkable possibility, the big American asked if there was anyone present to stand and accept this man's testimony.

I don't know where the bolt moving me came from. Without thinking, I stood and walked to the man, then told him my story. I remembered that day, that B-52 mission, that one time, that one navigation error of mine, that moment of searing doubt when I realized I had flipped the coordinates and entered the similar seconds of target latitude and longitude backward in the computer. But that was too late, after bombs away. The next day, target intelligence told me how far I missed the target box, told me we only destroyed a rice paddy. But I viewed our strike photos later by myself and saw one bomb crater too near the other village huts.

I was predictably reprimanded in front of the wing commander, but allowed to keep flying, grateful for no court-martial. This was wartime and we were short of bomber crews. I was never promoted again and eventually left the service, though my memories never did.

One of the great cruelties in war is that you never know anything for certain; you never know your part of the bigger picture; you never know what happened after you decided and acted; you never know if someone lived or died because of what you did or failed to do; you never know even their names. Doubt is its own devil.

I looked back and forth at the villager and the translator, finally saying to the entire gathering in my most inelegant words (beyond exact recall) that I was responsible for what happened. I made that navigation decision, that unforgivable error, and his child died.

There I stood in that moment, naked in guilt, ashamed to be human. I was ready to die and that, I suppose, gave me a little pause of peace, because my trembling began to fade and a strange ease fell over me. I raised my head, then reached down, helping the villager up. I didn't decide to do this; it just happened, as a waterfall flows. And so we stood there, eye-to-eye, connected without words as the soft flicker of fire washed his face and I saw him clearly, no longer identical to all Vietnamese. I saw him as unique as me.

Time again paused for something to happen.

Then I continued and explained that I, and no one else, was responsible for what I did and what happened to his child. That was not my intention, I said. My intention on that mission was to destroy my enemy's will to fight and to help my combat brothers on the ground, nothing more. I told him I did not do this to satisfy a personal vengeance. I told him if I could, I would change the past and somehow save his son. I told him of my own fatherhood, of my own loss of a child— not to minimize his hurt, but to share a common one.

Finally, standing there bleached colorless by unrelenting flames, I asked what I could do for him. I stood there remembering, accompanied by the silence of the gathering, the crackling brambles, and a dawning clarity, less alone. Whatever happened next, I had already gained a sliver of something, even if a screaming humiliation or physical attack followed.

There I saw him as simply another suffering human being. I knew his pain was not so much about the other person, me, or about the traumatic events beyond his control that connected us. I knew his pain, like mine, was internal and self-directed, even if he did not. I told him the heart of the matter, the heart of his anguish: "This tragedy is not your fault. You did nothing wrong." His eyes blinked, struggling to comprehend that new truth beyond the facts. I said it again, slower for translation, then again, and again. Slowly, his face opened up and his eyes flooded away the relief of decades. He knew. At last, he knew that he simply needed to be heard. And I knew it, too.

Once more, time skipped away from me, and the man gestured with an open hand and uttered the most remarkable and unexpected words ever wished for. "You, American," he said, "you and I are much the same. We seek something tonight. You, American, I forgive. You deserve no blame. I tell you, American, you meant me no wrong. War makes us all suffer no matter what we do, isn't it so?"

Our communication in fire was all so simple, so stunning in its spare beauty. His look transformed from grief to profound relief, almost a joy crinkling at the edge of his eyes. I saw the weight of years lifting off his shoulders, and he looked taller to me and stronger than before. Perhaps he saw me changed, too, as much as I felt changed.

As we stood there in the flaming bramble light, I nodded and put my left hand on his right shoulder. Then he smiled and slowly placed his left palm in the center of my chest, and our embrace became inevitable.

You could say that villager and I came to this jungle, this night, in this firelight, in this moment of our lifetimes, to realize the same strange truth. You could say we both understood a great shared learning in words. You could say we both found our different ways out of hell.

The great change I found for me that night was really about the very secret, deep, and unexpressed fear of my dangerousness, that core fear so well disguised, unknown even to those who loved me most and still do. All the irrational, stupid misery I've held onto since my war was still eating me slowly, damaging my private respect, and keeping me from the man I expected to be.

That fear of myself, my greatest darkness, is gone. There is no longer that shadow in me I dread. All my effort to fix me is unnecessary, replaced by a new energy drawn toward light, indifferent to the past, a slow, sweet ease my thoughts and body welcome—and no words can express it. Now I can be without care, without old wounds, relaxed as in sleep, yet awake, as if life met death inside me and settled their conflict.

After our shared ceremony about that fire, I accepted the truth that my soul not only survived the war, but remained intact all along. There I learned my true story: I have the power to forgive myself and reclaim who I am and my connection to the world. My life is simply a matter of continuous belief in me, a belief that I can accept the affection of others with a gentle ease and return it the same.

"What's past is prologue," Shakespeare said. This day and the days to come are my proof. I am alive again, brightened by one star-filled night of bramble fire in a once dark jungle, gone.

Mr. Harden retired from government science after combat in Vietnam. He has lived in Georgia, California, Massachusetts, Missouri, Virginia, Guam, Thailand, and Okinawa; wandered to Japan, Sri Lanka, Bhutan, England, Mexico, Panama, France, and Italy; and studied yoga in India extensively. He still travels and writes mostly of love, war, childhood, and personal growth, favoring poetry, essay, children's books, family history, and lyrics. You can see some of his early photography and writing at http://www.jayharden.com.

Katherine Bell

The Sulphur Sink

Every night, we boil our tap water so that it's hot for baths. The water goes into the cheap aluminum pots I bought at a yard sale, and we watch as it rolls and bubbles on the stove. We put oven mitts on our hands and slowly carry the pots up the stairs one-by-one from the kitchen to the bathroom, where we pour the water into the tub and watch it steam up a big cloud as it meets the air. Then we do it all over again, until we have enough warm water to soap up our bodies and clean the specks and grains of dirt off our skin.

My daughters don't complain, but sometimes I wish they did. I know they want to be normal and have a mom who doesn't wake them up in the middle of the night with her screams. They'd rather have a mother who doesn't forget what time they need to be picked up after school or which of them is the one who likes to go to the library every weekend. But they don't complain about me. They don't complain about anything.

Two weeks after we bought the house, the hot water heater stopped working, and I couldn't afford to buy another one. One week later, it rained. That was when we learned that the roof had holes no one told us about. There was one hole about the size of my fist, which would push rain through like a funnel. We put a bucket underneath and switched it out regularly whenever it rained, but the other holes, the tiny pinprick holes, made a mist and turned our upstairs bedroom into a rainforest. Then, in September, the first frost of the year cracked our siding, and we could feel the wind on the inside whenever it would blow on the outside.

One day in November, my youngest, Denise, brought home a book called *Little House on the Prairie.* I was sitting at the kitchen table, waiting for the oven to warm so I could put in the store-bought pizza. Denise dropped the book in my lap. "I'm just like Laura," she said.

I reached for the book, thumbed through its pages. "What do you mean?"

"It's like living in the old days," she said. I didn't understand why she was smiling so proudly. "We can make do with less. Laura didn't even have running water."

She twisted her brunette curls around her finger. Her pink shirt was just barely too small for her, and her jeans were ripping apart at the knees. "Oh honey," I said. Her smile faded away and I couldn't look at her anymore. She left me sitting at the table alone with her book in my hand.

The wind was fiercest in January, and the four of us had to snuggle together in my bed to sleep where it would be warm. It reminded me of Fort Jackson, the nights the unit—especially me, Max, Maria, and Swanson—would stay up too late seeing who could do the most shots without throwing up, and falling asleep wherever we passed out, all despite our 04:30 First Call. My daughters will never know about that part of me.

I would wake them up every morning with a new round of screams. Jenny, my oldest, shook me awake each morning. I would come to in her arms with the last scream on my breath and freeze, paralyzed from the mix of the dream-world and reality colliding and coagulating in my brain. One night I dreamed she was alongside me in the Humvee wearing a flak jacket and kevlar helmet. When the IED exploded, like it does every night in my sleep, I lost my grip on her wrist, and she started sliding away from me, dead or dying.

When Jenny woke me up, I didn't know where I was, and I couldn't stop screaming, but finally I realized I was in bed and she was safe. I hugged her so tight I thought her internal organs might implode, but she didn't push me away. She just hugged me back and stroked my hair and whispered in my ear. "It'll be okay, Mom. You'll be just fine." The rest of that night, I couldn't shake my reality away from my dreams, so I hid away in the living room, enveloped in blankets and reading *Little House on the Prairie* to keep myself awake.

It seemed that the things I wanted to remember I forgot, and the things that I wanted to forget stayed with me. Those phone calls: "Mom, where are you? Lucy's play starts in thirty minutes." "Mom, you need to go to the grocery store today." "Mom, I'm not going to be home for dinner tonight, so please don't forget to take your medicine." Jenny's memory is strong because mine is not. Some evenings I had to run out the door, remembering just at the last minute that I had to attend Denise's Mathlete competition or Lucy's theater production.

Lucy wants to be a dancer. She's tall, slim, and graceful like one, but I can't afford to buy her dance lessons and the troupe in town doesn't offer scholarships. She tried to learn on her own—watching lessons on YouTube in the library after school, taking notes, and practicing on the makeshift barre she built out of aluminum cans and duct tape in the basement. It's not the same, though, as being a part of a dance company and learning with other girls. That's why it has been so important for me to be there for her, and it hurts when my brain allows me to forget how much dance and performance mean to her.

When I was deployed for fifteen months, they lived with their father because the court ordered him to provide custody. Living with that man for over a year must have been enough for them to be happier with me in the cold and the filth of a broken-down house. I've faced bomb-strapped Iraqis, but I can't ask my daughters what happened while I was gone. The bits and pieces they've shared have made me uneasy, and I imagine that they were fighting a war with their father while I was fighting a war in a foreign country. Still, they had hot water.

They also had salads and cookies and pocket change to buy candy and magazines. They had internet, wifi, and cable. Jenny saved up for a few pedicures. Denise could purchase her own books, rather than be a slave to the library. Lucy bought a leotard and ballet slippers. They may not have had much, but at least they had some material comforts. It's more than I can do for them.

Only once did I suggest they move back in with him. I was instantly silenced by three pleading looks around the dinner table. "No, Mom," Denise said. "I don't want to go back there. I want to stay here with you." She left her seat, pried open my arms, and forced herself between them. As I brushed her hair out of her eyes, I knew she would never tolerate such a suggestion again. Jenny and Lucy stood and joined the bear hug. Together we all felt whole. The kitchen around us was so silent I could almost hear their thoughts. We were different members of the same team. Team Harrison. I stifled the urge to shout "HOOAH" at the dinner table.

While I spent most of the winter cold and screaming, the worst day was Valentine's Day. It marked the date of my divorce to the kids' father. It stood as a yearly reminder of the two soldiers in my unit that we lost that day. Danny O'Heren would celebrate his third birthday without his mother and my best friend, Maria, for the second year in a row because she was one of the ones we lost. Throughout the day, I vacillated between sleep and distraction, between pillows and *On the Banks of Plum Creek.* I had trouble staying focused on the pages, but whenever I would close my eyes, I would hear the roar of the IED as it tore through the convoy and upended our Humvee.

I'd see the way Maria's face changed in seconds from laughter to seriousness to pain. When I looked down and there was a crimson mess where her left leg had been, I remember that I gaped at it before taking action, and it felt like I was in some Hollywood movie where the camera was zooming in and out and going from slow to fast motion without stopping. The Humvee came to rest on its side in a dusty rut about twenty miles south of Baghdad. Sun streamed in as Max pried the door open for our rescue. I refused to let go of Maria, so the bulkiest soldier, Norton, with Max's assistance pulled us both out of the transport and went back for the others. I couldn't even tell him who else was alive. I hadn't looked at anyone but Maria.

With the girls at school, I had no one to keep watch over me, so I mourned Maria in my own way, opening the photo album we'd made together with photos from Basic, one of the ones we rushed to finish after we got our deployment orders. Maria's mother kept one album. I stole the other from her house after the funeral. It is a tiny piece of the reason I neglected to call her husband and son that day.

I counted the hours I had left until my daughters would come home from school. Finally they did, Jenny with a bouquet of roses, Lucy with a box of chocolate, and Denise with a bag full of cards and candy. Did I send her to school with Valentines to hand out to the others? Jenny saw me frowning and went to the coffee table to retrieve the box of red and pink-hearted Valentine cards that I'd forgotten we picked up at the dollar store. My muscles relaxed; I felt better. "Did you girls have a good day?"

Lucy handed me the box, a medium-sized red heart. "This is for you, Mom." She set it in my lap. I brushed my hand over the embossed packaging and tore the plastic away.

"Do you know how long it's been since I had a piece of chocolate?"

The girls nodded. "Since you bought the house." Jenny looked around the living room. She saw the paint on the ceiling that was chipped and peeling. She looked at the used purple couch which clashed with the Goodwill-purchased teal armchair, and she knew the coffee table was small enough to be an end table. I know she did, because that's what I saw every time I looked through the living room. We had a TV stand, but we didn't have a TV. It had become a coat rack for the girls to lay their tattered outerwear upon when they came home.

"What are you going to try first?" Lucy's voice brought me back to myself. I glanced from her to the box, and removed the lid and brown paper layer of protection. All of the pieces were either light or dark brown with two pieces of white chocolate mixed in between. They were shiny, gleaming chocolates, and I could feel my mouth water as I looked them over.

"Which one would you recommend?"

Without hesitation, Denise stepped forward and pointed to a round, light-colored truffle. So I picked it up and popped it in my mouth. The minute it started melting, I felt something I hadn't felt in a long time, something hard to describe, but the closest I could come would be happiness. It was fleeting, lasting only a few seconds, but it felt real. That feeling might never show up again.

I handed the girls the box, they chose their morsels with consideration and thoughtfulness. They weighed their options and chose strategically, trying to maximize the flavors of chocolate that each person could taste. I watched as Denise took control, speaking to the principles of division and reason. "If there are twenty candies total and there are four of us, then we each get five. Mom and I don't like white chocolate, so by default, Jenny and Lucy each get one of the white ones. That leaves nine milk and nine dark. But, Lucy, you don't like dark, so the rest of your four are milk. There are five milk left and three people. Who likes milk just a little more than dark?"

As she talked, she lit up. Math was easy. She could use facts to reach a decision. I wondered how such a smart girl could be related to me, the woman who relied so heavily on instinct to make decisions in a war-zone. I prayed Denise would never have to face making a decision about whether to save her best friend or to protect herself. With that kind of choice, I never even had a chance to think.

Jenny called me on my cell phone during my VA appointment. The brick lit up and danced around in my pocket as I was sliding my pants over my hips, ready to make the two hour drive back home. I reached down, grabbed it, and answered.

"Mom, you need to come home," Jenny said. It was a command and an order.

"I just finished up at the VA, and I should be home by seven." I wanted to stay calm.

I could hear her sigh. She knew there was nothing more to ask of me. "I'll see you then," she said.

While I pulled the phone from my ear, I heard her add, "I love you." I would have said it back, but it was too late. I was already pushing the button to end the call.

The one comfort in our lives was the car. It was a relatively new sedan, but picking up miles quicker than I'd liked from all the trips back and forth to the VA hospital. It was the one thing I got to keep in the divorce. Once a week, I would take a bucket of suds and soap and scrub the interior and exterior of the car. It was mine. I would do whatever it took to keep it looking nice and new as long as possible.

I drove up and down the mountain roads, through the budding oak, red maple, and cherry trees, until I made it back home as the sun set. Our twisted gravel-paved driveway, sinister as the shadows fell, led to the house, which looked clean and stately on the outside, disguising the problems on the inside. From the way Jenny had spoken to me on the phone, I knew that nothing good would greet me as soon as I opened it. After I killed the engine, I sat in the driver's seat psyching myself up. "Come on, soldier. You can do this. You've been through so much, one more little thing won't kill you. Let's GO SOLDIER! HOOAH!" I was my own drill sergeant.

Before I got out of my car, I took one deep breath and let it out slowly. Then I walked from my car, up the front steps, and pushed open the wooden door. All of the lights downstairs shone brightly, but those upstairs were dark. Through the illuminated hallway and into the kitchen, I crept, listening for my daughters' hushed whispers that quieted as I approached.

They all sat around the kitchen table, Denise looked from Lucy to Jenny as though she was the mastermind behind whatever plan they'd concocted. Lucy's hands were folded in her lap, but I could hear her picking at her fingernails. Jenny wouldn't look at me, with her hands crossed over her chest.

"What is it?" I looked from daughter to daughter.

"See for yourself." Jenny stood. She walked past me to the sink and turned it on.

Something yellowish sprayed everywhere, like an invisible thumb was pressing up against the spigot. It reached the ceiling, dripped over our cabinets and the floor.

"STOP!" I yelled, and turned off the faucet. Then it hit me. The rotten egg sulfur stench. It came in through my nostrils and burned my eyes. Immediately, I flashed back to Iraq, back to the time when I was trying to push Maria's patella back into her leg so that I could make sure she'd have her kneecap when the medics came for her. Her skin turned white as each drop of blood hit the sand. She knew she was losing too much blood. She pulled me close. "Take care of your girls," she said. I said nothing. I focused on tying off what was left of her leg to stem the bleeding, but we both knew it would be a waste. That stench hit me, the chemicals in the IED smelled like gut rot and I teared up for the wrong reason. Maria cried. She babbled incoherently until I placed a finger across her lips. Then she cried, and I just cradled her head and cried with her, shaky, ugly and harsh. I will never forget that she died with tears in her eyes that moistened my fingers as I closed them.

Then I was standing in the kitchen with the smell lingering in my nose and tears streaming down my face. My girls stared at me, frozen in time. They didn't know what to do next. I didn't know what to do next. The sobs came fast, faster than I was expecting, and I sank to the floor, on my knees as if in prayer. I didn't have anyone to pray to, though, but that one action prompted my girls to move. They joined me on the floor. Denise grabbed my right arm; Lucy grabbed my left. Jenny came over. She sat down right in front of me and crossed her legs. She took each of her sister's hands, forming a circle.

"Mom," she said. Her voice was even and calming.

Denise looked up at me, her eyes wide. "We need some help, Mom."

"We can't live like this anymore," Jenny said.

I nodded and wiped the tears from my cheeks. "I'm so sorry, girls. I'm so sorry."

Even though they knew they deserved more, they loved me anyway. Lucy rested her head on my shoulder. Then, for what felt like hours, we sat together like that, in a circle on the kitchen floor, and made plans for the future.

Katherine Bell is the daughter of a Navy veteran and granddaughter of two World War veterans. Currently she works with the military non-profit Operation Homefront as a Public Relations Assistant. She obtained her Bachelor of Arts in Creative Writing from the University of Tennessee in 2010 and has worked with writers Margaret Lazarus Dean, Tom Paine, and James Mathews. She writes and maintains a blog called "We Write Together" with her boyfriend and writing partner.

Frederick W. Cutter

Something's Wrong

The airfield of Pope Air Force Base rose into view as trees and build-ings flew past at over a hundred miles an hour. The Boeing 737 shuddered as it touched down, promising a return to a normal life, as though I should be coming home. My wife Constance now waited for me at the passenger terminal in the same self-designed, home-sewn dress she had worn for all my return flights.

We had come to call it her Welcome Home dress.

Cheers erupted when the aircraft stopped and the seatbelt light switched off. The anticipation set off yet another throbbing headache.

I kept my seat as soldiers clad in desert camouflage uniforms exited the plane. Something was wrong. I couldn't put my finger on it.

Something was very wrong.

I stepped outside and squinted in the mid-August sun that scorched the airfield. Ripples of heat blasted the air as I staggered down the steps. I almost lost balance and fell. I stared at the concrete, my head spun. Again. My eyes focused, and I was back in southern Iraq staring at an ocean of sand inter-rupted only by highway asphalt. I climbed into the passenger seat of the convoy gun truck as Aguilar took the driver's seat, once again frustrated he lost the "paper, rock, scissors" drill over who would drive on our return con-voy from Al Basrah into Kuwait on the Highway of Death. I couldn't breathe from the overpowering heat inside the vehicle. The roar of the vehicle's engines drowned out Aguilar's complaints. I laughed. Be a fuckin' man and drive us out of here.

I shoved Aguilar out of my mind. Almost home. Not quite, but almost.

A palpable energy radiated from the unit. The aircraft engines faded behind us as the welcoming crowd's cheers intensified. Wives, parents, and children waved Welcome Home banners and signs written in crayon, finger paints, watercolors, markers.

Constance stood to the left of the passenger terminal entrance, just far enough from the crowd that I noticed her, but she . . . wasn't wearing the wel-come home dress, but a violet blouse and black slacks I didn't recognize.

We stood in formation just outside the passenger hangar as the brigade deputy commander, a lieutenant colonel, gave the welcome home speech. He stood, tall and trim, chiseled expression hardened by two decades of service, as he rambled. Great job. America owes you a debt of gratitude. You wrote a check for our freedom in your own blood. Observe a moment of silence for the fallen. Then he gave what I called the "don't beat your wife or kick your dog" safety lecture. Counselors and chaplains are here for you.

Bullshit.

My vision blurred, I barely heard the command: "Fall out!"

Finally.

Something is wrong.

The formation fell apart as the men scattered to look for their families. Constance and I embraced, and her warmth overpowered the pain in my head, for the moment.

Where is the welcome home dress?

Experience taught me we would spend another hour in the hangar to receive safety briefings, reintegration processing, and gluttonous servings of chocolate cake, oatmeal cookies, sub sandwiches, and chicken wings. I wasn't hungry.

I turned in my M4 carbine and M9 sidearm to the unit armorer, a nervous, awkward boy barely a summer out of high school. He knew nothing of the horrors of the world.

How long had Constance been rattling off the latest updates of life from home?

The commander released us from the hangar, and Constance couldn't have said it better: "Andrew, let's get the hell out of here."

Constance led me through the parking lot. Home was only twenty minutes away, a residential retreat in a gated community south of Fayetteville.

But something was wrong. This last return trip was different from the others. Most soldiers threatened to explode with joy at the prospect of coming home. I felt . . . nothing.

Something is so very wrong. I wanted to go home, but I felt nothing.

Constance suggested lunch at Calypso's. "It'll be fun," she said, her not so subtle code phrase for we are going to do this like we have after all your deployments. I wanted her to cook for me at home, and afterwards . . . but after nearly a year overseas, I was done fighting. I am done with battle. I don't have the energy left.

We reached her Hummer in the passenger terminal parking lot. "Do you want to drive?"

I shook my head.

The nearly flat sands of southern Iraq flashed by my passenger window as Constance gabbed the entire way to Calypso's about how she had redecorated my den. Aguilar wouldn't stop blabbing about how he lost the paper, rock, scissors drill for the seventh straight time. The collage of destruction left over from the first Gulf War flashed by my window—the skeletal remains of Iraqi armored tanks and vehicles. I hated driving convoys almost as much as I missed Aguilar's annoying whine over the last fifteen years of our friendship.

"I think you'll like the new décor, honey." Constance poked my shoulder to get my attention, and I recoiled. "It's everything we've talked about doing with the house."

The Calypso's parking lot and front entrance was crowded. I fought panic. I'm exposed to a hundred people I don't know, with no means to project the capability that I would defend myself against the mere perception of threat.

The restaurant had an open patio for guests that preferred the outdoor experience. I wasn't one of them, but Constance tugged me to the patio. "Honey, let's eat outside."

Calypso's changed its layout. Most of the tables still seated four but were now covered by white linen with a single rose and vase in the center. Constance followed the hostess through the post-lunch crowd. The server seated us on the patio overlooking the parking lot, where the honks of rush-hour traffic competed with the overlapping conversation of a score of other patrons.

Without looking at the menu, I ordered my Greek Delight routine: an appetizer of Saganaki and an entrée combo of Dolma, Souvlaki, Broiled Scampi, and Mousake. I had ordered that same entrée since Calypso's opened ten years ago. I looked up to ensure the waitress understood my order, and she smiled with sympathetic regret.

"That entree isn't offered anymore. Can I suggest alternates that will be just as good?"

"I'm sure you'll like the new menu," Constance said without looking up.

I ordered some random appetizer and an ice water, and waved the waitress off.

Constance evaluated the second half of the first page of entrées. I excused myself to wash the last of the deployment from my hands and face, while reaching below my seat for my weapon. It wasn't there, and I almost panicked.

Constance didn't notice.

At least the restroom was still in the same place. I washed my face. I didn't recognize my reflection. I left the restroom and stood for a moment in an air vent's heavenly current. Aguilar turned up the air conditioner in the vehicle, which blew freezing air to compete against the hellish desert heat. Sweat had soaked through my uniform, had dripped into my eyes from under my Kevlar helmet. I removed my sunglasses and wiped my face with a hand towel. Aguilar kept talking, but I couldn't hear him unless he shouted over the roar of the engine and air conditioner. A flash of orange light from his side of the vehicle . . . the highway spun upside down and my helmet slammed into the door. . .

Through the post-lunch rabble, over a dozen tables bustling with activity like a Baghdad bazaar, I could see Constance still examined the menu. My appetizer had already arrived, and she still hadn't ordered.

A year ago I would have invented conflict between the menu items to pass the time while she decided on her meal: And the house salad is having an argument with the scampi. Chocolate Martini and Doctor Pepper are arguing in the next room, I mean on the next menu page, over which should get to dip their fingers in the cheesecake. I don't need to invent any more conflict.

She didn't even notice me when I sat down.

Constance drummed her fingers on the table and rocked her head from side to side as she contemplated the menu. I reached for the Saganaki, and it was cold. I tossed it back on the appetizer tray. At least the water had ice. I picked it up, sipped, clenched the . . . the full glass shattered and water splashed on the table and soaked both our menus.

"What was that?" Constance looked up, startled, and for the first time, she was really looking at me. So were a dozen nearby patrons, their mouths half open with half chewed food, their hands frozen in mid air with forks and spoons and knives.

I realized I had squeezed the water glass just a little too hard.

"Andrew," Constance said, and she pointed at my right hand.

Blood pulsed from cuts in my palm and dripped to the floor.

I felt nothing.

I picked up the silverware linen, let the silverware clatter to the floor, and wrapped my palm. I pushed through the waiting line for the restroom. Blood soaked through the cloth when I reached the sink. I washed my hands again. The bleeding wouldn't stop. The blast shredded Aguilar's left arm, neck, and face. There was so much blood. The still-running air conditioner and my ringing ears drowned his gasps for breath or the last words he struggled to speak. I pulled him onto the highway as others from the convoy ran up to us. The light dimmed from his eyes.

Someone tapped my shoulder and asked something about whether I was okay.

I jumped and nodded. An older gentleman stood by, his gaze fixed on my palm, on the gashes that still pulsed blood that dripped into the sink.

"Are you sure? I saw what happened," the old man said.

"I should have been the driver."

"What?"

I left the bathroom. Patrons and staff stared at me.

I stood beneath the air vent. It felt almost as good as the vent in my den—the vent in the combat support hospital in Kuwait where Aguilar and I had been transported. The surgeon team rushed me out of the operating room, but I couldn't leave. I wouldn't leave. A nurse almost suffered a broken arm when he put a hand on me to escort me out.

A busboy swept my broken water glass while another toweled the stone floor. I couldn't raise my eyes from the floor of the clinic as the convoy commander himself told me Aguilar didn't make it. Nurses tended to my otherwise minor scratches that have since healed.

The manager stood beside Constance; he said something and she smiled. I waited for the busboys to leave before I returned to the table.

"How's your hand?" the manager asked. "Need a doctor?"

I held up my self-bandaged fist and shook my head.

Constance said, "Andrew, the manager here offered to comp us since you just got home. Isn't that really nice?"

"I haven't been home yet."

Constance apologized to the manager and asked him to give us a moment, but he examined me with a dark, piercing gaze, and I felt like a man accused of beating his wife.

I faced off against Constance. "Did you decide what you want to order?"

"Let's call it a day, honey. I'm sure you want to get home and clean up your hand, get some rest." She smiled. "Maybe take a shower and. . ."

"Where's your menu? I thought you wanted to be here. This is what you wanted."

Constance leaned to her left and retrieved her purse from the floor. "Honey, it's been a long day. I'll take you home." She rummaged in her purse for the car keys.

I held up my injured hand in protest, like a cop demanding the cessation of traffic. "Just one question first. Where's your welcome home dress?"

She looked at me, puzzled. "You don't remember?" She leaned forward. "Andrew, I told you maybe a month ago that the dress was ruined by the dry cleaner. We talked for, like, an hour about it."

I shook my head. What the hell is she talking about? I rubbed my temples. Another headache loomed.

"Andrew, are you okay?"

I pounded my bloodied fist on the table; the silverware rattled and the flower vase tipped over. "What kind of a dumbass question is that?"

Constance's expression froze and her eyes shadowed. "What happened to you?"

A crushing pain erupted from the back of my skull, as though a sadist squeezed my head open with a nutcracker.

She stood. "Let's go."

The manager returned to our table. "Please, you are welcome to enjoy lunch on us today."

"And why did you redecorate the house? Why the hell do you change my home!"

"Sir, please sit," the manager insisted. "You are making a scene."

Constance's eyes moistened and her lip quivered. "I promise we talked about this also, only a few weeks ago. . ."

The manager patted my shoulder. I gripped and twisted his wrist and shot my fist into his elbow as he dropped. He flopped on the floor and screamed, and I released his wrist. A nearby waiter stared wide-eyed and wailed something about calling the police. Every eye in the room was on me now . . . a woman shrieked at the manager's disfigured forearm bent back into his shoulder.

Constance recoiled as I reached for her. She pulled away.

The crowd backed away from me, stares of suspicion, of fear, of horror.

Two police cruisers and an ambulance turned into the parking lot and stopped before the entrance. A convoy of armored gun trucks roared on the highway, a quick reaction force to destroy the insurgency that infested the barren desert.

Two patrolmen approached, one with handcuffs already poised, the other aimed his weapon, as though I could care about his shaking grip and whether he would even hit me at this range.

"Sir, put your hands on your head, turn around!"

I knew then what was wrong, what was so very wrong.

I had survived.

Fred Cutter is a career soldier currently stationed at Fort Bragg, NC. He enlisted as a combat medic and later received a commission as an artillery officer. He lives in Fayetteville, NC, with his family.

Sheree K. Nielsen

jimmie (pier)

Sheree K. Nielsen is the author of *Folly Beach Dances*, a "healing coffee table book of lyrical photography and poetry where people, sandpipers, dogs, and beachside structures dance with the rhythm of the shifting sand and changing tides." An award-winning writer, photographer, and poet, her publications include *Missouri Life*, *AAA Midwest*, *Southern Traveler*, *Carolina Go!* and countless anthologies, newspapers, and websites. Follow her at www.shereenielsen.wordpress.com and on Twitter @ ShereeKNielsen and @Follybeachdance.

Jay Harden

For the Arc Light Fallen

Mr. Harden retired from government science after combat in Vietnam. He has lived in Georgia, California, Massachusetts, Missouri, Virginia, Guam, Thailand, and Okinawa; wandered to Japan, Sri Lanka, Bhutan, England, Mexico, Panama, France, and Italy; and studied yoga in India extensively. He still travels and writes mostly of love, war, childhood, and personal growth, favoring poetry, essay, children's books, family history, and lyrics. You can see some of his early photography and writing at http://www.jayharden.com.

Jay Harden

War's Shiny Things

Dominika Wrozynski

Retrieval

The desert has taken you, though right now you lie
in our bed. Your body will not cease its Hanging Man
pose, part of the tarot deck you never learned to read.

In sleep, you are louder than awake, your septum still
deviated, and I wonder how it is that you can really
come back from war. I imagine you return one limb

at a time, one joint. First your legs cease running,
then your toes spread out in sandals you haven't worn
in a year. You stop biting cuticles and allow your hands

to rest on the leather of the steering wheel, on the small
of my back, on the cat's fur. But some things take longer,
and I can't always find the quick wink. Instead there are

tendons I'm afraid will pop like over-strung guitars, sinews
that twitch at the start of a lawnmower. That's when I think
you'll never come back, a nomad lost in shifting sand dunes.

Dominika Wrozynski is Assistant Professor of English at Manhattan College in the Bronx, where she teaches creative writing and literature. Her most recent work has appeared in *Crab Orchard Review*, *Spoon River Poetry Review*, *Saw Palm*, and *Rattle*. Her husband, Todd, served three tours overseas in the U.S. Military, both in the Navy and in the Army.

D.A. Gray

Whistling Past the Graveyard

A platoon, last week scattered across seven bases,
reconnects in a circle around a makeshift grill.
From metal trailer steps, faces above the flame
look disembodied, look uneasily calm,

look the way they looked before R and R,

the memory of which, like the warmth of an abandoned bed
has begun to fade. For a moment I wonder
if the strangers back home find solace,
now that I've kept one of two promises.

Tonight, though, stolen mess hall chicken
rests on the grate, on a sideways metal drum,
the bird's skin, unlike the human kind,
takes its sweet time browning over flame.

Voices shift in the night, from mission to missing
home. "My wife," says one. "My boy," says the next
before a hand pulls a mix of GI spice
we call gunpowder, so much pepper the fragments

that miss send pyrotechnics from the coals
toward the sky.
That is when the klaxon sounds
in the distance and two newbies fall face down,
army training still twitching in every muscle.

The rest of us watch the speed with which these soldiers
drop, maybe hurl fingers and F bombs at an unseen God.

We turn silent when a whistle passes overhead
then out of range; then we turn the meat,

because, if tonight's the last supper,
damn if we're going to let it burn.

D.A. Gray recently retired from the Army after 25+ years and spends his time as a full-time graduate student. Gray has published one book of poetry, *Overwatch*, Grey Sparrow Press, November 2011. His writing can also be found in *Poetry Salzburg Review*, *Grey Sparrow Journal*, *Bellow Literary Journal*, and *Spark*, among other journals.

Paul Hellweg

Ghosts

The dead from that war so long ago
continue to haunt.
I wish it were possible to speak with them,
but I know not what language,
English, Vietnamese, French, or perchance
ghosts speak in tongues not understood by the living,
boughs whispering in breeze,
wind wolves sighing through grasslands,
call of redtail hawk.
I wish I could understand,
I wish one would speak to me, maybe
the burned boy who lived nine days, or
the gut-shot PFC called upon to endure twenty minutes,
or the lucky one, killed instantly, one bullet, one heart.
All dwell deep in my skull, reclusive,
not coming forth to tell what I want to know.
Were one to speak up, he might be angry,
having expected a seven-course dinner
but served only a mess of pottage,
resenting, perhaps, my surviving, and
surely questioning the point in coming home intact
only to live like the street, without joy,
fortified with beer and Scotch,
thick with longing,
heavy with inertia.

Paul Hellweg has had more than 200 poems published since his 2009 debut. His poetry
has been nominated for both the Pushcart Prize and multiple Best of the Net Awards.

Interviews

Sheree K. Nielsen
Meet Jimmie McInnis—Bronze Star Recipient

I met James "Jimmie" T. McInnis completely by accident. Strolling one fine morning on the Sunset Beach pier in North Carolina, I came to check on my husband's fishing efforts and snap photos of his "big" catch. I never made it to the end of the pier. Instead, I found another man more captivating.

After spotting the gentleman's leather wheelchair, I noticed his navy-blue hat littered with countless medals. Bright, gold-embroidered capital letters emblazoned on the arc of the worn cap read, "Bronze Star." Directly underneath was stitched "Vietnam Veteran" in red.

The veteran's face showed age underneath those cool aviator sunglasses and behind that neatly trimmed silver goatee. Two pens poked out of his light-blue polo shirt pocket, and a silver medal hung around his neck. Wrapped tightly around his right wrist were four plastic bracelets—white (which said something about veterans), two black, and a red and blue two-toned, sporting stars. I could only make out the words "Step Up For" on that one.

Jimmie, reading his newspaper intently, simultaneously was keeping an ever watchful eye on his fishing poles directly across the pier deck. I approached him, extending a handshake, and introduced myself. We exchanged names. Then I thanked him for serving our country so proudly.

After chatting with Jimmie for a while, I'd discovered he was a three-time Vietnam War veteran with stints from 1967–68, 1970–72, and later again in 1972. He served from 1964–1980 in the Army's 25th Infantry Division, with base camp in Cu Chee, Vietnam. If anyone knows anything about the 25th Infantry, you realize these guys were tough as nails, with nicknames like "Tropic Lightning," "Electric Strawberry," and the Cu Chi National Guard (during the Vietnam War).

Studying the veteran's cap, I recognized the shoulder-sleeve insignia, red outlined by gold, with the shape representing a taro leaf, native to the Hawaiian origin of the Army's 25th Infantry Division. A yellow lightning bolt symbol sat dead center of the insignia. This was pinned directly next to the Purple Heart.

He spoke briefly about how he received the Bronze Star and Purple Heart. While in Vietnam serving near Vung Tau, a camp ammunition dump was blown up by a V-device. "As the dump was exploding," Jimmie said, "I didn't stop to think—I was just called to action." He pulled four of his fellow comrades from the remains of the fiery dump.

Suffering bouts of PTSD in the past, he's been to the Fayetteville, Virginia, Veterans Administration hospital for treatment. It's helped him sleep and cope better.

"The worst you can do is just not talk about it," Jimmie says.

Jimmie was duly awarded the Purple Heart and the Bronze Star for "being a hero in action" in Vietnam—the medal closest to the Medal of Honor—from Lyndon B. Johnson.

His children have carried on the military tradition—one son is now retired from the Army, another son was promoted to sergeant major in the Army at El Paso, Texas. His grandson is currently serving in Somalia as a 1st Lieutenant in the 82nd Division.

By far, my favorite pin on Jimmie's cap of honors is the silver Christian fish symbol which proudly displays Bible verse, John 3:16: "For God so loved the world that he gave his only Son, that whoever believes in Him, shall not perish but have eternal life."

Jimmie hails from Evergreen, North Carolina. One of life's greatest joys is fishing with his wife from the gray, weathered Sunset Beach pier. His secret to catching good fish—"fish bite" bait from Wal-Mart! (Shush. Don't tell him I told you so.)

Sheree K. Nielsen

Jimmie McInnis

Sheree K. Nielsen is the author of *Folly Beach Dances*, a "healing coffee table book of lyrical photography and poetry where people, sandpipers, dogs, and beachside structures dance with the rhythm of the shifting sand and changing tides." An award-winning writer, photographer, and poet, her publications include *Missouri Life*, *AAA Midwest*, *Southern Traveler*, *Carolina Go!* and countless anthologies, newspapers, and websites. Follow her at www.shereenielsen.wordpress.com and on Twitter @ ShereeKNielsen and @Follybeachdance.

Robert B. Robeson

Interview with a Warrior:
The Wound That Never Heals

It is well that war is so terrible, or we should get too fond of it.
—*General Robert E. Lee*

John N. Seebeth, III, is a unique, intelligent, and conscientious American. At 66 years of age, this former U.S. Army, specialist five, flight medic has observed and experienced extensive pain and suffering in his lifetime. He's a combat survivor with an important story to tell of things he's learned through the cold and hard realism of armed conflict during the Vietnam War in 1968–1969 and through other personal events up to the current day.

Our interview took place in Seattle, Washington, far from the sound of artillery, mortars, and small arms fire of days gone by. His 5-8, 140-pound frame belied his numerous acts of courage on the battlefield. He was seriously wounded in the throat by enemy North Vietnamese Army AK-47 rifle fire on August 22, 1969, approximately 30 miles southwest of Da Nang, South Vietnam. As a 20 year old, Seebeth had already been responsible for saving a significant number of military and civilian lives during his nine months in Southeast Asia. He was a member of the 50-man, 236th Medical Detachment (Helicopter Ambulance) unit stationed at Red Beach on the shore of picturesque Da Nang Harbor.

When Seebeth was a youngster, as the oldest of three children, he recalls playing war with other kids in his Philadelphia, Pennsylvania, neighborhood. They had a lot of fun, but the kids who were "killed" or "wounded" always made it home for dinner. In those days, he understood few of the realities of war.

The flip side of any perceived "glory" aspects of combat is deep sorrow. It's sorrow for yourself, your comrades, and others whom you've witnessed being wounded or killed in what may encompass nonstop daily action and violence. It wouldn't be until he was 19 before Seebeth experienced this latter fact in real time. That's when he would become a prominent participant in the most hazardous and debilitating competition ever created by mankind. It's an event in which one group or nation—always fighting on the side of "right"—competes with another group or nation by simply killing the most competitors on the other side, in all-out hostilities through any means conceivable, and by causing the most damage to their land and infrastructure.

When asked how he was raised, Seebeth paused for a moment before answering. "My father was a machine operator in a bakery, a lower middle class, blue collar worker," he began. "I grew up in a rough neighborhood. My parents divorced when I was about 13 or 14 years old. It was very traumatic leading up to that. I've essentially been on my own since I was 14."

After graduating from Bensalem High School in 1966, Seebeth and his friends decided to go into the military because they felt there was nothing to do around their community. He joined the Army, and all of his friends joined the Marines. It's something he still laughs about.

"My grandfather had been in the military and was in the Battle of the Argonne Forest, from September 26–November 1, 1918, in France during WWI," Seebeth said. "American casualties totaled 117,000, the French lost 70,000 men, and the Germans had 100,000 killed. It was the greatest American battle of that war. When he got back home, he was never the same mentally or emotionally. My father served in WWII. I'd always wanted to be a Pennsylvania State Trooper when I was younger, so I tried to join the Army as a military policeman," he continued. "I took the MP physical twice, but I was too short. So I decided to become a medic and went to Fort Sam Houston in San Antonio, Texas, for ten weeks of my initial medical training."

After finishing the course at Fort Sam, Seebeth was sent to West Germany. In Baumholder, he was assigned to a ground ambulance company that had 40–50 ambulances. He worked six days a week in the dispensary or helped pull maintenance on the vehicles. He performed these functions for a year and wasn't pleased with the experience. In 1968, his company was withdrawn from Europe and sent to Fort Polk, Louisiana.

"Fort Polk was also a negative experience for me," Seebeth admitted. "So I thought I had to get out of there. That's when I heard the Army was recruiting for the 236th Medical Detachment (Helicopter Ambulance) unit. They had six helicopters and needed a medic for each of them. Joining the unit would mean having to go to Vietnam. I was aware of the war that was going on, but it was very abstract to me," he added. "So I thought, well, what the hell. I'll go over there and do my little bit . . . my patriotic combat duty, since that was in my family history. I was accepted by the 236th, after being interviewed by the first sergeant. I was transferred from the ambulance company and started getting ready to go to Vietnam."

Seebeth arrived with the entire 236th Medical Detachment at the Da Nang, South Vietnam, U.S. Air Force Base on Thanksgiving Day of 1968. He was 19 years old. The unit flew in on a USAF C-141 decked out with weapons and full military gear. They were finally in the combat zone and quickly assumed their flight duties and mission of providing aeromedical support to those in their 5,000-square-mile area of operation. He remembers his maiden medevac mission as an unreal experience.

"We landed near some armored personnel carriers for a wounded Vietnamese soldier," Seebeth said. "When I jumped out, enemy fire kicked up sand beside the chopper. That was my first recollection that this was for real. I think that was the fastest I ever moved. I took the patient and literally threw him on the aircraft. Then I dove into the cargo compartment myself. That sand kicking up was just like in the movies."

He was soon temporarily attached to the 54th Medical Detachment at Chu Lai, a port city on the southern coast of I Corps, about 55 miles south of Da Nang. This "Dust Off" detachment had been there awhile with experienced flight medics who provided him with on-the-job training. The Dust Off name had become a call sign for all U.S. Army helicopter medevac missions in the country. Since the countryside, in many areas, was often dry and dusty, helicopter evacuations in the field continually blew dirt, dust, and shelter halves around the ground troops. This Dust Off call sign continued throughout the remainder of this war.

Another fact of life in combat was the possibility of becoming a prisoner of war. This was brought to Seebeth's attention in a vivid manner one day when his crew picked up a dead American who'd been discovered dumped by the enemy in the jungle.

"We picked up this guy who'd obviously been tortured to death," Seebeth began. "He'd been out in the jungle for quite a while and had eroded. They'd bound his arms and legs with baling wire and had cut off his hands and feet. The wire was up against his bare bones. It was a disgusting and revolting sight. The stench was overwhelming. That mission was really devastating to me because I was new in-country and I had a low tolerance for the aspects of pain," he continued. "So, later, this business about the possibility of being captured and tortured like that was something I had to deal with many, many times in my mind lying on my bunk. I kept thinking of how I'd react if I were ever captured."

He still doesn't think this possibility could be overstated because, not long after that, he was involved in a crash on a hoist mission. This made the thought of being captured by the enemy and becoming a POW even more real.

"One day we got this call for a priority mission," Seebeth said. "It was in Elephant Valley, southwest of Da Nang. An Air Force helicopter had crashed not due to hostile action. A couple of American advisors with a Vietnamese patrol had radioed to evacuate one of their guys who had gotten sick. When they dropped a forest penetrator to get him out, the helicopter had engine failure. It crashed and burned. The crew consisted of a Vietnamese pilot and an American crew chief. They had a few injuries but nothing real serious."

Seebeth's crew soon took off with a hoist in their aircraft. The pilots were a captain, who was aircraft commander, and a warrant officer copilot. Two crew chiefs were strapped into canvas seats on each side of their Lycoming jet engine. Seebeth, the hoist operator, wasn't strapped in or plugged into the intercom system so that he could talk directly to the pilots. This was a major error. The two crew chiefs were using the only intercom cables in the cargo compartment. Seebeth was forced to have one of the crew chiefs relay his comments and directions about the hoist and patients to the pilot and the pilot's comments back to him. The time this took would create a devastating dilemma for all of them.

"As I'm bringing these two guys up from the clearing to our aircraft on the jungle penetrator," Seebeth said, "I'm informing this crew chief to tell the

Specialist Five John N. Seebeth (right) of the 236th Medical Detachment (Helicopter Ambulance) rests between missions at Landing Zone Baldy with crew chief Jerry Southard, one of the two crew chiefs who were in the crew with Seebeth during their hoist mission crash not long after this photo was taken in 1969. *Photo courtesy of John Seebeth.*

pilot to hover 'left' or 'right' to keep these patients directly under the hoist. Suddenly the hoist cable hit one of our skids and the penetrator moved out of my view. The aircraft had drifted too far, and the cable must have gotten hung up in the trees. This bled off engine rpm. As I was lying on my stomach looking over the edge of the deck, all of a sudden there was a rocking motion and the cable snapped. It whiplashed up into the main rotor blades and suddenly . . . there were no rotor blades above us. They'd disappeared."

Seebeth grabbed the two springs behind one of the pilot's cockpit seat and hung on as the aircraft spun straight down and crashed. Both men on the jungle penetrator were instantly killed.

Their aircraft commander was thrown through the windshield, smashing one hip, while the copilot was trapped momentarily when the instrument panel was crushed by the impact against his armored seat. The two crew chiefs were left hanging from their seats. Seebeth had to forcibly unlock their seatbelts so they could drop down and get away from the aircraft. They were all afraid it might catch fire.

One of the Americans in the ground patrol informed them that they'd heard gunfire not far away. He thought the enemy might be on the way to the crash site. That's when Seebeth recalled the tortured American POW and knew they had to get out of there. A little later, a Marine Chinook helicopter arrived, and a jungle penetrator was dropped down to extract them. This didn't make Seebeth comfortable after what had just happened to the other two unfortunate soldiers. But it was their only way out. He and his crew were flown to the 95th Evacuation Hospital on China Beach in Da Nang for medical treatment and evaluation.

Seebeth related story after story about patients he'd treated under the worst of circumstances. This was something all Dust Off medics and crews had to deal with. Many of their patients were beyond human aid and found a speedy easement of their suffering in death.

"It weighed on me a lot when patients we went after died," Seebeth admitted. "There is so much going on at the same time, so many screwed-up people, you just looked at them to see who was the worst and did what you could for all of them while attempting to block out the rest. In the beginning, I just felt overwhelmed. Sometimes we might pick up 15 or 20 Vietnamese at one time and they'd all be messed-up." Seebeth's eyes filled with tears frequently as he recounted various missions and experiences. "You wanted to do something on the way to the aid station or hospital, but where the hell do you start? Or with people who are burned. Sometimes the only intact skin on them was under their combat or jungle boots. It seemed like you could never do enough. That's why some of the crew chiefs were cross-trained to help us and became efficient medics, too."

In late July of 1969, a new operations officer—a captain—arrived to join their unit at Red Beach. Seebeth was on the aircraft that flew over to pick him up at the 95th Evacuation Hospital pad on China Beach, beneath the ominous shadow of Monkey Mountain to the northeast.

Grabbing this pilot's overloaded duffel bag, Seebeth effortlessly slung it over his shoulder and directed him toward the idling helicopter twenty yards away. War was now a new reality for this captain, but Seebeth had already experienced more than his share of it. Like so many others this operations officer would get to know in combat, Seebeth seemed to have been born old and experienced in the ways of life and death.

What both of them didn't realize, at this moment, was that the following month would dramatically alter their lives. Yet this pilot often stated that he'd never forget Seebeth's smile that first meeting. It always seemed to be present whether they were involved in good or hard times.

Seebeth was placed on the medic and crew chief flight roster, by the unit top sergeant, to be a part of the next crew assigned to field standby duty at their battalion aid station at Landing Zone Baldy—25 miles south of Da Nang—beginning on July 20.

"The medic who had already been out there for a week came up to me," Seebeth said, "and wanted to stay out because there was a lot of action going on. He asked me to switch standbys with him, since I owed him a favor. That week he'd already had an IV bottle shot out of his hand in the air and apparently hadn't had enough of it. I'd already had a premonition that something bad was going to happen to me. And I was tired, my year tour was getting short, and a lot of stuff was hitting the fan out there, so I thought I'd just wait

80

this one out. I told him 'okay,' and then went to lay down on my bunk for a while."

Before the other crew left for their field site, Seebeth thought about the decision he'd just made.

"As I lay there, I kept thinking that it was really 'hot' action out at Baldy," Seebeth said, "and if he gets himself killed, I'm not going to be able to deal with that. So I got up, went to operations, and told him I'd changed my mind. 'No, I have to go.'"

The new operations officer had also assigned himself to field site duty with Seebeth that week as a rookie peter pilot. These four crewmembers bunked together in an oppressively hot hootch about thirty yards from the aid station landing pad and ten yards from the aid station entrance.

Sitting on his bunk that first afternoon, between missions, this captain talked to Seebeth who was resting on the other side of their Dust Off hootch. Seebeth had a high-pitched voice, and he used his hands to gesture a lot when he was talking. This time his words took on a serious note, perhaps because of his previous premonition of bad things to come or because he understood his odds in combat were getting worse from all that had already happened to him. He spoke rapidly and brought up the possibility of their being shot down.

"Well, sir," Seebeth said, "if we ever go down you can count on one thing."

"What's that?" their copilot asked.

"That I won't leave you alone out there," Seebeth replied. "Especially if you're hurt. If I have to die, I want to go trying to help someone or attempting to protect my buddies."

At that moment, it sounded a bit overdramatic to the captain, even though they'd already taken enemy fire on their first few missions. For many embraced by the arms of direct combat, soldiers often *don't* think the worst will ever happen to them. They see it happening frequently in battle. But it's always to someone else . . . never them.

What Seebeth's medevac crew wasn't aware of was that they had already been thrust into the middle of a major battle. It involved 4 regiments of the U.S. Army's 196th Light Infantry Brigade, 2 battalions of the U.S. 7th Marines, and batteries of the U.S. 82nd Artillery that provided fire support from four firebases located 30–35 miles southwest of Da Nang around the Hiep Duc settlement. Dust Off crews referred to this area as "Ulcer Alley," because more aircraft were shot up or shot down near there than anywhere else in their area of operation. This collection of Americans would be facing 1,500 Communist soldiers.

In the following 2½ days of devastating action, Seebeth's crew evacuated 150 wounded Americans from the Que Son Valley around Hiep Duc on 42 missions, 15 of which were "insecure." This meant that the ground troops couldn't guarantee the safety of the landing zone or they were low on ammunition and couldn't provide sufficient covering fire.

On a majority of these insecure missions, helicopter gunships weren't available to cover their unarmed aircraft because there was too much action requiring their services in other parts of this battleground. So their only alternative was to go in alone, since most of the wounded wouldn't have survived if they'd waited for gunships to arrive.

During the morning of August 21, their UH-1H (Huey) was shot up by enemy AK-47 rifle fire while exiting another insecure landing zone. A burst of fire ripped into an oil can their crew chief kept under the copilot's armored seat spraying oil over his Nomex flight pants. Another round locked him in his shoulder harness when it clipped a wire on the unlocking device attached to the left side of his seat. Many more rounds penetrated other parts of the aircraft.

"One of those three patients was wounded for the second time on our way out," Seebeth said.

They deposited their patients at the Baldy battalion aid station and waited while another helicopter was ferried out from Da Nang for their use.

On the morning of August 22, their crew was returning to LZ Baldy with a wounded American when they received an urgent in-air mission for another American who'd been shot a couple of times, the most serious of which was a back wound. The ground troops were in close enemy contact and low on ammunition.

"Our aircraft commander decided it would take too long to fly back to Baldy and then back out again," Seebeth said, "so he decided to drop off our current patient at LZ Center, because he was ambulatory. Then our copilot called for gunship cover. The guns said it would take them ten or more minutes to get to the grid coordinates of this 42nd mission for our crew. When our pilots made contact with the ground unit and told them the gunships couldn't be there for ten minutes or so, their radio operator became agitated and replied, 'This guy's going to be dead in ten minutes.'"

"I was smoking a Lucky Strike," Seebeth recalled, "and I'm thinking, *I don't want to go down there but I know we have to.* I'm feeling real bad."

Their aircraft commander made the decision to go in alone and began his diving tactical approach toward a red smoke grenade burning in a small landing zone surrounded by jungle. The pilots knew it was going to be a tight fit whether they got shot at or not.

"As we dove down," Seebeth said, "I depressed my intercom button and muttered 'God go with us.' I'd never done or said that before."

The new crew chief, because the replacement bird had been borrowed from the 571st Medical Detachment from Phu Bai north of Da Nang in I Corps, later noted that Seebeth had held up two crossed fingers when he said that. He'd never done that before, either. Perhaps intuition had warned him.

Their aircraft commander barreled toward the landing zone at 120 knots and did one of his patented 180-degree turns, with a hairy flare, to a dead-hover just above the surrounding trees. Then he began hovering down next to the still smoking grenade.

"About this time I'm starting to get off the deck of the chopper to help load the patient," Seebeth said. "I hear automatic weapons fire and something grabbed me by the throat and spun me around. I knew something was wrong, but I didn't know what. There was no pain. So I started to talk over the intercom and nothing came out. That's when I went to my throat with my hand. When I pulled it back my hand was covered with blood. That's when I knew things were serious."

Two infantrymen hurried toward their aircraft and loaded an African-American staff sergeant into the cargo compartment next to Seebeth.

"I'm sitting there and these two guys are looking at me really weird," Seebeth said. "I can imagine what I looked like with my throat hanging out. As we took off, that's when I had an out-of-body experience. I was looking down at the helicopter from above the rotor blades, but I could hear and see everything that was going on. I fought to get back into my body because I knew I was dead if I didn't. I'd already taken off my body armor and flight helmet and motioned for the crew chief to start an IV on me. But he's all shaky and tried to cover my wound with gauze bandages, which only cut off my oxygen."

Their copilot turned around in his seat and said, "John, you're going to be all right. We'll get you out of here." He knew Seebeth wasn't dead, at that moment, but he realized he was a lot less alive than he'd been five minutes before.

"I tried to start an IV on myself," Seebeth said, "but I'm going into shock and there was no way this was going to happen. And then I got really angry. I couldn't believe that it was *my* turn. I'd been dealing with stuff like this for what seemed like forever . . . and now it was *my* turn. My wound was swelling fast and I was beginning to suffocate."

That's when Seebeth recalled a mission he'd flown earlier in his tour for a severely wounded Vietnamese woman.

"This mama-san was really messed-up," Seebeth said. "The bottom part of her face was gone. There's this big gaping hole. The front of her neck and chest were gone, and she was motioning to me with her hands that she couldn't breathe. Nothing is bandaged and I'm working real close to her body. Her brown eyes are bugged out of her head. It was gross. And when I got hit, that's what I thought I must have looked like. Now here I am; I can't breathe. Same thing, you know. It repulsed me. I think the image of that poor woman saved my life because that horrific scene kept me going."

The enemy had shot out two of their three radios. Only their FM radio was operable. At the Baldy landing pad, two litter teams were waiting. Seebeth waved them toward the other patient, leaped out, ran into the aid station, and jumped up on a litter supported by two wooden sawhorses. He waved for a doctor he'd worked with on other patients to start working on him. He knew time was of the essence.

Seebeth kept mouthing the words *I can't breathe*. He was fighting to live. Then he began kicking his legs in frustration. That's when their copilot held his legs. There was no time for pain-killers. This doctor said, "John, you know what I have to do," and began a tracheotomy with a scalpel. Seebeth looked at the copilot, and his lips moved silently with another *I can't breathe*, as tears began running down his cheeks—mingling with the mucous and blood that covered him and those nearby. He suffered bravely until passing out.

After initial surgery at the 95th Evacuation Hospital in Da Nang, Seebeth was judged to be capable of being evacuated from the war zone. Days later, he was flown by a 236th Medical Detachment helicopter to Da Nang Air Force Base for further surgery in Japan. The crew that flew him over said that when his litter was removed from their helicopter, Seebeth raised two fingers to form a "V," and then he raised his other hand. In it he waved their unit patch—a patch that exhorted "Strive to Save Lives."

They said that Seebeth was smiling beneath the blanket and plastic tubes. The two pilots had to look away. They were all crying. Even in combat there

236th Medical Detachment (Helicopter Ambu-lance) unit patch. *Courtesy of Robert B. Robeson.*

is time for love to grow, and his comrades loved him for what he was . . . one of the best medics they'd ever seen.

This special aidman left his mark on the hundreds of patients he'd treated under the shadow of death. He endured his wound the same way, fighting but humble. His memory within their unit would be watered by tears and warmed by the smiles of yesterday.

Their crew was recommended for the Distinguished Service Cross by a one-star general—the nation's second highest award for valor—but all four crew members received the Distinguished Flying Cross instead.

Seebeth's wound required a series of twelve operations over thirteen years to reconstruct his throat. A skin graft from one thigh was used to create another larynx. The first words that he uttered with his new larynx were "Jerry Bell." This was the Army surgeon who gave him back a voice.

On October 3, 1982, Seebeth and his copilot had their first reunion since that August 22, 1969, mission when he was wounded.

As they reminisced about that day, the pilot asked Seebeth if he recalled what he'd said to him after he was wounded.

"You said, 'John, you're going to be all right. We'll get you out of here,'" Seebeth recalled.

"That's right," the copilot replied, "but I realized later that you couldn't have heard me because you'd already taken off your flight helmet, and you haven't talked to any of our crew since then. That's how I know your out-of-body experience was real. You could hear and see everything happening in the aircraft even though you weren't plugged into the intercom system at that time."

War has the unique ability to act as a vehicle of emotion, anger, fear, triumph, and sorrow that are all aspects of any combat action. A soldier *or* civilian cannot go through war without tallying up a few scars, regrets, or anguish. It's not possible to go through life unscathed, either. Take these lessons, confront them the best you can, and move on. Though John Seebeth's physical throat wound will never heal, in addition to the reality of witnessing the suffering and deaths of patients that have touched his being permanently, he never gave up. His psychological and emotional toughness enabled him to deal with the tragedy and despair that has encompassed a good portion of his life. He's an example of how one person's spirit can triumph over pain and cruelty and how humanity and love can still reign in the depths of that hell on earth known as *war*.

Postscript

John Seebeth has a 100% VA disability, but he's still accomplished remarkable achievements. He attended Ocean Community College in Toms River, New Jersey, from 1971–1973. Within its 3,000-student population, he met a large number of Vietnam veterans. He helped organize these former military members into the largest social organization on campus. It became a national fraternity at the end of his freshman year.

His efforts gained him visibility with other students and the administration. His self-worth returned. He was elected student body president his sophomore year. Seebeth was so popular that nobody was willing to run against him. This had never happened before in the history of that college. The college president selected him to address his graduating class. He was also president of the Veterans' Club, a member of the varsity tennis team, and named to the "Who's Who of American Junior Colleges."

Seebeth has earned two college degrees and completed extensive graduate work in sociology and race relations, which included volunteer work for a year in a mental hospital and extensive volunteer time working with troubled youth.

In addition, he's run marathons, bicycled from Seattle, Washington, through Baja California, from Seattle to the Arctic Circle, and all around Europe. He's kayaked on the open ocean, received an award from Washington's governor for his work with veterans, and helped develop a rubber vest that fits around his chest and neck to prevent him from drowning while involved in water sports. The VA has evaluated this device for tracheotomy patients.

How do I know that all of this is true? Because *I* was the operations officer and copilot who shared those missions with Seebeth from August 20–22, 1969, at LZ Baldy in Vietnam.

John Seebeth testing an experimental rubber vest in a swimming pool that he helped develop for tracheotomy patients, after the Vietnam War, so they could be involved in water sports without drowning. *Photo courtesy of John Seebeth.*

Lieutenant Colonel Robert Robeson flew 987 medevac missions in South Vietnam (1969–1970). evacuating 2,533 patients. Seven of his helicopters were shot up by enemy fire and he was shot down twice. He's been decorated eight times for valor, in addition to being awarded a Bronze Star and 26 Air Medals. He was operations officer and commander with the 236th Medical Detachment in Da Nang. Robeson retired from the U.S. Army with over 27 years of service.

Fiction

Amanda S. Cherry

A Nickel Requiem

The trumpet, wailing its last plaintive notes of Taps, leaves the grave site in utter silence. It makes me wonder for a moment if I have gone deaf, the silence is so complete. I strain to hear the squeak of the windshield wipers on the limousine that brought your coffin to its final resting place. Their rhythmic beat calming me, centering me, grounding me away from losing myself completely in grief. Even that soothing sound has left me in silence. I feel alone in the stillness.

As my eyes flutter open under the weight of so many tears, my sight drifts over a dark sea of mourners. Their black umbrellas shield them against the misting rain like dark feathers forming a protective shell, keeping their sadness from escaping into the ether. It was overwhelming. I want to run. I want to run through the crowd of mourners watching them ruffle and flap away like a murder of crows, their words of sympathy and encouragement cawing into the distance, as I disappear from this place of death. But I stay, the tips of my heels piercing the soft ground beneath my feet, rooting me in this spot until it is over. Until you are under the same ground where I sit, my head bowed in grief.

From above me, I hear, "On behalf of the President of the United States, a grateful nation, and a proud United States Army, this flag is presented as a token of our appreciation for the honorable and faithful service rendered by your loved one to his country and the United States Army."

I look at the blue nylon of the flag being held with white-gloved hands directly in front of me. I focus for what feels like an eternity on the tightly woven threads that create the white stars. Standing behind me, your sister gently rests a hand between my shoulder blades, her soothing touch brings me out of my lull. Moving her hand to rest on my shoulder pulls the strings of my numbed arms; they reach out to grasp the flag.

The weight of it surprises me, heavy, solid, lying in my lap with the same weight of your head when it rested there. A flash of memory hits me before I can stop it, and you are here, smiling up at me. It's during our Sunday morning ritual of completing the crossword, and we are laughing over a four-letter word for swearing. I said oath; you thought I said oaf. It brings a smile to my face until I realize it was one of the few memories I have left of you. There would be no new memories now and the old ones will start to fade.

The priest speaks in a mellow voice, "We now commit Logan's body to the ground; earth to earth, ashes to ashes, dust to dust, in the sure and certain hope of the resurrection to eternal life."

"This now concludes our service," comes the soothing voice of the funeral director. "Family and friends are invited to gather at Ruby's restaurant after the service."

The mention of Ruby's brings back a flood of other memories. Every

Saturday morning we'd drive into town to Ruby's diner. I'd order a coffee, you'd get a large milk, and we'd split a cinnamon roll. Your letters from Iraq reminisced about those mornings. The cinnamon rolls warm from the oven, big as your head and twice as sweet. Sweet icing, warm dough, melting cinnamon overflowing the dinner plate too small to contain even one. When Ruby heard you were being deployed, she promised to send a cinnamon roll every week. True to her word, the guys in your unit devoured them like wolves on a fresh kill. You wrote to me with a warning that they were all coming for a visit, so they could have one of Ruby's rolls fresh from the oven. None of us thought to prepare for them being here and you being . . . gone.

The darkness envelops me, as the black clothed mourners come to offer words and gestures of sympathy. I smile bleakly, grasping the warmth of hands that pass in mourning, nodding as the murmurs of sympathy hang in the cool air between us.

I fight the urge to run.

I fight the urge to scream.

I fight the urge to dissolve into a puddle of weeping.

Gratefully, the large crowd dissipates into smaller cells of friends and family reconnecting in their grief, leaving me to my own enveloping sadness. Their distance reminds me how alone I feel without you. A few car doors slam shut, as the acquaintances, the patriots, the official representatives, and your older family members take their leave to gather at Ruby's. Others linger, like me, unable to let go of you just yet. Your sister, Susan, stays at my side, a quiet sentry against the pain I was sure would assault me, leaving me as dead as you were now.

"I'll be right back," she whispers squeezing my hand. I watch as she crosses the cemetery toward a group of men nearby. She walks with the same military bearing you had in each stride. The men she approaches are gathered in a tight circle. Some are dressed in dark suits. A few others wear dress blue uniforms that mirror the one Susan is wearing. I draw in a sharp breath as I notice two familiar faces: Specialist Miller is sitting in a wheelchair, and Sergeant Ramirez's arm is in a dark blue sling that matches his uniform. I can see in their faces they are just as haunted by your absence as I am, perhaps more so. Miller pulled you out of the vehicle before being shot in the spine. Ramirez held you in his burnt and broken arms as you passed from this world. I feel as connected to them in your death as you did in life. We are all warriors fighting our battles. As Susan approaches, they open their small circle; a few hug her; they all greet her as the old friend she is to them.

I stand, on less than steady ground. Miller takes point. His wheelchair grips the wet grass with force, bringing the whole group toward me. The whole group falls into a V-formation, flanking Miller. Their march toward me isn't even marked in half-time; their Drill Sergeant would be screaming. It's more of a saunter than a march, with some obvious limping as well. When they finally arrive, Susan resumes her position by my side, a reassuring hand resting on the small of my back. The six men in front of me are introduced, each of them connecting you to your Army service. Some knew you in Basic Training, some through AIT-Advanced Individual Training, most from the unit you served in while in Iraq. Miller wheels himself directly in front of me, taking my hands in his. I sit down so I can look directly at him.

"We promised Sergeant Reed we'd mark the occasion," he said. "You're welcome to join us if you feel up to it."

I can't speak. I merely nod my head in the affirmative.

"He didn't lie about how gorgeous you are, Mrs. Reed," one of the guys in civilian clothes says as the few standing near him punch him playfully. "What she is—"

"You are such a jerk," Ramirez shoots back. "She's six months pregnant and just buried her husband. Get a grip, dude."

"What? I meant it as a compliment," he chuckles. "You know how Reed was always bragging about how beautiful she is—I mean, he didn't lie."

"Sorry," Susan laughs. "Bullard doesn't spend much time around women. He forgets how to be polite."

"Only because you don't count as a woman," Bullard shoots a look at Susan.

"Oh, I'm not a woman am I?" Susan asks. "Is that because I can kick your ass?"

We all laughed. It feels good to laugh and joke again. It is comforting to be with these guys, to be treated like someone other than your pregnant widow. Ramirez struggles to open a backpack one of the guys has brought with him. No one tries to help him; it is an unspoken understanding among these warriors that struggle is good for the body, mind, and soul. If he had wanted help, he would have asked. His struggle rewards him with a bottle of Jack Daniels. Someone else pulls out eight shot glasses, and another person cues up an iPod to a familiar song list, the one I made for you before you left.

The group gathers around Miller and I as we sit across from your coffin. As if by direction, they each begin to share stories about you. Some I'd heard countless times; others were new to me. After each story, the bottle was passed, the shot glasses filled, and then drained in your honor. The strong smell of Jack Daniels mixes with dirt and grass, keeping me in the moment. With the forethought only Susan could provide, her glass and mine are always filled with water. The person telling the story pours the contents of his glass on the ground, symbolically including you in the ritual. After six rounds of stories and shots, the iPod falls silent as does the group.

"*Jeremiah was a bullfrog. . .*" Miller's baritone voice sings, breaking the silence. "*Was a good friend of mine.*" Others join in the chorus of your favorite song.

Just as the last note falls into the space between us, we close ranks. There are hugs, pats on backs, handshakes, and promises to keep in touch as each member of the group makes their departure, some to Ruby's, some to places unknown. Car doors slam, engines rev as silence falls around me again. The rain stopped, and the sun is trying to pry itself away from the darkness of the clouds. The light doesn't reach me, unable to reach past my sorrow and grief.

Susan, Miller, and Ramirez remain behind. Ramirez shifts his weight from one foot to the another. Susan and Miller give each other knowing glances. It's becoming obvious they're waiting to say something to me, but don't want to begin. Susan breaks the silence by announcing she'll wait for me in the car.

"You'll be okay?" she asks. "The guys have something they want to show you. I'll wait for you in the car."

She walks away, Miller produces his smart phone. He cues up a video, placing it back in my hands. "Reed—I mean Logan—had a message for you. He made us promise to play this for you when we saw you."

"We were going to show you earlier," Ramirez explains. "But we thought you might not be okay with other people seeing. It's for you, no one else."

I push play, and your face, dirty, bloodied, and pained fills the screen. I drop the phone. Miller picks it up and places it in my hands. My breath catches in my lungs as your smile, your beautiful smile breaks the floodgates holding my tears in check. Your voice echoes in my heart like an old song I haven't heard in forever. I strain to hear your words as the roar of the Medevac helicopter in the background nearly drowns you out. Your last words to me, and I can barely understand them. A surge of anger presses against my chest. Anger that you're gone. Anger against those who killed you. Anger at you, for being who you are and that your last words to me will be a constant reminder of what a wonderful man I've lost. Anger that our daughter growing inside me will never meet you.

I listen to those last words, reassured those last thoughts are of me and my happiness. I'm convinced the promise you've asked me to keep will never be kept.

* * *

"You used your last breath asking me to keep a promise to you," I tell your grave. "There was a part of what you asked me to do, that I just couldn't. I guess you knew. You knew it might take me awhile, so you've given me a push. At least I hope this is what you've done."

I sink to my knees on the damp ground near your headstone. I lean against the cool marble the same way I used to lean against your solid chest. The stone presses cool against my forehead, making me miss your warmth even more. With my index finger, I trace the lines of your name carved into the marble, Logan Michael Reed. The droplets of rain form rivers under my touch, like tears of the angels, you'd tell me. The pennies, nickels, dimes, and quarters left on the arch of the stone catch the sunlight playing hide and seek with the clouds. The sight of them soothes me, knowing others have been to visit you, so I leave them undisturbed.

The last time Susan visited your grave with me, she told me the story. "When a fellow soldier visits a grave, they leave coins as a way of telling the family they've been to visit," she said. "The tradition began during Vietnam to protect everyone from reactions an unpopular war would cause. Pennies from a friend, nickels from someone who trained with you, dimes from those who served in your unit, and quarters left by the men who were with you when you died."

At first I found one or two pennies during my daily visits, which baffled me. Once Susan explained, I found them comforting, knowing you weren't alone, realizing people were remembering you. Occasionally I find a dime or two. After Ramirez's visits, a quarter can be found resting on your headstone. Normally just pennies find their way there, little reminders of your legacy, like pennies from heaven.

"When our daughter Lucy Helen Reed was born, it meant I had to stop coming every day. I had a life to live, with a newborn baby, eventually a part-time job and the daily business of life; I could only spare you one day a week," I tell your headstone. "I'd come every Sunday to tell you about the life I was living without you and how much I missed you. I looked forward to Sundays so I could tell you about Lucy's first words, her first steps, and her first tooth. I'd complain about work or how the plumber overcharged me to fix the leaking faucet. You are here with me, listening, laughing, or hugging me tight. But it wasn't what you wanted for me."

The leaves rustle as a breeze caresses my face, the same way you would brush your hand along my cheek in a tender moment. "During one of my Sunday visits, I noticed a nickel on your headstone. For some reason a nickel brought me solace. I was curious, though, after the third week of finding one on your headstone about who was leaving them. Someone else, someone who knew you in the Army, was visiting every week. I wanted to meet them, to thank them. As long as they remembered you, you were still alive. But you and God must have discussed the timing, because it didn't happen quickly."

"Ramirez and Miller showed me the video you made," I say. "My first thought, I'll never be able to move on from loving you, you can't ask me to."

I sit up on my knees, steadying myself with one hand placed above the grooves of your name in the marble headstone, the other on my chest. I touch your dog tags hanging near my heart and automatically wrap my fingers around them. As always, I feel you here with me, listening.

"But you did," I begin. "You asked me to find someone else who would love Lucy and me as much as you do—did."

I close my eyes to stem the tide of tears gathering behind them. With a deep breath I sense your calm presence surrounding me. This place, being here always makes me feel at ease. I realize being here, with you, is the reason I met Nate.

"For three years now I've done my best to *not* keep my promise," I say. "I kept telling myself I wasn't doing it on purpose, but maybe I was. I just never believed I could find someone as wonderful as you. I mean, your dying words to me were all about finding my happiness again. About finding someone to love me and letting myself love someone new. You were and will always be my big damn hero. I think you've done the impossible and that makes you mighty."

I find myself smiling, because I still quote from your favorite show. Parts of our life together will never leave me, and that brings me comfort.

"So if this is you," I smile. "I mean, if you had anything to do with Nate Thomas coming into our lives, give me a sign."

I look to the gray clouded sky, expecting a lightning flash or a rumble of storm clouds as they move to the west. You miss your cue, and I seem foolish for expecting such a literal sign.

"I never believed in fate or magic or even angels, until I met you. Now I think all of those things are possible. I believe you are with me when I come here to visit your grave. I believe you watch over Lucy. She learned about guardian angels in Sunday daycare and thinks you are her personal guardian angel. Every night before she goes to sleep, she'll say her prayers and then kiss your picture. She says, 'Good night, Daddy angel.' That's what she calls you."

"I think you are watching over both of us. I think you are the reason I met Nate. You knew him, you grew up with him. Susan says you two were inseparable as kids. Then he moved away, and you all lost touch until you met again at Basic Training. He was coming once a week to visit your grave; he was the one leaving the nickels. He started visiting you as soon as he got back from Afghanistan. He wanted to be at the funeral, but he didn't learn about it until he got back months later. He's out now, of the Army, so that's good. You made me promise not to fall for another soldier; you didn't want me to go through the grief again. So I won't—go through that again. He is a fireman, so I couldn't completely resist the element of danger. He's also a paramedic and is using his GI Bill to go back to school. He's studying to be a nurse. He said you'd give him grief, but he's really good—he's really good at helping people. He's just a good guy.

"I met him at Ruby's. Lucy was throwing a temper tantrum because I wouldn't let her have chocolate milk. He sat down at the table across from us and started making faces at Lucy, making her laugh; she completely forgot about the milk. Can you imagine? Me having a peaceful meal out with a two year old. I wanted to kiss him. You remember how Lucy went through her phase, where every time I took her out to eat she'd dissolve into screaming fits. I was amazed at how this complete stranger kept her so calm. I offered to pay for his meal. Of course he wouldn't let me. We chatted, and he said he knew you growing up, went into the Army the same time you did. He recognized you, he remembered you, made me want to spend time with him. Maybe because he soothed Lucy out of her screaming fits. I don't know, I didn't think about it, I can't explain it. I just did it.

"I don't think either of us had any intentions toward each other at first. After meeting him I went back to Ruby's every Saturday, at five o'clock, hoping to run into him. He told me later he did the same thing, hoping to see me again. I guess we both kept going, showing up at Ruby's on Saturday at five o'clock, because remembering you helped keep you alive for us. He'd sit at his table, I'd sit at ours. Eventually, Ruby sat us together. She said that she was getting tired of cleaning two tables when we'd just end up sitting together eventually anyway.

"I started looking forward to Saturdays, almost as much as I looked forward to Sundays. We would just sit and talk for hours. We talked about you, about Lucy, about our hopes and our dreams. He's the one who's pushing me back into photography. He sent some of my photos of Lucy to a professional photographer friend of his, and now the guy wants to hire me. Nate says I should start my own studio, photograph newborns and kids. I dunno—it's not hard photographing Lucy, but other people's kids—I'm not so sure. He believes in me, he encourages me, like you used to.

"On the subject of Lucy—she's got Nate wrapped around her little finger. He loves her so much and is so good with her. She loves him right back. That part makes me a little sad, knowing he's here, and you're not. I wanted you to be the one who makes her smile and laugh when she's having a tantrum. I wanted you to wipe my tears away on her first day of school. I wanted you to be the one to help her with her math homework someday, because we both know I won't be able to. I wanted a photo of you in your suit and tie with her in her graduation gown. I wanted you there to intimidate the boys she decides to date. I wanted you to be the one to walk her down the aisle, when she marries the man of her dreams, someone like her angel Daddy. But you're not here—and he is. And I think it's because of you that Nate is here."

I look across the cemetery to see Nate walking toward me with Lucy; her little porcelain hand is wrapped around one of his larger calloused fingers. She kneels to pick up a flag from another grave. They're several yards away from me, far enough that I can't hear the conversation, but I can see it playing out in mime. Nate is telling her no, the flag doesn't belong to her, she should put it back. She stomps her foot, her free hand flies to rest on her hip and I'm sure her bottom lip protrudes defiantly. I can almost hear her say NO! as she walks, away her blonde curls bounce with each step. Nate looks at the grave, looks after the retreating form of Lucy; with a slump of his shoulders he follows her like a scolded puppy.

She takes a few steps, stooping to pick up rocks from the ground. She likes rocks and treats them as precious jewels. Susan gave her some crystals from Turkey, and now she believes all rocks can be grown into crystals. Soon her hands are full, and she gives the flag to Nate freeing her to pick up more rocks. Nate, with one eye on Lucy tottering back to me and another toward the flag-less grave, turns away from her briefly. He respectfully places the flag back where it belongs and dashes after Lucy. When he gets to her, he scoops her up in his arms. His blonde hair matches hers, his blue eyes sparkle like hers—anyone seeing them would think they were father and daughter. Her pink tutu catches the breeze, fluttering around her chubby legs as Nate swings her in a wide circle. I can hear her high pitched squeals of delight. I smile at the sight of our daughter with the man I've come to love. Turning back to the headstone I lay my hand on the cool marble.

"I think I'm finally ready to keep that promise I made to you. So I just have to ask you, are you okay with this? Because I think I'm in love with him."

"You are?" Nate asks from behind me. Smelling of sunshine and baby shampoo, Lucy rushes into my arms. "You're in love with me? You know you've never said it."

I stand with Lucy in my embrace. Nate opens his arms to hold us both. Lucy wraps her pudgy little limbs around his neck, kissing his cheek. I lean into his embrace. I close my eyes and inhale the scent of Irish Spring covering the smell of smoke that he never seems able to wash away. "Hazard of being a firefighter," he told me once.

"I do," I whisper in his ear. "I'm sorry I haven't said it. I guess I'm waiting for Logan to give me a sign—to give me permission. I know it's weird, but I need his approval."

"I understand," Nate kisses my forehead. "I totally understand."

"Mommy!" Lucy shouts. She is balanced on Nate's shoulder, pointing behind him at the sky. "Mommy look—rainbow!"

"You're right, sweetheart," I say. "It is a rainbow."

I look over Nate's shoulder to see not just a rainbow, but a double rainbow. One for each of his girls, I think to myself. Two fully formed rainbows reaching from the horizon into heaven, their colors more vibrant than any rainbow I've ever seen.

"Is that a clear enough sign?" Nate asks glancing over his shoulder.

I shake my head yes.

Nate gently sets Lucy on the ground. He moves forward, grasping my hand and placing his free hand on your headstone. "I promise you, buddy, I will do everything in my power to keep your girls happy. I will spend everyday of my life making sure they know how loved they are. I won't let them forget you and I won't let you down, because I love these girls. Let's face it, bro, you've got great taste in women."

I laugh. Then I smile. It's not the first time since your funeral I've smiled. But it's the first time since your death that I feel a smile fill my whole heart. Tears come to my eyes, but this time they're tears of joy. I look up at this man I love. "I love you Nate. I do love you."

Amanda Cherry recently graduated from Concordia University with a BA in English. She joined the military, serving as a Medic and Public Affairs Specialist for the Iowa Army National Guard. In 1996–1997 she was deployed to Bosnia, where she honed her skills as a journalist and editor working for US Army Europe, USAEUR. As a veteran, Ms. Cherry's military service inspired her to pursue her passion for writing and photography.

Finally home, an F-16 Pilot receives the ultimate gift, hearing his daughter say "Daddy" for the first time ever.

Kimberly Billington is an expectant mother & wife of an Air Force F-16 Fighter Pilot. She resides in Phoenix, Arizona, with her husband and their two silver labrador puppies. Although considered a 'jack of all trades' in the media world, she most recently worked as a television producer and journalist in tv news before switching hats to work in the freelance world as a media specialist. Kim was born and raised in Detroit, MI, where she attended Eastern Michigan University for her undergraduate degree and Specs Howard School of Media Arts where she specialized in Broadcast Journalism/TV/Radio and Film. A former collegiate athlete, she loves to stay healthy & active in the Phoenix mountains, her family is her inspiration.

The Renegade Robinson

"War is foolish," my dad said over his newspaper one night, glasses pushed to his nose. "Don't you boys get caught up in all this patriotic excitement. You're going to become doctors and lawyers, not have your guts scattered across three countries."

These words of wisdom were spoken to us in the aftermath of the Pearl Harbor attacks. After this historic event, the people of our country seemed to go into a frenzy. American flags spontaneously appeared overnight, and now you could not step outside without seeing one in the lawns of every neighbor. People lined up down the streets and overflowed recruitment offices trying to enlist. Patriotic songs played non-stop on the radio. In town, the only topic of conversation was the war. Everyone talked about war. The men, the women, the old ladies in sewing circles, the children who played hopscotch outside the ice cream parlor, the convicts, the mentally ill. War was on everyone's mind.

Everyone, that is, except my father.

My father was a banker and worked downtown. He made 20,000 a year, an assurance that his wife would never have to work. (Hypothetically, of course; he'd never let her work, even if we were starving.) He lived in a big house in Cherry Creek, Colorado, and had five well-rounded, successful children. (Well, almost. I had a retarded younger sister who lived in a sanatorium upstate. Speaking about her was a strict taboo.) He had everything he could ever want, and was content with life. He couldn't understand the obsession with war. War was not a concern for him. All my father was concerned with was raising his family and running his business. He believed those were the essential aspects of life, not running off and shooting guns in foreign lands. All the young punks running off to enlist were stupid.

My three brothers agreed wholeheartedly with him. They were going to be doctors and lawyers, white collar men, just like my father. They didn't need war to distract them from their full potential.

"Let the scoundrels of the country get themselves blown up in the south Pacific," my father said. "My sons won't join the war."

My brothers nodded in agreement. I shifted nervously in my seat.

"What if we're drafted?" my younger brother Dewey wanted to know.

My father simply chuckled and shook his head. "I'll get you out of it then," he said. "There are ways. Working a respectable job gives you a lot of connections; don't worry about the draft."

I looked at my father. "How can you possibly get us out of the draft?"

My father's smile vanished and his eyes narrowed. He spoke sharply. "Don't speak to me to me like that, Tommy Robinson. Remember that time when I got 'breaking and entering' removed from your police record?"

My father and I didn't see eye to eye. While he believed in hard work, education, and religion, I liked to take life as it came at me. I was more hot tempered and combative than him, and he stopped at nothing to try and coerce me into being like him. When I was 16, a friend of mine had tried to make a move on my girlfriend. Naturally, the only thing to do was enter his home in the middle of the night with the intent of inflicting physical harm. Unfortunately for me, his high-strung mother was at home and dialed the cops. Breaking and entering was placed on my previously surprisingly spotless record sheet. My father, being the clean-cut, hardworking man he was, somehow managed to get it expunged from the record. He had then tried to take me under his wing and teach me banking. But a 17-year-old hothead like me doesn't take to banking lessons so easily. I quit after the first week. He yelled at me for wasting my life, and I yelled at him for wasting my time. We just didn't get along.

That night, the radio news report talked about the thousands of new recruits signed up. My heart leapt and raced.

"Hey, Dewey," I said, looking at my 8-year-old brother. "Are you going to join the Army when you grow up?"

Dewey made a face. "No way! I'm going to be a banker."

"What! And miss out on being a hero?"

"Dad says only punks join the army."

"What's wrong with being a punk?"

Dewey thought for a moment. "They don't have jobs," he said. "And they don't have wives or take baths."

I sighed. Another victim of our father's ruthless indoctrination. I felt sorry for him.

Sometime later, I took a seat on the couch next to my 14-year-old brother, Martin. He was reading a book but I spoke anyway.

"How long do you figure it'll take us to beat the Nazis, Marty?" I asked him.

Martin looked at me. "Excuse me?"

"The Nazis," I said. "Hitler. How many weeks do you think it will take us to kick their asses? Two? Three?"

"Why should I care? I'm not involved." Martin went back to his book. He pushed his glasses to his nose and for a second was the spitting image of our father.

I didn't even bother talking to my oldest brother. Ricky had spent the night at the kitchen table, fully engaged in a conversation with my father about taxes and homeownership. Ricky was 18 and engaged to a cute, ditzy little girl who lived down the street. They were getting married next month and then moving to Denver, so Ricky could attend law school.

Even later that night, when house was asleep, I quietly got out of and bed and snuck to my closet. I threw some clothes, shoes, socks, and a carton of Lucky Strikes into a burlap sack. I found my jacket on the floor of my room

98

and grabbed $50 from under my pillow. Tiptoeing through the silent house, I left a brief note of explanation on the kitchen table. Slipping on my shoes and jacket, I quietly shut the front door and ran down the dark, snowy sidewalk.

I was leaving to fight for my country.

I am 15 years old and live in Oregon. My great-grandpa served as a pilot in WWII, my grandpa was in the Navy during the Vietnam War, and my aunt was in the Navy during the early to mid-90s and spent some time stationed in the Middle East. Because I have so many family members who have served in the military, I grew up hearing war stories. Their stories inspired me to write my own.

Two GIs didn't want to wait in line for chow at the chow hall. The
soldiers coming in from Kuwait made the line extremely long. "They need
to regulate this shit," the first GI, who was thirsty, said to the other. The first
man was tall and had a thick neck. He looked like a football player. The other
man, his friend—not so much. He was short, white, and scrawny. He also
wore the standard-issue, birth-control eyeglasses.

The first GI, the football player, wanted to walk down to haji-mart to buy
himself some soda. "Come on," he said to his friend. "I'll buy you a cold
one." As the two men treaded the white, dusty gravel, they joked about the
transient soldiers and their freshly pressed BDUs. "They should have to eat
shit like we did the first few months. Teach 'em a lesson," the football player
said.

Haji-mart was a row of shanties situated off of base in back. The shanties were made out of wood, crude wooden poles with a plastic tarp or straw
overhang. Some of the stores had a metal chain-link fence standing at base in
front. All sellers were either men or boys, who sold soda, bayonets, DVDs,
old Saddam currency, new Iraqi currency, foreign coins, canceled stamps,
uncanceled stamps, travel guides in German, English, French, makeshift
flags, fans, t-shirts, burkas . . . you name it, they had it, and if they didn't
have it, they promised to get it for you. Before haji-mart was cordoned off
with row upon row of concertina wire, one GI bought himself a fat Iraqi
whore for five minutes.

The football player surveyed the stands before starting to barter. He took
his boonie cap off and fanned himself. It was blistering hot out. On days like
these, buyers had to be wary. The soda cans would burst if haji left them out
too long in the sun.

The scrawny GI was not one for bartering. In fact, he hated it. When the
local in the dirty white thawb offered to sell him two blue, ice-cold cans of
Pepsi for a dollar each, he went ahead and bought them both.

When the football player saw this, he said, "Uh-uh, wait, I can get
those," he pointed at the two blue cans, "both for a dollar. Give 'em to me,"
he motioned with one hand. "Watch."

He relieved his friend of the bone-chilling cans, demanding that the haji,
who had ripped his friend off, give a dollar back. The merchant's name was
Sadiq. Sadiq, who was smiling, suddenly wasn't smiling anymore. He didn't
like this GI, who was named "the impertinent one" by the other merchants.

"Give me the fucking dollar!" the GI demanded.

Sadiq was not a man of great means or intelligence, but he was not
dumb. He also had a wife and two children to feed. "La," he said, shaking his

Haji-mart

head "no" as he spoke. His head was slightly bowed. His countenance was one of great suspicion, distrust.

The frail, lanky, yet big black mustached Iraqi Policeman on guard sensed a problem and stepped forward.

"What the fuck do you want, numb nuts?" the black GI turned toward the IP and asked.

"Come on, man. Forget it. Let's go," the scrawny kid pleaded.

"I bet this guy here is this fucking camel jockey's bitch." He pocketed one can in his left trouser cargo pocket, while shaking the other one up in his other hand. "Man, I hate these fucking sand niggers," he said through gritted teeth.

Opening the can up on the IP, he whipped its sugary contents out, throwing the half empty can at Sadiq afterwards. The IP's eyebrows sharply rose with anger. Having already taken a step back, he switched the fire selector of his AK off of safe. The second GI saw if not heard this and cried out: "Noooo!!!" He clasped his hands and arms down around the IP. A shot pierced the air. The black GI clutched his leg and let out a sharp, pain-filled cry. He jerked his head back and up. A hot scalding rush filled the wound. His eyes squinted. Dropping to one knee, he slapped at his nine-millimeter. Pulling it from its holster and cocking the hammer back, he fired, hitting his friend first in the arm. When the friend fell away, he fired two more shots, causing the IP to drop down to the ground, wide-eyed, mouth agape, gasping for air.

The football player let his hands drop to his side. He had a tired look on his face. He then plopped down in the blood-spattered dirt, dropping the pistol before clutching his leg again.

A guard tower supplied with an infantryman overlooked the area. The shots jolted the man in the tower out of his sleep. Seeing the men lie desperately on the ground, he cried out for a medic. The merchants by this time had already fled. The IP who was in his late thirties or forties stopped breathing before the medic arrived.

Jeremy Warneke

Abu Ghraib

Jeremy Warneke is a veteran of the Illinois Army National Guard. He served in Iraq immediately following "mission accomplished" and subsequently received a BA from Sarah Lawrence College. He was previously an unpublished writer.

The Unique and Revealing Short Timer's Calendar of Sergeant Carl "Pig" Higgins

How did a runt like buck sergeant Carl "Pig" Higgins (twice promoted to staff sergeant—and twice busted back to an E-5, three-striper) earn the nickname "Pig"? I bet that back in 1965, when our unit landed in Vietnam, he weighed no more than 150 pounds. He looked 16 years old, with reddish hair, and an over-ripe tomato complexion, thanks to pale skin roasted by sunburn. Thousands of Howdy Doody freckles dotted his cheeks and forehead—maybe shit stains from a swarm of gnats that alighted on his face seeking helmet shade from the brutal Vietnamese heat and humidity. Still, nothing about him, at first glance, suggested porcine verisimilitude. Nor did his perpetual "I know something you don't," shit-eating grin or his shifty little green eyes darting back and forth, looking for opportunities to cheat, gyp, con, or sweet-talk anybody out of anything of interest or value.

This farm boy from the mountains of west Tennessee was the evil twin of Huck Finn on the inside, but regulation uniform-perfect on the outside. His fatigues were always starched and immaculate as if fresh from a laundry, the crease on the pants sharp enough to shave with.

He even managed to keep his spit-shined combat boots gleaming in all weathers, even during monsoon season, when the rest of us wallowed ankle deep in the red mud of Tay Ninh Province, about a hundred kilometers (80 miles) northwest of Saigon, near the Cambodian border.

Carl was crafty and sly, rather than smart, also said of pigs, when I think about it.

Also, his up-turned pug nose, showing the inside of his nostrils, did resemble a pig's snout. And he snorted like a pig when he laughed, so he tried not to laugh, and covered his mouth when he did. Between snorts, he giggled a high-pitched "te-he-he-he. . . ," worse than the snort. I just had another idea. Maybe the Pig nickname came from his predilection for women who were "at least an ax-handle wide," a sexual preference he didn't reveal to me until about 9 months into our 12-month Vietnam tour. We were both artillery surveyors who, in crews of six to eight men, used special scopes, poles, and measuring tapes, similar to equipment used by civilian surveyors to map roads, proposed building sites, etc. But our job was to put artillery batteries on the map with a precision that made their fire more accurate. As various field operations were launched, one or more of the brigade's three 105 millimeter batteries (6 guns each) were airlifted by big double-rotor Chinook helicopters to positions from which they could support the infantry. Then we surveyed the battery in, providing precise coordinates, so the cannon jockeys knew exactly where the guns were on the map. This gave the battery a better chance of hitting targets, usually designated by forward observers who had visual contact with the enemy. The observers would radio in the estimated coordinates of the enemy position, then radio back adjustments after each volley was fired, until the target was knocked out, if all went according to plan.

As crew chief, Pig was my boss. We didn't like each other much, but one day back in base camp, relying more on his authority than friendship, he asked me to do a favor that would call into play my artistic credentials as a failed art school student.

To explain the favor requires some background that combines superstition with psychology, wishful thinking, and a Vietnam war tradition few civilians know about.

Once a soldier had three months to go on his 12-month Vietnam tour of duty (13 for Marines), he was considered a short-timer. This status provided a degree of happiness at the prospect of going home, especially for draftees who usually arrived home without enough time remaining of their active duty commitment to justify another posting, so many, like myself, were given an early out—like parole from prison. However the dark side of short time was the superstition that short-timers, by some perverse twist of fate, were much more likely to be killed or wounded. Many soldiers believed this and they turned extra-cautious, often concocting phantom injuries or ailments that would hopefully exempt them from patrols and other dangerous assignments.

But there was a singular psycho-sexual weapon employed against the 90-day hex: the short-timer's calendar. This consisted of a pin-up girl, usually scantily clad, drawn in cartoon style, yet voluptuous enough to turn on deprived and depraved troops.

These fantasy women varied considerably in body type and attire in order to appeal to wide-ranging tastes. But all had one thing in common. Each was criss-crossed with a fishnet of 90 numbered squares corresponding to the last 90 days of the soldier's tour. Each numbered square was shaded or crossed out as it passed into hopefully uneventful personal history, counting down like a secular advent calendar, to the final day one. You can guess where that square was located. Day 1 was, most importantly, the day of departure, via the "freedom birds"—private company airliners that brought us back to the states. They were leased by the government, complete with crews, including highly popular stewardesses.

Some particularly talented and imaginative soldiers turned their paper ladies into works of art, using sets of colored pencils or watercolors sent from home. There should have been an art exhibit of the best at MOMA, or the Metropolitan, or at least at a famous folk art gallery or museum. But most of these paper companions were tossed on funeral pyres of burning shit in steel drums next to the latrines, ripped or wadded up, and otherwise disposed of before departure as the prospect of the real thing loomed in the near future.

But Pig with his double-wide tastes in pulchritude had no chance on the commercial market of landing a paper doll to his particular tastes. That was where I came in. He wanted me to draw a customized lady Goliath who could, if real, literally smother him between her mountainous breasts. I complied by creating a brazen centerfold of bulbous beauty, a plus-sized Amazon who totally infatuated our little Napoleon. He confided that she was more voluptuous than his current wife who measured a mere one-and-a-half axe handles wide. Inadvertently I was afraid I might have sown the seeds of marital dissension by inflaming his ambitions beyond reasonable expectation.

I felt a little better when our headquarters battery clerk, James Dillon, a conservative and somewhat prudish Boston Irish Catholic, suggested that the short-time women were mere vessels who were in fact possessed or inhabited by guardian angels who argued passionately for their assigned charges in Purgatorial Courts of military life and death. Dillon's views did not prevail but they did help de-sexualize the short-timer calendar girl ritual just a little. In fact, I must confess that not all short-time calendars were women. One favorite was a GI helmet in profile which I thought more accurately reflected the defensive nature of the last 90 days, as did another icon of homesickness—a cartoon of a confused tortoise, with the 90 days carved into his shell.

Carl "Pig" Higgins did make it out alive, so I guess my exotic artwork was vindicated. I also got out alive and in fact, was married within a year to my wife of 47 years, JoAnne. Near the date of our second anniversary, on a Sunday morning, our doorbell rang.

When I swung the door open, our humble portal framed none other than Carl Pig Higgins in civvies, passing through St. Louis to San Francisco, then on to his second tour in Vietnam, a fate few army careerists or "lifers" could avoid. He had, as I feared, tossed over (figuratively) his wife—now judged insufficient at one-and-a-half axe handles wide. His dissatisfaction was no doubt fueled by the fact that he'd met a woman who measured a whopping two axe handles wide. She became his second or third wife after the divorce. Since it was a Sunday without much going on, we went to a friend's house to drink beer and play pool. Of course Pig's visit was not strictly social. He borrowed $50, which I knew I'd never see again. Nor, I was sure, would I ever see or hear from Carl Pig Higgins again. And, sure enough, I didn't.

Tim Leach was an artillery surveyor (82C10) with Headquarters Battery of the 82nd Artillery, 196th Infantry Brigade, based in Tay Ninh Province northwest of Saigon on the Cambodian border. He then moved south of Cu Chi, north near the DMZ where he finished his tour as artillery liaison with a Vietnamese Popular Forces Unit—a posting he attributes to a desire to get rid of him. He went onto a safer, more lucrative career in journalism, advertising, public relations, and university teaching of PR and media relations. His first book of poetry, *Icarus Flees the Garden of Earthly Delights*, will come out next May, published by Word Tech LLD.

It's Time to Let Go

The air felt as crisp and clean as sun-dried cotton sheets. Jay had reached the ripe old age of eight. When I handed him his birthday present, he tore through the wrappings and cardboard box and pulled out a Red Ryder BB gun. Its black barrel ended at a wooden stock the color of molasses. A strip of rawhide dangled from a ring on its side.

Jay dashed toward the back. With his gun in one hand and a pack of BBs in the other, he hit the door without stopping.

A minute later I heard yelling. I ran down the steps, taking two at a time, and sprinted toward the pecan grove. There under the tree house knelt Jay. He'd shed his cap, and his blond hair whipped in the wind. The bottom of my hunting jacket puddled around him.

In front of him lay the ugliest thing I'd ever seen. It looked liked a wadded-up, dirty dish rag. At first, I thought he'd found a possum, what with that tail stripped clean. But a closer look revealed a dog, a puppy actually. Fleas gnawed from one end and mange spread from the other. They met in the middle. It turned out partly terrier, mostly pointer, and all ugly.

"He needs help, Daddy. Can we keep him? Can we? Please," Jay pleaded through a slight overbite. His blue eyes teared in the wind.

What was I to do? Hell, it'd be dead in a few days anyway, so I said we could.

Jay whooped like a Comanche, scooped the puppy up, and carried it into the house. His BB gun lay propped against a pecan tree. Had I known that puppy would come crawling up, I could've saved myself the eight dollars I paid for that gun.

Pretty soon he had a name and was eating more than Jay. Even healthy, Flash looked as ugly as a root to everyone but his new owner.

Those two grew up together and wouldn't be separated no matter what. One day, old man Hacker backed over Flash with his John Deere. Wasn't Hacker's fault, but Jay let loose with all the rage an eleven year old could muster. Hacker begged to pay the vet bill, but I couldn't let him.

We took Flash in, and Jay stayed with him at Doc Phillips's for three days and nights. Wouldn't leave 'til he knew Flash would be okay.

Flash took care of Jay, too. One night right after his sixteenth birthday, Jay complained of a stomach ache. Turning down his mama's hot apple pie, he went straight to bed. About two o'clock that morning, I heard Flash pacing outside our bedroom. Panting and thrashing his tail against the hallway wall, he led me straight to Jay's room.

Jay's forehead burned to the touch, and he'd tucked himself into a ball. With Jay in my arms, I struggled out the front door. Rose wrapped her blue raincoat over her pajama top and jeans, and led the way. Flash, right at our heels, jumped into the bed of my Ford truck, and the four of us tore down Highway 41.

After we knew Jay'd be okay, Rose and I stood in front of the hospital and watched the sun pour like honey from a pitcher over the roof. Doctor Daves walked up and said that if we hadn't got Jay in when we did, his appendix would've burst, and he might have died. I shivered more at that thought than at the November morning's chill. With my arm around Rose's shoulders, we walked along the cracked walkway leading to the graveled parking lot.

We'd left Flash pacing in the back of the truck. As I reached for the door, he blasted my face with warm foggy breath. I scratched his head and told him, "You did good."

When Jay graduated from high school, wouldn't anything do but that we bring Flash. Since it was outdoors, I agreed. I wore my grey suit with a fancy tie. Rose wore her best Sunday dress, the beige one with the fishnet lace around the top. And, of course, Flash sat there, proudly part of the crowd, slobbering on my pants leg.

A couple of months after graduation, Jay got his letter. I told him to join the Guard, but he wanted in the regular Army. The war in Vietnam raged strong, and he felt compelled to go. I fought the Germans for three years during World War II and knew the feeling well. Actually, I felt proud to see him join, though I never breathed a word of it to Rose.

Flash and I took Jay to the bus station. I shook his hand and paused awkwardly. It didn't seem enough, so I hugged him close for a long time and told him I loved him. Flash got in one last lick. Jay waved through the Greyhound's dusty back window as it lurched down Route 27 headed for Fort Benning.

Four months later he came home for Christmas all spit and polish and wearing the finest looking green Army uniform you ever saw. He even wore a medal. Said it was for the National Defense. Of course, he had the expert marksmanship badge, too. Jay always held a steady aim.

He hadn't been home more than three weeks when, through a mouthful of mashed potatoes, he said he was leaving for the war.

I felt both sick and proud. But his mama, shoot, I didn't know a woman could hold that much water.

That night in bed, while the gas heater hissed, Rose said, "Earl, can't we keep him here?"

I thought a minute then said, "You know better. Besides, it's time to let go."

When he left, it felt like a part of me had been sawed off, but I believe Flash missed him most. He didn't eat for two weeks. I thought that fool dog would starve himself to death. His ribs looked like sheets of corrugated tin. Finally, he ate a platter of grits and scrambled eggs that Rose fixed him. Before long she was feeding that hound better than me!

Jay was "getting short" when his last letter came. Like in all the others, he wrote he was doing fine. He went on to write that, as the senior man in his squad, he walked point.

Wrote that things were hard on 'em. They'd heard that people in the States were burning the flag and saying how the soldiers didn't have any right being there—as if the soldiers were the ones who decided to have the war in the first place. Went on to write that it was tough enough fighting the NVA and Viet Cong, and that the soldiers needed all the support they could get from folks at home.

Since then, I've reread that letter until its pages are as wrinkled as the bark on the pecan tree that cradled Jay's tree house.

We'd no sooner sat for supper when the doorbell rang. I asked Rose, "Who could that be?"

She shrugged her shoulders and I walked to the door. The sight of the sergeant standing beside the chaplain made me heave.

Jay was coming home alright, but in a plain grey, government-issue coffin. I believed my heart would burst and knew Rose's would. We asked for a military funeral. Jay would've wanted it that way.

All we could do was sit and stare at that box. Imagining Jay inside was too hard. When Dr. Cutts finished, I heard, "Ready . . . Aim . . . Fire!" Shots rang out. Then the bugler played taps.

It's funny the things you remember at times like that. The sergeant in charge is the one I recall. He stood well over six feet. He wore his salt and pepper hair cropped close on the sides and flat on top. Skin the color of well-cured leather stretched tight across his face. On his right sleeve, gold cloth bars climbed from cuff to elbow. He moved like a hunter but had the eyes of the hunted. From the rainbow of ribbons on his chest, I understood why.

The soldiers folded the flag covering Jay's coffin into a tight triangle and hand it to the sergeant. He turned toward us and with sure, steady steps approached Rose. She held her face like a concrete statue.

He bent forward and placed the flag in her lap and with a soft Southern drawl said, "Ma'am, this flag is presented to you on behalf of a grateful nation as a token of our appreciation for the honorable and faithful service rendered by your son."

Rose's mask crumbled, and she heaved overdue sobs. The sergeant stood erect and rendered her a slow salute. Then he walked away.

I was surrounded by friends, relatives, and a wife I loved, but I was never so alone. Suddenly, my lap filled with a warm familiar weight. Flash's eyes gazed up, glanced toward the grave, then returned. I patted his head and whispered, "Me, too, old boy."

The day finally ended, and Rose and I faced the night alone. Those who are hell bent on always finding a silver lining say things look better in the morning, and that may be true. But you can't prove it by me.

Bending down, I lit a fire. Using the poker as a cane, I pushed myself up and plodded to the back. The spring on the screen door groaned as I nudged it open.

Jack Frost had dusted the brown grass a powder white. The smell of burning kindling hung in the air. A ribbon of smoke waved overhead as the bare limbs of pecan trees clawed a grey stained winter's sky. I placed my hands in the small of my back, pressed forward, and stretched to my toes.

I whistled for Flash. Nothing. Then I called. Still, nothing. What led me I can not say: just a feeling. Remembering the first time I saw them together, I trudged through the weeds toward Jay's tree house.

Flash lay cold and still, right where I'd first seen him as a pup. Through the icy November air, I could hear Jay's excited voice pleading, "He needs help, Daddy. Can we keep him? Can we? Please."

For the last time, I stooped and stroked that flea-bitten bag o' bones I'd grown to love so much and said, "Reckon so, Son . . . hell, he'll be dead in a few days anyway."

Tom Davis's publishing credits include *Poets Forum, The Carolina Runner, Triathlon Today, Georgia Athlete, The Fayetteville Observer's Saturday Extra, A Loving Voice Vol. I* and *II, Special Warfare*, and Winston-Salem Writers' POETRY IN PLAIN SIGHT program for May 2013 (poetry month). He's authored the following books: *The Life and Times of Rip Jackson*; a children's coloring book, *Pickaberry Pig, The Patrol Order*; and an action adventure novel, *The R-complex.* Tom lives in Webster, North Carolina.

Homecoming

Sean Taylor

Captain A. Sean Taylor enlisted with the Iowa Army National Guard on October 24, 2002 at the age of 35. He deployed to Bagram, Afghanistan, with the Iowa Guard from August 2010–August 2011 as the Medical Operations and Plans Officer for the 334th Brigade Support Battalion. Upon returning from deployment, he transferred to the Army Reserves, where he currently serves as the Public Affairs Officer for the 649th Regional Support Group.

Jeffrey Paolano

The Corpsman

The Start

The round enters above my wrist tumbling its way up my forearm converting the muscle to milled meat. The ball exits above my elbow, although I do not feel it. Corroborating evidence is the hole in my triceps and the sleeve of my blouse.

I see it although there is no sensation, no pain. The arm is numb, hanging limp, the blood now pours down over my flaccid limb.

My right hand still grips my piece. I can still fire, still fight, still make a contribution, still support my squad. I am not out of it yet.

My mind bathes everything I see in crimson.

The world has never before appeared to me blood red as it does now. I marvel at this, examining the strange sight. I try to see past the rufous, see again the green, yellow, and brown, but the bloody red permeates all.

Crapman reaches up, grabs at my K belt, and tries to pull me down. I look down at him with languid curiosity. His lips stretch wide as they scream a word repeatedly. "Corpsman, Corpsman," the meaning slowly emerging from the miasma so that now I look about me in wonder. *Who is wounded? Who requires assistance? Whose life or limb is in danger?*

With frightening ferocity, the Corpsman tackles me, knocking me to the ground. His body shields mine from additional harm as he pulls my combat bandage from the rubber band encircling my helmet. He sprinkles antiseptic powder on my arm, wraps the bandage about the hole and retrieves my morphine vial which he rubs between his hands before ferociously slamming it into my thigh.

His features are blurry to me, bathed in crimson as they are. I cannot make him out, could not identify him in a line up, and would not know him at a picnic. This will not do; I must know his facial contours.

He pulls me up by my right arm, slings me over his shoulder, and trots to the evac huey. He flips me deftly onto the chopper deck.

The empty morphine vial is secured to my blouse collar by its needle.

I stare intently at his face, forcing myself to see through the cerise, to sear his countenance onto my memory so that I may never forget him.

This man risks his life to save mine. The Corpsman will repeatedly risk his life this day as he has done on previous days and intends to do on future days.

I escalate the pressure on my mind, forcing a clearing away of the red fog. I am rewarded with a dimming of the crimson and the emerging definition of his visage. The picture is almost clear. I nearly have a grip on his mien when suddenly his right eye disappears, replaced by a bloody, gooey, pulsating mass. His head is blown aback, which drags the remainder of him with it. I see only his body flying backwards. With the bird lifting, the deck edge extinguishes my sight line.

I see, hear, feel no more, blackness envelopes me. My will to observe weakens, overwhelmed by the drug and the debilitating effects of shock.

The Race

Sliding onto the leather seat, a slide the like I'd made a thousand times, I raise my hand to attract the barman.

"Hi, I'll have a Jameson neat, thanks," I give a glance up and down the bar to ascertain target density then swing around for a view of the whole room.

My left hand remains nestled in my lap only to be raised and revealed in the face of the greatest necessity. The Navy saved the arm and the hand but so much of the muscle tissue was destroyed, the appearance is off-putting.

I take a pull on the liquor that I already know will be the cause for my blackout around midnight. Without the depressing effect of this drug, sleep would be unattainable for me.

Just behind my eyes, the memory of the Corpsman persists, preventing sleep, inducing alcohol consumption, the root cause of emotional outbursts.

Together these factors have prohibited the forming of strong family ties, neither with my wife nor my children. They have underwritten an irascible demeanor at work, irritating to my colleagues but a decided contributor to my success.

At times my fantastical historical rehash is such that I actually blame the Corpsman, in my replications, for surrendering his life in exchange for mine. I find I cannot forgive the Corpsman for the slur he has bequeathed to me. Further, I cannot forgive myself for having failed to imprint his topographical visage on my memory. As a result, I am unable to pay due homage to him, and this failing eats away at the remainder of my being, eviscerating what character I should be hauling along life's way.

The effect is a constant polluting of my spirit. I imagine the foul, bitter taste. I am compelled to retch into my mouth unexpectedly. I wash away the bile with water but the acidity remains.

In this manner, I have stumbled through life these many years.

I have prospered financially more through the expediency of discovering the ease with which money may be acquired than any other factor. The only effect is an increase in disdain in which I hold those who are unable to realize this modest goal.

The horizon is bleak. It's as though I look out upon the heaths, uniform in their composition, unremarkable in their verdure and lacking in sustenance. There is no appeal in such a future, no reward awaits me. No realization in exchange for a lifetime of striving.

My space is on the third floor of the parking deck, with easy access to the elevator that conveys me to the floor on which my office is located. Without reason, I turn and walk down the slanted exit decks until I reach the ground floor.

I deceive myself by thinking my intention is to retrieve a cup of coffee at the shop on the corner. However, I neither regularly drink coffee nor need to obtain my own. My secretary would provide the beverage in a porcelain cup upon my request.

No, this is something else. There is meaning here, purpose. I am meant to make this pilgrimage, meant to pursue this deviation, meant to discover a new path.

On the street, a girl sits on the curb with her feet in the gutter. She appears to be sleeping, nodding off really; a doze would be more accurate. Possibly she's in the throes of a substance-induced stupor. In any event, her circumstance is precarious.

She appears to be detritus, apparently having been on the street for a time. Her boils, pocks, and tattered clothes suggest the ravages of the life.

The building employs a private security force, and one of their number closes in just now. Just as I notice her, just as I approach her, just as I appear on this spot. *Do I feel the Corpsman's breath? Is he speaking to me?*

I address the security man. "Good morning, this lady appears to be in distress," nodding towards the woman with as sincere an expression as I am able to muster.

The security man looks at me in a quizzical manner. He may not recognize me, but he recognizes the clothes, the brief case, and knows to be polite and amenable. *Failing to treat a suit just right could result in a lot of unnecessary trouble.*

"Sir, I was just thinking the same thing, that possibly it would be fortunate if I got her inside and notified the authorities. They would know best where she could get the assistance she requires," he said, smiling broadly, confident there was nothing in his monologue the suit could find offensive although his motives still eluded the guard.

I look at the security man, trying my damnedest to discern his sincerity. *Would he in truth see to her needs, did he have her welfare foremost, or was he positing for my benefit and would cast her aside at his earliest convenience?*

Peeling from my roll, I hand over the bills, saying to him, "I want this woman cared for, and I believe you do too. Take this money and use it to aid her. Here is my card, let me know what has happened to her and what else I can do to help her," I try my best to contrive an expression that conveys I am in earnest and believe that he is too.

I'm enlightened. I experience a substantial sense.

He looks down at the money and the card as he grasps them, more than a week's pay at his ten dollar an hour rate. *Here are clothes for the kids, something for his wife, the payment of overdue bills. No one hands money out to assist him, but this druggie on the street gets rewarded.*

The machinations are unfathomable.

Jeffrey A. Paolano was honorably discharged from the U.S. Navy as DK3 in 1968.

Moments: Forgotten

It's 3:00 in the morning and I'm lying awake in my bed. Normally, for a man my age that wouldn't be unusual. On any other night it wouldn't be for me, either. Tonight was different. The dreams that I fought so hard to forget for all those years have come back. It seems the older I get, the more I try to forget—the more I remember.

I was jarred from my sleep by another dream. The dreams are never exactly the same. Sometimes I'm alone and other times I'm with people I don't recognize. When there are others with me, they're shouting and then the shouts turn to screams. Tonight I was alone while I was being pursued by the faceless person dressed in black. That part is nearly always the same. I am stumbling backward, firing my weapon, but it doesn't seem to do any good. The figure just keeps coming.

Now I can feel my body shaking. I'm screaming at myself that this is only a dream and I'm trying to shake my head to wake up. The figure just keeps coming and I keep shooting. At one point the figure raises a long sharp blade into the air over my head as I stumble backward and fall. I jerk my hand up in front of my face to block the blow. My right hand strikes my face and I wake up. Now I'm lying on my bed, shaking in a cold sweat, again. I throw back the blankets and take a deep breath.

As I lie there, I notice one thing that has become common in most of the dreams. It's the smell of the jungle. The damp, musty smell is always there. Even after all of these years, I can still smell it. I sit up slowly and swing my legs out of the right side of the bed. I fumble to get my slippers on, as I peer through the dark to find them. The only light in the room is coming from the the light green glow from small bulbs on my computer and my digital clock. There's a closet straight ahead with a small window at the end. The moonlight is adding some small amount of clarification to the shadows.

I lift my head slowly to face the closet. As soon as I do, my heart rate takes a leap. At the end of the hall is the silhouette of a figure standing in front of me. Just as quickly, my heart rate falls back a few beats. It is the robe I'd hung up the night before. The moonlight from the window is casting the outline that had given me the start.

I stand up and turn to the right. I'm facing a row of windows about four feet off the floor that run over my bed. I reach out for the cord that would draw the shades up to expose whatever is out there. I pull my hand back to my side. What if this is the dream and when the blinds go up I see the jungle? The thought rocks me. I extend my hand again. I slowly pull down on the cord. I can feel the cold air that's been trapped between the blind and the glass. It rushes down over my hand and jerks me back to reality.

The blind rises slowly, and I don't see the heavy green foliage bathed in moonlight that my mind expects. My eyes slowly focus on the snow-covered leaves of the dark red oak outside my second-story window. Past the leaves on the tree, I can see the frozen lake covered with snow. The moonlight casts strange shadows over the rough surface. The swirling wind on the snow creates flashes of light back into my eyes. They're too much like other flashes I'd seen at night so many years before. My heart rate climbs just a little.

I reach out and give the cord another tug, and the blind drops back down. I stand there for a moment staring at the closed blind. What if it had been the jungle? What would I have done then? I turn back to my left and sit on the edge of my bed with my face buried in my hands. After a few minutes I sit up straight and look at the clock on the night stand. It's 3:11 in the morning. I can't go back to sleep, now. The dream will just come back and I'll be back in the jungle. I sit for several more minutes before I drop back onto the bed.

I take one more look at the clock. It's 3:15. I can only shake my head. I'm seventy-one years old. These dreams stopped a long time ago. Why do they have to come back now? These are moments to be forgotten.

Dan Bradford served a tour in the U.S. Navy and a second tour in the U.S. Air Force. After leaving the military, he studied mechanical engineering and construction management. He took up writing while at Sandia National Labs. He's written three science fiction novels, three children's stories, and a western. Dan resides in northern Minnesota with Sherry, his editor, best friend, and companion. He has three daughters and nine grandchildren. In the near future, he hopes to move to Las Vegas to continue his writing.

Poetry

Losing Self

First, whittle a wooden doll in the shape
of all you believe. As you carve an expression
on its face, think of values you espoused
in the cozy clutch of a restaurant booth.

When you dig foxholes in sand and wait
for tank treads to crush breath from your lungs,
craft a second doll that is a hollow shell in which
the first can nest. Patrol at night. Try to sleep

through day's heat beneath canopies of buzzing flies,
tension drip-drip-dripping like a faucet in sweaty dreams.
Build another shell, then another yet, when you cross
into Iraq. Crawl through bunkers, point your muzzle

into dust-choked haze, hoping no one senses your fear.
Bury that beneath another layer. When medics strap
green compresses to blooming fissures on a comrade's chest,
build another yet. Let anger guide your hands.

Pour a molten stream of hate into an outer skin of iron.
Obscure features of everything contained within.
Harden into a sledgehammer. Pound on doors,
on enemies, on loved ones after you come home.

Bill Glose is a former paratrooper, Gulf War veteran, and author of the poetry collections *Half a Man* (FutureCycle Press, 2013) and *The Human Touch* (San Francisco Bay Press, 2007). In 2011, he was named the *Daily Press* Poet Laureate. His poems have appeared in numerous publications, including *Narrative Magazine*, *Poet Lore*, and *Southern California Review*.

David R. Bublitz

break down

when my father says I love you
he's field-stripping an M16
the hand that holds mine
while we cross the street
is thumbing the magazine release
button pressing the bolt catch
pulling the charging handle
locking the bolt to the rear
checking the chamber to ensure
the weapon isn't loaded
when he asks me about my day
he's striking the bolt release so he can
move the bolt forward for disassembly
the pins in his eyes pivot and takedown
just above the safety selector switch
press the pin charge the weapon
press the pin charge the weapon
receivers separate upper and lower
as I explain why in the grand scheme of things
nothing at school really seems to matter
he flips the upper receiver around
on the table and pulls the slip ring
until guards fall away careful
to balance the charging handle
retrieve the bolt carrier group
remove the charging assembly
he says a man will do what he has to do
using the charging handle to push in
the buffer detent pin and release
the buffer and action spring
it isn't until the bolt carrier
group is stripped
the firing pin
the bolt cam pin
the bolt
the bolt carrier
the firing pin retaining pin
the extractor
it isn't until the bolt carrier
group is stripped until he finally says

reattach the top and bottom hand guards
reconnect buffer and action spring
reposition action spring in lower receiver
reassemble bolt carrier group
replace bolt carrier group
reinstall charging handle
realign receivers
clear your weapon
for your own protection,
send the bolt forward
without looking back

pull the trigger

David R. Bublitz

Mutually Assured

desert funeral
practices
are practical
you bury
your dead
within one
day of passing
it turns out
it doesn't matter
how you go
bullets
rockets
left out
in the heat
all bodies
explode

David R. Bublitz is the son of a veteran. David has completed an MFA at the Oklahoma City University Red Earth program. He teaches journalism courses at Cameron University in Lawton, Oklahoma, while advising for the student-run CU *Collegian* newspaper.

Milton Ehrlich

VA Hospital

Red Cross volunteers bring flowers to the living.
A Sergeant Major makes sure hallways are spit shined,
reminding a patient of how he had to see his face
in mirrored boots, stolen by a butcher from Bensonhurst,
who went AWOL during basic.

He thinks of a homesick woodsman from Berwick, Maine,
who was dressed down for calling his rifle a gun
instead of a piece. He broke down and wept,
and pissed himself on the barrack floor.
Discharged as a section eight: "Unfit for military duty."

Paunchy patients wearing VFW jackets and caps
adorned with patches, pins, and campaign ribbons,
shuffle down halls searching for waiting rooms.
They mingle with the young, like fathers and sons,
swapping stories about Anzio beach,
landing at Inchon, siege of Khe Sanh,
and bloody chaos from Baghdad to Baquba.

Bodies mangled by roadside bombs sit with glazed eyes
extending lobster claw arms, turning pages in old magazines.
A wheelchair-bound weekend-warrior stares where his legs used
to be, as he waits for a new pair. A volunteer agonizes about what
to say when a guardsman says, "I really like your shoes,
I used to wear them all the time." A gangrenous stink
drifts down the hall as a much older patient is cleaned up for a new fitting.

The hospital is a messy bureaucratic battlefield
with wounded managing the wounded,
victims of post traumatic stress assigned to watch
the suicidally depressed, and disengaged clerks
who can't be bothered to report black mold and mice running rampant.

Indifferent staff try to look busy carrying clipboards,
as they mindlessly gossip at the coffee machine.
Brain-damaged soldiers wander a maze of trapezoid walls
of hospital halls that murmur ghostly pleas for the help of a medic.

Loopy on percocet, patients withdraw to their rooms,
resentful and disenfranchised, under orders not to talk to the media.

Milton P. Ehrlich, Ph.D., is a psychologist and a veteran of the Korean War. He has published poems in periodicals such as the *Wisconsin Review, Antigonish Review, Seventh Quarry, Descant, Shofar Literary Review, Christian Science Monitor, Toronto Quarterly Review, Huffington Post,* and the *New York Times*.

Paul Hellweg

Dance to the Dustoff Waltz

Fear of flying no more
wounded
medevac swooping in
rotor blades whooping it up
in the key of A major
trembling violins and staccato horns,
rising.
Tracers red and green arcing
brass casings spent
sunlight reflecting
too bright, too bold, too much
no pain.
Blood sanguine and sticky
shimmering on hands, legs, abdomen
no pain.

On a litter, four men running
scrambling for their lives and mine
someone stumbles, goes down, I roll off.
It's OK, I think, I don't mind.
Just get me to the bird before she's hit
get me to the supermarket, coffee on sale
get me to Reno, prostitution still legal
get me anywhere,
just get me the fuck outta here,
and they do
sliding me in next to our platoon sergeant,
swathed head to thigh in battle dressings
our very own mummy, moaning softly
I look to the crew chief, my eyes beseeching
lift off, lift off, lift off.
The bird does, and we don't get hit.
We clear the tree line, joy surging
every cell, fiber, synapse, as
eagles vie with Valkyries for our souls,
and Wagner provides the overture.

Paul Hellweg has had more than 200 poems published since his 2009 debut. His poetry has been nominated for both the Pushcart Prize and multiple Best of the Net Awards.

D.A. Gray

Staring, Miles Away

The world wants Hollywood in single takes
but zeroes on a jagged scar again
carving down his face, not the shrapnel but its wake.
No blast remains, only dirt and burnt skin.

Some wait for stories of bullets and muzzle flash
that never emerge, only smoke's rise, an orange
glow of cigarette become columns of ash.
A soldier's eyes will the world off the page

into view. The stare connects the man miles away
and though his scar has faded pencil thin
a gleaming shines from that look like desert fire.
The Kevlar and nylon don't hold his face in place
but a silence deafens when asked where he's been,
looking always beyond your head, whites of his eyes
form shapes you will try—and always fail—to read.

D.A. Gray recently retired from the Army after 25+ years and spends his time as a full-time graduate student. Gray has published one book of poetry, *Overwatch*, Grey Sparrow Press, November 2011. His writing can also be found in *Poetry Salzburg Review*, *Grey Sparrow Journal*, *Bellow Literary Journal*, and *Spark*, among other journals.

Rat Bastard

Having done a most despicable thing
Humping ammo on Dexedrine
While I was with my
60 mike mike mortar team
In the summer of Sixty-eight

I find it
Difficult to articulate
Let it out of my mouth
That I would hydrate
While them poor sons of bitches
Dropped their rucks and 782 gear

& when they made contact
I hung back
And skated in defense of the rear
That's where
In the iron armpit buttress
Of a tualang tree
I developed a big time
Paradigm of cottonmouth from the speed

Wee white, cross top tabs,
Mailed to me from Berkeley
Where my brother would eat them
On the all-nighters cramming
For his exams in Russian
And Chinese philosophy

& all the while
They were getting hammered out there
The 1st and the 3rd
Bushwhacked by Sir Charles
And his rank and file tribe
Of jungle brother nationals

Adorned in a wardrobe of shrubbery suits
Affixed to the sweat of the goldenrod flesh
Naturally concealed from the sights

And the plight of our grunts slipping
On a slimy prolapse of roots

Out there under the wet
Of the heavy mountain steam
Rutty-slick
On a sloppy chocolate track of trails
Switch-backing portions
Of its jungled cordilleran reach

Draped in the myriad stirrups of vine
Lianas shared an unshorn border with Laos
Out on the impervious side of its tropical spine
Slightly shy and two klicks south

Of the Seventeenth where I
So bloated myself on their warm canteens
While they fought-off a force
Of invisible monkey warriors
That was the kind of
Miserable rat bastard I'd been

A kid I'd phased over with
Laid upon me
The glass-eyed horror
Of his shocking first-kill glaze
Bored a rabid hole into my conscience
& straight on back
Into my rat bastard face

Fred Rosenblum was born in St. Louis, Missouri, served with the 1st Marines in 1968–1969 Vietnam, fueling most of what has appeared in numerous publications over the years. He currently lives with his wife of forty years in San Diego, California, where they enjoy a very therapeutic existence in the warm California sun. Fred's first collection of poems, *Hollow Tin Jingles*, was released in February 2014 by Main Street Rag.

John Parker

sugar's out

excerpt from Labellum Danang, *submitted on behalf of John's family by Greg Bachar*

Snake in the summer and dog in the winter. Pharmaceuticals also sold well. This particular briar patch was full of thorns and yellow-jackets that kept us from getting the best raspberries. Any unusual movement set off a harsh alarm. The rhythms of the bush had to be disciplined into my every step. If daydreams descended on me, they had to be shed like autumn leaves. The very best sharpshooters could aim a round at a particular button of a shirt moving slowly in the haze at about 200 meters. The button would explode before one actually heard the bark of the rifle. The wearer of the shirt would be in immediate need of a tailor. Several of the boys had cut their teeth on hunting rifles and had devised many unusual ways of unbuttoning a shirt with a bullet. When it wasn't the leeches, it was some Victor Charlie trying to take a chunk out of an unsuspecting calf just before the downed foe's rigor mortis set in. He would take that bite even if he had more rounds in him than Sugar Ray Robinson. That single bite might mean a ticket to Japan but if the bite came from one of the hookers who got her teeth through the first few layers of skin, then Our Lady of the Resurrection Hospital in Chicago was the next stop. Fruitcakes came in the mail; lemon peel and all. One of them could be washed down with a can of fruit cocktail or a cola. Well-meaning relatives thought they were just the thing but brown bread would have been a better choice and gone perfectly with our baked beans. During the monsoon everyone looked like a wet dog and smelled like one. The skin on our feet curled up like thousand-year old peaches. Dry socks brought a better price than nylons from the priciest Parisian boutiques.

John Parker was born in Worcester, MA, in 1948 and served two tours of duty in Vietnam, where he worked as a Marine Corps interrogator. John earned a Bachelor's degree in English from UMass, Amherst in 1977 and was awarded the M.F.A. in English and Creative Writing (Poetry) in 1993, also at UMass, Amherst. During his long tenure in China after leaving Amherst, John taught literature and English language courses at Fudan University, Shanghai University Fine Arts College, Shanghai Jiotona University, and City University of Hong Kong at SJTU.

London Burning
1939–1945

Even now I can hear that thrum . . . that sound high above
That made me numb in those days long gone by
When they crossed the Channel far up in the sky,
And panic-stricken search lights began their pencil weave
Too late for many, those left must grieve.

Caught between the hell that was sky and earth
Of bombs there never was a dearth.
The guns brought in from coastal shores helped guard the city:
The Enemy was at its door. Awakening at night sometimes I still can hear
Those awful bombers, of yesteryear.

For those with no concept what war can bring, think of a simple thing.
You take for granted the water you drink, the tap you turn on at your sink.
The road you walk upon, the car you drive.
But if in a war you manage to stay alive
You will accept the fact that things won't always jive.

The gas mains will probably be gone and water and sewage mixed. . .
And ONE lit match and you've blown yourself to bits.
And when you are all in hell together you have to do your share
Even when it means giving something that you can barely spare.

It most certainly will be, you will not drive a car—
To walk is what you'll have to do, even if it's far.
And nothing will ever be the same again, you can bet on that!
But if you are lucky and survive the blown up sewers, polluted water
And toilets that never work; and then there's the shrapnel through the window
That killed the dog. But that was friendly fire, just a quirk!

Of gas mains broken where one match will take you off!
And before you've got things straightened out more bombs come from aloft.
Bombs in daylight: a reminder lest you forget what bombs at night
Are really like. And along with all the rations and all the queues for food
You will always have a hunger, for there never is quite enough food.

You will tell yourself that you are brave,

It's the only thing to do while trembling in the dark of night
In a bomb shelter, praying for one more day,
Or even two.

In 1941, Lilah Pearce, at age 17, volunteered for the Women's Land Army. She became one of England's Land Girls, who replaced the farmers sent to war and helped feed her nation and military for the duration. She married an American sailor and came to the U.S. in 1946, leaving her beloved country and family forever. Lilah is an artist in St. Charles, Missouri, and a veteran of the Senior Olympics and Missouri Choral Society.

Charles H. Johnson

I Came Back

I came back
because I learned how to survive
in the infantry
in the jungle
in sweat-soured fatigues.

I came back
because I learned how to lead
men into combat
how to deploy after a chopper insertion
how to clear bunkers
how to set up an automatic ambush
how to radio for a fire mission
how to call in a dust off
how to smoke three packs a day
how to burn leeches off my skin.

I came back
with a Combat Infantry Badge
on a uniform I was advised
not to wear after landing in California.

I came back
to realize after 43 years
I still could recapture
my childhood innocence
and fascination with life
despite all the death
I learned how to inflict.

I finally came back
after so many years
away from home.

Charles H. Johnson

He Did Not Belong

He did not belong on a battlefield
yet he joined to go to war anyway
marching behind a line of men
struggling to stay in step
with the siren cry of a bugle.

There were no heroics.
Only bugs and mud and food
that tasted like leftover memories.

He did as he was ordered
but always with a twist
that kept him around
to fight another day.

And fight he did.
Just enough to return home alive
to see the picture of peace
he had dreamed of on the battlefield
though his mind was now a puzzle
lacking edges and a frame
to keep all the pieces together.

A graduate of Rutgers University, Charles H. Johnson was a 1st Lt. infantry platoon leader in the 1st Cavalry Division (air mobile) in South Vietnam in 1970-71. He continued to serve in the Army Reserves after the war. In the 50th Armored Division, he had been a mechanized infantry captain company commander before leaving the military in 1983. He is a 2013 second place winner of the Allen Ginsberg Poetry Awards and the 2011 New Jersey Poetry Prize winner. His third poetry collection, Smoke Signals, was awarded a 2010 Paterson Poetry Prize for Literary Excellence. His second book, Sam's Place, about his Vietnam experiences and published in 2006, won a literary excellence award, also. A retired newspaper editor, he also is a Geraldine R. Dodge Foundation Poet in the Schools. He lives in Hillsborough, N.J., with his wife Lainey.

Andrew R. Jones

Old Friend

Hello old friend. It's been quite some time since you've come around. I've been well without you, but I must admit, there are times I miss you.

Giving you the control you had allowed me to not take responsibility. "It's not my fault, it's my PTSD."

The tears. The screams. The dark rooms and dramatic scenes. Broken walls and broken hearts.

Like a high-explosive rocket impacting a brick wall, you blew apart my support structure. You cut the rope to the bridge that connected me to each person I ever cared about and more importantly, the ones who cared about me.

I was your POW. Bagged, tagged, and segregated. To your table of torture I was tied, subjected to nightmarish forms of cruelty causing others to perceive me as a monster. An unrecognizable beast of unpredictability.

But a day came when all of that changed. Do you remember that day? 'Cuz I do. Very well as a matter of fact. I was beaten, scarred and tired, but with my last breaths I cried out for my Savior, my Lord.

"End this and take me home, or set me free and guide my journey." As if they were a child's toy, your rusted chains broke from my wrists and ankles and I embraced my freedom. I realized I never had to be your prisoner, I was always free to go.

But I had to make that choice.

Our time together was enjoyable for a season and I will always miss the misery. But eternal life and happiness is what is meant to be. So this is goodbye old friend. Goodbye forever.

You're no longer welcome in my life or in my home. And don't worry, it's not you, it's me. I'm no good for you. I actually desire to smile and I know how much you hate that.

So be on your way, I'm a free man today.

Andrew R. Jones

The RPG

They say you can hear it coming,
The RPG. I used to agree until the day
It hit me like that moment you realize
Your parents had sex the day you were conceived.

An instant of surprise which stopped time and
Although I was lifted up, the moment was
Not so uplifting. Brick became dust and
Silence became silent as combat became clear.

To the Gunner who saw me—this life
Or the next—we'll meet again. I want to
Say I'll return your rocket,
But chances are,
I'll shake your hand.

Andrew R. Jones is a Marine Corps combat veteran of Iraq (2003). Andrew is published in *Outrageous Fortune, Canyon Voices, Veteran's Writing Project, International War Veterans Poetry Archives, The Traveler, The Gila River Review, The War Writer's Campaign* and *The Blue Guitar.* He is also the author of *Healing the Warrior Heart* and *A Warrior's Crown.* Andrew is pursuing an English (Creative Writing) degree with ASU in Phoenix, Arizona.

Ashley Henley

The War Behind Closed Doors

My soldier left the battlefield,
with many wounds still unhealed.
He no longer wages death in a far-off land;
he has been labeled a broken man.
As the wife of a wounded soldier,
my devotion to God, my family, and my country remains unwavered.
Behind closed door battles rage every night.
Patiently I often wait until the morning light.
My wounded soldier is not home.
His missions are unclear and often he simply roams.
As dawn approaches jingling keys ripple my waves of anxiety,
as I tremble in the dark awaiting whom I will see.
My combat earns no badges or medals of honor.
Daily I fight in this war behind closed doors.
My mission, through enduring faith in God above,
is to never give up, never leave behind the man I love.

I am a mother, a teacher by profession, and the wife of a wounded soldier by the grace of God. We married two weeks before he left for his tour of duty in Operation Iraqi Freedom in 2005. Our son was conceived just two days before my husband boarded a plane for Iraq. Enduring the entire pregnancy without my husband, while simultaneously completing my Master's Degree, was truly a challenge, but nothing could have prepared me for the challenge I would face upon my husband return from war. His transition to civilian life has been a long, hard journey for our family, but we have survived. Our family's strength is gifted to us by the Lord above, and we are truly blessed to share our story of love.

Bruce Sydow

My North Star

I was born in an amniotic ocean,
a salty fluid of life,
buoyant and sustaining.

But I swam in oblique angles,
and like a dolphin racing a bow,
I darted to avoid the centerline.

I joined the Marines
searching for discipline
and direction.

I lost all purpose after Vietnam
and became a wayfarer
seeking respite from the storm.

Convulsed in night terrors,
I was ready to take sail
to any distant shore.

By an act of serendipity,
I crashed into a safe harbor
and her welcoming arms.

We collided like two oceans,
a boiling vortex of currents,
a Cape Horn of love.

She waited patiently for the calm
and steered me toward the horizon
as I thrashed in the water.

In the end,
I stayed true
to her charted course.

She is my first-mate,
my moral compass,
and the navigator of my heart.

Bruce Sydow. *Photo courtesy of the author.*

Bruce Sydow was decorated with the Combat Aircrew Wings, United States Air Medal, and Cross of Gallantry for his service as a door gunner in a Marine Corps helicopter attack squadron in Vietnam. He holds a master's degree from the University of Washington, Seattle. He taught at Chapman University and St. Martin's University, among other colleges, was elected Professor of the Year twice, and received the Excellence in Teaching Award. He has been published widely.

Carl Palmer

don't

I did it
reenlisted
stayed in the Army
for the money
times were tight
not many jobs
even if I had the education
long welfare lines
friends out of work

but I wasn't an infantryman
didn't wear a steel pot
carried no weapon
never slept in a foxhole
there was no war
I was a peacetime soldier
a radar technician
on a missile site
with unarmed missiles

now there's Iraq
you've already been there twice
once to Afghanistan
you'll have to go again
you ask what I would do
ask if you should reenlist
don't
please don't
don't ask

Carl Palmer

left unsaid

as I enter his room
he focuses upon me
silently begging me not to ask
of his absent roommate

empty bed freshly made
side table tidy and neat
surrounding area cleared
of anything personal

in that part of the VA hospital
where soldiers go missing

Carl "Papa" Palmer, retired Army, retired FAA, now just plain retired, lives in University Place, Washington. He has seven chapbooks and a contest-winning poem riding buses somewhere in Seattle. Carl's poetry is in both *Proud to Be* volumes I and II.

Charity Tahmaseb

The Boys' Club

Saudi Arabia, January 1991

In the early morning, steam rises from fifty-five
gallon drums. Old Spice and menthol
ride the breeze.

The men never falter in this ritual.
By the time the sun's heat touches
the air, all that's left behind are
dots of shaving cream on sand.

The scrape of razors sounds like grit
against metal, and that razor-burn red?
The men wear it like a badge of honor

I watch them,
my feet itching to creep closer.
Would the captain lend me
his shaving cream?
Or would I have to bring my own?

Could I kick off my boots, roll my pant legs,
and hike a foot on the rim
of the drum?

And if I carved up my legs like they do
their faces, would that be enough?
Or are there other rituals to endure
to be a member of the club?

Charity Tahmaseb has slung corn on the cob for Green Giant and jumped out of airplanes (but not at the same time). She's worn both Girl Scout and Army green. These days, she writes fiction (long and short) and works as a technical writer.

Charlie Sherpa

Suburbistan

The snap, crumple, and pop of small arms fire
arrives through the sliding door I have cracked
open to the spring as I breathe in
the earthy black steam of liquid breakfast.
"The sound of Freedom!" I mutter happily to the trees,
an old joke from when we first moved to Suburbistan.

The red flag will now be up on Post, and the easy morning sun will rake
long shadows behind the paper silhouettes. Sergeants will herd their smoking
  soldiers
in waves back across the road. There, they will first click in their zeroes,
then move as individuals toward their qualifying rounds.
At all times, they will take great care to keep their weapons pointed up and
  downrange.
They will take all orders from the tower. Lunch will be an M.R.E.

Now routine, the weekend noise has faded into
the distant soundscape of our lives, only occasionally called to attention
like the late 9 o'clock train ("Was that the a.m. or p.m.?"),
rescheduled Friday Night football games ("Isn't it Thursday?"),
and the Civil Defense test that happens at 12 noon
the first Saturday of each month, rain or shine.

Odysseus had himself lashed to the mast
and told his men to plug their ears with wax
to avoid the Sirens' call. Instead, I stand on my deck, listening,
sipping, wearing a bathrobe, wishing that I could grab my musket
and run toward the sound of the guns
one last time.

Charlie Sherpa is a pseudonym for Randy Brown. In 2010, Randy Brown was preparing for deployment to Eastern Afghanistan as a member of the Iowa Army National Guard's 2nd Brigade Combat Team, 34th Infantry "Red Bull" Division. After he dropped off the deployment list, he retired with 20 years of military service and a previous peacekeeping deployment. He then went to Afghanistan anyway, embedding with Iowa's Red Bull units as a civilian journalist in May–June 2011. Brown writes about military topics at: www.redbullrising.com.

Chelsie Meredith

At 3:53 am, I wake after rolling over in my sleep

And not pressing into your body.
Getting up, I walk to the kitchen
aghast at empty moonlight.
Thought I'd find you, water glass
in hand; but then, I remembered—
deployment.
                    *

And on the phone line, our silence
lessons, warsilence, silencefugue.

Chelsie Meredith teaches in the Rhetoric and Writing Department of San Diego State University and acts as a managing editor for Six Arrow Press, a small literary press. She has publications in *Pleiades: A Journal of New Writing*, *Mosaic: Art and Literary Review*, and *Litconic: A Pincushion of Literature*.

David S. Pointer

Launchpad Central

That persona non grata graduate degree
allowed me to float atop many troubles
like a space pathogen, a speck not seen
above banished jobs or blast concussions
endured by next-gen significant others and
to understand sturdy psychological endurance
can be eroded constantly by the weight of
at-homeland-economic-underhandedness and
hoof marks leading to little stress bombarder
check stubs tiny by elite choice with so much
permafrost filling that my lucky regeneration
by small press poetry scribbled by Inkville-ite
buccaneers marginalized as much or more as
enlisted veterans made me feel like reentry

David S. Pointer was born in Kansas City, Missouri. He served in the United States Marine Corps from 1980–1984 as a military policeman.

Domenic James Scopa

Has-Been Highway Sign

The sign is pocked with bullet holes.

My grandfather would shoot
the highway signs of backcountry Virginia,
prone in the pickup bed
of his antique Ford Ranchero
he planned to will to me,
testing if he was still accustomed
to recoil, muzzle flash, and gunpowder smell.

I do not know that much
about the Korean War,
except that he received a terse prosaic
from the Draft Board notifying him
that he would have to leave his farm life:
his pond with trout and fattened catfish,
the mooing of his cows with swollen udders,
insistent as cicadas singing till they die.

It took sixteen days to travel
to the country nicknamed
"land of mornings calm,"
the mornings anything but calm.

He wrote that "The Forgotten War"
would never be forgotten,
nor his farmer friends still there,
their bodies unrecovered,
themselves now fertilizer for Korea's chilled soil.
Whenever my grandfather gets a chill,
he thinks their souls are trying to seize his attention.

The sign lies tire-printed as a testament
to those who did not heed its warning,

as if to say *slow down, slow down, slow down.*

Domenic Scopa is a student at Suffolk University and will be graduating in April. He was recently accepted into the Vermont College of Fine Arts, and will attend there in June to attain an MFA in Poetry and Translation. He has worked closely with a number of accomplished poets including National Book Award Winner David Ferry and Washington Book Prize recipient Fred Merchant. He is currently the assistant poetry editor of *Venture* literary magazine and has been published in literary journals numerous times.

Dominika Wrozynski

Record Keeper Of All You Want To Forget

1.
I know there are charred bodies
in those pictures you won't let me see.

I know what it means to investigate,
though not what it means to drive across
the Kuwaiti border in the back of a humvee
with a bull's-eye on its back, with the Kevlar
vest your parents sent you underneath
a starched white shirt.

Your crew cut and khaki pants do not belong
here—Kuwaiti men don't often have red hair.
But the general likes you, soldier, likes the way
you do things,

he says, and presses a coin into your palm—
a general's coin: it smells sterile,

you think, like a surgeon's scalpel. It's an honor,
he says. A heavy honor,

you think. An honor to be given this coin,
he says. An honor to document the dead,

you think, to add new names you make every effort
to pronounce to the list.

And now you are tied forever to these angry,
pale hills dotted with oilrigs—giant clumsy
beetles, burrowing deep into the land.

I'm not surprised when you do show me pictures
of the Kuwaiti skyline—skyscrapers that rival those
in American cities. It's beautiful,
you say, when there are no explosions.

2.
Your lens zooms in on the woman's hair, framing

her face just so, or the bias of a crocheted shawl
that cuts a black swath across her waist. Either way,
you won't focus on her legs, no longer there.

You want to know her name—her Arabic name—
not the translation.

You want to hear the syllables that still belong to her,
want to weave their husky silk into a shroud.

You wonder if your name has a translation,
if you exist in Arabic, if you could have been born
here. You could certainly die here,

you think, and they will write your number
on a metal box, and it will only matter to your parents
then, who will engrave it on prayer cards.

If your commanders ever check these pictures
you never take, this woman will be long gone,
buried by her brother who never wanted to meet
you, who wants you to do your job and get the hell out
of his city, while the smokestacks continue pouring black
clouds, and your nose bleeds at least once a day.

Dominika Wrozynski is Assistant Professor of English at Manhattan College in the
Bronx, where she teaches creative writing and literature. Her most recent work has
appeared in *Crab Orchard Review*, *Spoon River Poetry Review*, *Saw Palm*, and *Rattle*.
Her husband, Todd, served three tours overseas in the U.S. Military (both in the Navy
and in the Army).

Jeremy Warneke

Tampa

Jeremy Warneke is a veteran of the Illinois Army National Guard. He served in Iraq immediately following "mission accomplished" and subsequently received a BA from Sarah Lawrence College. He was previously an unpublished writer.

Doug D'Elia

Counting M-16's a Part in My Sheep

The rumors were spreading like mountain wildfire.
The M-16 rifle was reported, "failing to extract."
In civilian terminology, they jammed.

Word spread from an advance platoon
that 72 men went into battle and only 19
came back. Most of the dead were found
with their M-16's broke down next to their bodies.
They were trying to fix them when they were overrun.
Overrun like Santa Ana's troops swarming the Alamo.
Jim Bowie fighting back with his knife,
and Davey Crockett and William Travis
with their rifles butts. I don't want to die like that.

So, I keep cleaning my damn weapon,
day and night, obsessively.
I empty the chamber,
remove the magazine,
lubricate, separate, clean,
sweep, loosen, then reassemble.
I do it all day long; I do it till I get blisters;
then I do it some more.
I do it at night before I sleep,
then I do it some more, in my dreams.

I want to remind them that this isn't the fucking Alamo,
I want to tell them I need a weapon that works!
I'm not going out there. I'm not!
It's one dollar for opium, a stinking dollar,
and five dollars for a vial of morphine,
pot is cheaper than cigarettes, and a seed planted
in this climate matures in a week.

I'm tired of thinking about death.
Tired of thinking about Davey Crockett.
I need to relax. I need to get high. I need to zone-out.
I need to close my eyes and hear the Miracles,

or the Temptations, or Led Zeppelin.
I need to hallucinate. I need dream nonsense.
I need to stop counting M-16's a part in my sheep.

Doug D'Elia was born in Massachusetts and served as a medic in the Vietnam Theatre. He is the author of four books of poetry including *A Thousand Peaceful Buddhas* and *75 Klicks Above the Do Lung Bridge*, both inspired by the Vietnam War. Doug is an active member of the Syracuse Veteran's Writers group. His web site is dougdelia.com

Janelle Fila

Safe Place

The first thing the balding man tells you:
This is a
safe place
where you can let out your emotions
talk honestly and
candid
about your feelings and other feel good bullshit he learned
in the safety of a classroom while you
got pelted by mortar rounds
as you camped overnight in a hand dug trench.
He pushes his granny glasses up his
hawk nose
as you tell him how you almost
pissed your pants every time a man in a turban
walked within your target area and reached
into his robes.
How you prayed his hands came out empty
so you didn't have to shoot him in the head
before he blew himself
and half your squadron into
bloody pieces all over the marketplace.
That makes him uncomfortable, he says, as he scratches notes about you in
  the tiny
notebook on his lap.
You squirm in the seat
your right hand burning with the phantom pain
of an amputee.
You miss your closest ally
your only protection in a strange and violent land
but the government made you promise
to give up your gun when you came home.

Janelle Fila is a 32-year-old avid reader, student, wife, mom, and daughter of an Air Force Veteran. She is also the editor of youngADULTplatform, a new online presence of writers and readers of quality, honest fiction for teens and adults. This fall, she will continue her education with an MFA for Children and Young Adult literature.

Kaleb Cintonz

Our Heroes

People who fought for our freedom,
Protect us from harm,
Survived the war,
Died for our American dreams,
Live by a code,
Make us a better country,
Veterans!

My name is Kaleb Cintonz. I am 10 years old. My Grandfather was LTC Ronald Ralph Devitt of the United States Army. I wrote this poem on Veterans Day in remembrance of him. He taught me everything about bravery and sacrifice for one's country.

Karla Chapman

My Daddy Is My Hero

My daddy has a job to do
He says it's far away
He says it's real important too
Or else he would stay
I watch my daddy pack
His uniforms and socks
He puts my picture in his sack
And hands me a box
I open it up
As I let my tears fall
It's his picture on a cup
He got it at the mall
He gives me a bear
To hug and kiss good night
His favorite shirt to wear
To know everything's all right
It's now time for him to leave
I beg him not to go
He tells me not to grieve
He'll be back soon I know
My daddy is my hero
Fighting for the freedom we say is our right
My daddy is my hero
Fighting so we can sleep in peace at night
My daddy is my hero
A soldier who will fight until the world can unite

Karla Chapman grew up in the military, joined the military at 19, and married military. She has a deep respect for military members and their families. Her three children have become accustomed to military life, and constantly amaze with their strength and faith. Karla says she has been the child, waiting for her father to return, and now is the wife, encouraging and comforting her children as they wait for their daddy to return.

Liam Corley

Intelligence Report

Bottom line up front: *tonight*
the living sons harvest
poppy stalks, dry and sweet,
and burn the scant fields clean.

A mined road
extending from the village heart
leads to men smoking
in the hulk of a Soviet APC,
nodding as the conversation turns
to the next zakat,
who will pay
and how.

Fingering another spot
on the map, an elder cracks
pistachios. Shells pile up
on shura mats; each one speaks
to the unhelmeted commander whose hams
ache as he squats in the circle and weeks
after when he reports
to the scene of an unexploded IED.

One smiling face has valleys deeper than
the Korengal, lines marked by
years of squinting against the sun
and an enemy's silhouette.

Last to leave, he moves from pine
to pine, disappearing in the shade
of trees whose roots split rocks
to anchor in a hardened place.

Liam Corley

Father Jacob Gets His Limp

A limb of the soul, broken and refused, aches
when barometric pressure on the heart
recalls a moral wounding that mistakes
a loss inflicted for its willing part.

Irradiating thought, the pain escapes
in waves of guilt or innocence dismayed
from shrapnel lodged within synaptic tapes
that wake the dead whenever they are played.

How unforeseen the pang that splits our core
when gaming boys respectfully request
to know how many we have killed in war:
the one confirmed remains inside this chest.

What would we give to grieve them less? The truth?
That crimes abroad were born in callous strife
that codger, blogger, and protesting youth
daily sow in democratic life?

Returning as a patriarch at night,
alone, in pain, a concentrated debt
of foreign ghosts, of haloed fear, we fight
the bitter angel of a just regret.

The country's public sopping of our crime
is conscience pricked to life by brokenness;
when our distress compounds their sentenced time,
we blow the joint the angel turned to bless.

Liam Corley is an associate professor of English at California State Polytechnic University, Pomona, where he teaches American literature. Lieutenant Corley is spending 2013 to 2016 on military leave to serve as an instructor at the U.S. Naval Academy. He is a 2008–2009 veteran of Operation Enduring Freedom (Afghanistan).

Richard O'Connell

For a Dead Soldier

In the cathedral of your luck
You knelt and preyed on hapless girls,
Finding their pliant bodies warm
With the wine of real rituals.

You wrote your blood hurt on the ship
Going over—blamed our big drunk;
You wrote about your last good piece
Of luck: a round, rebounding blonde.

War is a lot like loving too,
A kind of fever and the swift
Coitus of the shuddering guns
Recoiling ends in the hot flesh.

From the Korean cold they fly
Your indestructible body home
While I compose an elegy
Of drunken days in our old room.

Richard O'Connell

Small War

Evil is statistical: a long range game of mind:
Programming the data: it's merely a matter
Of parallel logistics: a mythic country
Ground in the joint jaws of an identical cancer.

Look at the map: it's a lesson in dissolution.
It could go on forever if we're careful,
Diverting blood and the precise amount of terror:
The only treason: reason: quelling the confusion.

It's a matter of girding them: a bright meat grinder:
Of obfuscating all the nasty boring facts:
Those muddy faces fleeing towards you from vague fire,
Carrying their homes and the maimed on their backs.

Richard O'Connell lives in Deerfield Beach, Florida. He served in the U.S. Navy during the Korean War. Collections of his poetry include *RetroWorlds*, *Simulations*, *Voyages*, and *The Bright Tower*, all published by the University of Salzburg Press (now Poetry Salzburg). His poems have appeared in *The New Yorker*, *The Atlantic Monthly*, *National Review*, *The Paris Review*, *Margie*, *Measure*, *Southern Humanities Review*, *Acumen*, *The Formalist*, etc.

Robert B. Robeson

A Bad Trip

War is an off-note that sours the chords of life,
    a second-by-minute nightmare;
        flight from reality,
            self-defeating,
    sensing your entire life ticking down and
        wondering what new horrors
            the next day will bring.

Combat's a terminal overdose in the throes of another trip,
    often being "takee" rather than taker;
        mind-blowing experience,
            acute intoxication,
    surrendering your virtue to borrow a vice
        and paying a fiddler
            who's not playing your song.

War is waves of cold chills crawling through your flesh,
    body shaking like a vibrator;
        whispers that scream,
            inhaling danger,
    only marginally in control of any situation—
        struggling with confusing puzzles
            whose pieces continually change shapes.

Combat is a place where death is difficult to avoid,
    universally ruled by invisible forces;
        moral eyes blinded,
            zombie existence,
    wondering if anyone truly cares and discovering
        living is more courageous
            than striving to accelerate the dying.

Lieutenant Colonel Robert Robeson flew 987 medevac missions in South Vietnam (1969–1970) evacuating 2,533 patients. Seven of his helicopters were shot up by enemy fire and he was shot down twice. He's been decorated 8 times for valor, in addition to being awarded a Bronze Star and 26 Air Medals. He was operations officer and commander with the 236th Medical Detachment in Da Nang. Robeson retired from the U.S. Army with over 27 years of service.

Valerie E. Young

To My Fellow Vets

To all my fellow vets; it's time for us to elevate
Time to let go of our triggers; remove the tendency to self-medicate

Exhaling, tired of crying, seems that's all I tend to do
I feel like I'm losing my mind, not sure what is true

Constant thoughts, running through my mind, how do I make it stop
I just feel like rain, constantly pouring eventually it drops

Angry outburst at people, because they don't understand my pain
My past, military experience runs often through my brain

Who can I trust, enemies all around me; who is for real
It's like I am dying many deaths, now that's the real deal

Going to doctors, in hopes that there is a cure for PTSD
But only my fellow vets grasp my thoughts and really see

TBIs, insomnia, shell shocked, I'm panicky all the time
Maybe I need to go scream, go somewhere just to unwind

Constantly in isolation, avoidance of crowds, that's suitable 4 me
It seems that is a normal solution, but what's normal for me

We are trained "for discipline, or 1 shot 1 kill"
Not realizing what they turned on or what they instilled

Scared to go to sleep because nightmares are always there
I am frequently trying to avoid sleep but can't go nowhere

I have to catch myself because I am unpredictable
Not knowing if my mood would change, I'm feeling unstable

It's like people want us to fail, so many bets
No one understands my plea, my cries, but my fellow vets.

Valerie Elizabeth Young is a veteran of the United States Armed Forces, serving for ten years. She is mother to four-year-old son Sultan and three-year-old daughter Ver-TRUoz (pronounced Virtuous). She has a bachelor's degree in Sociology and Criminal Justice and is currently studying for a master's degree in Criminal Justice at Lindenwood University.

Wayne Bowen

A Tribute To Anthony Loyd

I'll whisper you a secret
If you promise not to tell
There is joy Over There
A pleasure in that hell

We cry to leave our lives and homes
And cry when we return
But in our hearts we feel
For There we'll always yearn

Over There our needs were met
Over There a simpler life
With KBR our mama
And Pentagon as our wife

They say that war is hard
That man craves just for peace
But having lived There for a time
I see that death still feasts

"My war gone by, I miss it so"
Is what Anthony did write
Of death, and pain, and longing for
The boredom and the fight

Once There, now Here
We lose and gain both ways
There never was a soldier true
Who doesn't miss those days

I miss my war, I do, but please
Don't send me back
I left too much of me There
That happy, miserable Iraq

Wayne H. Bowen served in Iraq in 2004, then at the rank of Major, with the 416th Civil Affairs Battalion. He continues to serve in the U.S. Army Reserve as a Lieutenant Colonel. Bowen is professor of history, chair of the Department of History, and director of University Studies at Southeast Missouri State University. He is the author of six books, including *Undoing Saddam: From Occupation to Sovereignty in Northern Iraq* (University of Nebraska/Potomac Books, 2007).

Milton J. Bates

As They Were

As you were!

The sergeant's voice was stern, peremptory,
unlike the weary drone he'd opened with:

This is Instruction Block Three hmnnn,
Chu Lai Combat Training Center hmnnn,
"Securing Your Perimeter" hmnnn . . .

The first mortar shell shattered his monotone.
It seemed to come from somewhere deep
inside the earth, burrowing furiously upward
until it punched the floor of the Quonset hut
where they sat in rows. The roof thundered
shortly after with the heavy hail of jungle stuff.

Hit the deck!

They hit it just in time to feel the second
blast along the full length of their bodies.
The floor bucked again, and the walls did
something they'd never seen before: the metal
folded neatly inward like a bellows pleat,
then folded out, as though the building,
too, sucked in its breath and then exhaled.

The roof rattled as before, and all was
quiet. Block Three would have to wait.
Perhaps tomorrow they would learn
how to secure a perimeter, how to hit
the deck with grace and dignity, how to be
as they were before the war turned real.

Milton J. Bates

Mantra

There it is, they said, and meant it,
when there was nothing else to say
about the village vaporized

by a misplaced bomb, the patrol
shredded by artillery support,
the short-timer wasted by a booby trap.

There it was when a letter from home
said there was no home to return to,
when a platoon went over the edge,

shooting chickens and children.
There it was whenever logic failed,
or justice. You could question

the whereness of *there* or the whatness
of *it*, but not the pure ontology of *is*.
Is refused to answer questions.

Syllables so often in their mouths
grew smooth and egg-shaped like
the pebbles along the South China Sea.

They chose streaked or speckled ones,
rinsed off the sand, and put them
in their pockets for good luck.

Milton J. Bates served as an army sergeant in Vietnam in 1970–1971. During a career as a professor of English, he published several nonfiction books, including *The Wars We Took to Vietnam: Cultural Conflict and Storytelling* (University of California Press, 1996). Since retiring, he has also published poetry in magazines such as the *Great Lakes Review*, *Midwestern Gothic*, *O-Dark Thirty Review*, *Peninsula Poets*, *Stoneboat*, and the *Wallace Stevens Journal*.

Essays

DeVonna R. Allison

The Summer of the Mouse

It was the summertime, 1986, and I, along with 2,200 other Marine reservists, was involved in a live-fire, combined service exercise on the Army post, Fort Carson, in Colorado. We were in the high desert, in the very shadow of NORAD (the North American radar defense compound), training for war, with the support of active-duty Army soldiers. The days were hot, broken by a mid-day shower that drenched any soldier or Marine unlucky enough to find him/herself away from shelter. My job was support-based, meaning I served behind the lines of engagement. I was with a Communications Unit out of Fort Wayne, Indian, (Det 1, CommCo, H&S Bn, 4th FSSG), and my "office" each day was the Communications Center, the heart of the exercise's radio and field telephone system. Daily I worked the main switchboard and the radio. I was a sergeant at that time, and the men I was working with were young and high-spirited. Pranks were not uncommon but never interfered with our duties.

One day, when the majority of the Marines were in the field engaged in training, I was given the task of rounding up a group of men to "police" the living areas of the tent city. With 2,000-plus people living, eating, and sleeping in a tented area, the potential for mess was great, and no entity hates disorder more than the United States Marine Corps. Off I went with a small detail of men to scour the empty tents, picking up anything that hadn't been left there by God Himself. Being in the desert, I warned the men to watch for snakes, who would be prone to curl up under the piles of empty MRE cartons we were gathering for burning.

While I mostly supervised the detail, I also spent my time going through the tents, kicking piles of cardboard before picking them up, "just in case." It was in kicking one pile of cardboard that suddenly half a dozen little desert mice came shooting out in all directions. My bloodcurdling scream split the desert air followed by the sounds of shouts and boots hitting the ground as my detail tore through the tents trying to find me. When they did find me, there was a moment of shocked silence as they skidded to a stop in the sand and beheld their leader halfway up the main tent pole, desperate to escape the vermin. That merciful moment of silence was followed by uproarious laughter and various rude comments. I slid back down the pole, trying to maintain some semblance of dignity as they ribbed and kidded me, saying I'd better request hazardous duty pay if I were going to continue to be sent on such dangerous missions as police details.

Soon we were back on track, and I hoped the incident would be forgotten as quickly as possible. Fat chance. The story of Sergeant Allison's disgraceful retreat in the face of her whiskered enemy made the rounds and I incurred even more ribbings. "What's that on Sergeant Allison's boot? A mouse?!"

The chuckling had hardly calmed down when one wag returned from a trip to Mainside, the commercial part of the base where the bank, post office, and shops were located, with a cat toy shaped like, what else? a mouse.

To his credit the Marine had picked out a particularly life-like caricature, even down to the real rabbit's fur that covered its vile little body. Suddenly, that mouse was everywhere. Staring at me from atop the field radio, peeking out of an empty can, perched on the switchboard. This went on for several days, and I prided myself that I was never once taken in. The Marines were disappointed at my lack of reaction but inventive in the places they found for me to discover the toy, always hoping to recreate that incident in the tent. Wherever I found the mouse, I would turn to face a group of Marines, all with their best "innocent choirboy" faces on.

After a few days of this, I found the mouse atop my can of Coke and drew the line. Holding the toy by its tail I held it up for all to see and, placing it in my pocket, announced playtime was over, let's get back to work. Their disappointment was palpable but short-lived as inspections loomed, and there was serious work to do. Many of them were called to act as radiomen to the inspectors who roamed the forward battlefield in jeeps, grading the Marines in the field on their action, and I was putting in long, late hours manning the switchboard and field radio.

On one of those late nights, I walked a quarter mile of the tent city, from the Comm Center to the women's tents at 11:00 at night. I was careful, as always, to stay in the very center of the aisles that passed through the tents at night, since personal attacks in the field were not unheard of. Lit only by moonlight, the empty tents loomed larger in the night; foxes squealed, yipped, and howled eerily in the darkness. I was relieved to reach my tent.

The women with whom I shared the tent were sleeping, so I moved cautiously to keep from disturbing them, stripping down in the dark, preparing for bed. I had removed my blouse and boots, and was standing barefoot in the sand in my pants and t-shirt, when I reached in to empty my pants pockets and pulled out . . . a mouse! Stifling a scream, I jumped back in horror and flung the thing from me, scattering the pocket contents across my cot. Where the vile creature had gone from there, I couldn't tell, so I grabbed my flashlight, and there, in the glow of the light, perched the toy mouse. Where a moment ago I was fighting back a scream, I now struggled to swallow my laughter.

They'd got me. Those Marines had finally given me the horrendous fright they'd been hoping for, and they weren't even there to see it. Nor would they ever hear of it. Until now.

DeVonna R. Allison at communications tent, manning a field switchboard, in June 1986.

DeVonna Allison is a freelance writer whose work has been published in various periodicals both in print and online. Recently she was a winner in the Southern California Genealogical Society's 2013 memoir writing contest and was an honorable mention in *The Binnacle* literary magazine's 2014 ultra-short competition. DeVonna and her husband, Earl, married while they served in the Marine Corps, have four children and one grandchild, and make their home in Southern Michigan.

Jarrod L. Taylor

A February Raid in the War on Terror

It was 1 A.M. Sleep this night had been elusive at best, coming in short segments between bumps and swerves that jostled us around in the cramped troop compartment of our twenty-ton tin can as we made our way toward the drop-off point for our mission. Boys in camouflage body armor, packed like sardines, leaned against one another. They moved and shifted, desperately searching for some small semblance of comfort, while trying to keep their legs and asses from going to sleep. A rifle magazine jammed into the inside of a thigh here, a hand grenade pinched a hip there. In the dim glow of my squad leader commo screen, their heavy eyelids slowly closed behind the lenses of their ballistic glasses. Heads bobbed up and down like pistons as the young warriors drifted off to sleep and awakened, startled, before their eyes drooped again. Gravity was especially cruel, pulling hard on the nearly 5 pounds of each advanced combat helmet adorned with tactical lights, d-rings, para-cord, camo bands, photos of wives and babies, and night-vision goggles, commonly referred to as nods.

Each of us fought a stiff neck, a sore ass, and tingling legs and feet when my gunner Sergeant Taaga opened the ramp. It was early February, and cold night air surrounded us as we stumbled out, rifles at the ready and adrenaline just starting to pump through our veins. We would have to worry about being tired and having aches and pains later, much later, when we are old and in our thirties. We had a mission to do.

The cold, winter night concealed our movement through a frosty grove of date palms. Our armored Stryker vehicle had deposited us along Iraq's Highway 1, at a spot some 30 miles north of Baghdad, leaving the last few klicks between us and our objective to be covered quietly on foot. The spikey trunks of date palms stood in uniform rows that disappeared into the glowing green darkness ahead. Dead and dying fronds hung low and out of place, making strange silhouettes in our night vision. Others reached up at us from their final resting places on the ground, their dry and hardened points like finely sharpened claws grabbing at our pant legs, at times puncturing fabric and flesh. Some found our faces, slicing and stinging our cold red cheeks. Decaying palm leaves, underbrush, and knee-deep ditches paralleling each row threatened at every step to give us away as we crept toward our target.

First squad was on point, walking in wide, fire team wedges, with Lloyd, their squad leader, directing from the middle. The infrared strobe light in his right shoulder pocket flashed every couple of seconds, invisible to the naked eye, but clear as day in my night vision. It lit up the palms around him, and left eerie snapshot profiles of the soldiers walking between us. I hoped they were on their game, since Lloyd's squad would be my over-watch when we reached our objective.

My alpha team walked between me and Lloyd's soldiers. Sergeant Fraleigh, who we often called Frolo, was at the front of his fire team wedge. Fraleigh was the best kind of guy to have as a team leader. He was a young sergeant, but he was big, loud, aggressive, and fearless. I watched him win our division's boxing championship long before he became one of my team leaders. He was the type of NCO who struck fear into the hearts of privates and Iraqis alike. No one wanted to be on his bad side.

As we walked, I spun around to check the spacing of my bravo fire team. My other team leader, Sergeant Jimmy Bridges, was walking at the apex of his team's wedge. They were doing exactly what they were supposed to be doing. I was proud of my boys tonight. Their spacing was perfect, and despite all of the obstacles, we were moving silently through the palms toward our objective. It all looked like a scene from a war movie or even a trailer for some new video game. Heavily armed soldiers moving through the darkness like silent ghosts. To the naked eye, the only evidence of their existence was the dim green glow that the night vision goggles left on their faces. All that was missing was a soundtrack by CCR and the thumping of helicopter rotor blades.

I turned back around and smiled at no one in the darkness. This was my favorite kind of mission. "Bravo Company, 1st Platoon, the 'Maggots' conducts a raid against target house, vicinity Iraqi Army checkpoint, in order to kill or capture enemy sniper." My boys, second squad, would be the assaulting element, while first and third squads were to provide support and security.

I couldn't remember a time when we had walked more quietly in the dark, and I was anxious to hit this house. Just days earlier our platoon had been returning to Camp Taji after a twelve-hour patrol, when we were directed by our battalion headquarters to support our sister company, Charlie, as they searched this very home. We had hoped to make it back in time for a midnight meal at one of the Camp Taji chow halls. Instead, we set up hasty blocking positions to prevent anyone from fleeing as soldiers from Charlie Company entered and searched the house. No one had tried to run away. We sat in an empty field watching lights come on in the windows of the house, and listening to the radio communication as the mission progressed. The occupants were cooperative, and there were no weapons or contraband found.

After several hours of waiting in the cold, we received instructions to hold our positions until daybreak, so that Charlie Company soldiers could search again during daylight hours. The temperatures had dropped below the freezing mark, and we sat there shivering, while frost formed around us. Finally, just before dawn, we were given permission to return to base. Charlie Company had found nothing in the home.

Now it was our turn to search this place. As we continued moving, I could make out the outline of a building through the palm trees. Lloyd, the first squad leader, whispered over the radio that he had the target house in sight. It was a pretty typical Iraqi home for this area. It was two stories with metal doors, a flat roof, and a sort of stucco exterior. There was a garage, a couple small outbuildings made of mud bricks, and a small fenced area with goats and sheep. It was quiet and dark as we approached.

We halted and waited for Lloyd to set up his over-watch position. As he set his men in place, I whispered radio checks with Sergeant Taaga; Sergeant First Class Arambula, our platoon sergeant, who had the medic; and Leo, the third squad leader. I had clear comms with everyone but Leo.

Where the hell was our reserve squad?

I walked over and knelt next to my Lieutenant. "Hey sir, I can't get Maggot 3 on the radio. Where the hell are they? I don't even see his strobe flashing behind us."

While Lieutenant Schardt, our platoon leader, tried to raise third squad on the radio, I heard brush breaking to our right. I turned around to see what or who might be moving, and the noise grew louder.

Then Leo called out, "Hey, second platoon, where the fuck are you?"

So much for noise discipline, I thought.

"My fucking radio isn't working," he continued, almost shouting.

By this point, we had practically announced our arrival. His squad continued tromping toward us, seemingly stepping on and breaking every stick and branch in the palm grove.

I quickly walked over and whispered through clenched teeth, "Hey, shut the fuck up. What the hell is wrong with you guys?"

Leo approached and started complaining that he had been trying to get us on the radio, and that we had just left his squad alone out on the highway. He went on and on about how he had somehow ended up on the east side of the road, opposite our objective, where he ran into another platoon's blocking position while trying to figure out our location.

Finally, we got ourselves organized, and Lloyd and Leo finished getting their squads settled into over-watch and security positions. Amazingly enough, there was no sign that we had disturbed the occupants of our target house. It appeared that we still had the element of surprise working in our favor, but this whole cluster set the tone for how the assault phase of this mission would go.

I signaled for my alpha team to move forward to the house. They spread out, crouching low as they ran quietly across the clearing to the front door of the house. I followed closely behind, and as we reached the corner of the front wall, the men automatically lined up in a stack. Most infantry fire teams have a breach man. In this team, it made sense for Frolo to be the door kicker. We had never encountered a door that he couldn't get through.

Sergeant Fraleigh stood in front of the door and looked at me through his night vision. I gave him a quick nod, and he took a step back with his left foot and then slammed the heel of his boot into the door next to the latch. It gave way, but the door didn't fly open like they usually did. He kicked again. Then a third time, and the plastic mount on his night vision goggles broke. They were hanging from the para-cord attached to the camo band on his helmet.

Frolo turned to me and said, "Sergeant T., my nods are down!"

"No shit! What the fuck to do you want me to do about it? Take care of it once we get inside."

He reached up and held onto the nods while he kicked the door again. It sounded as if someone were hitting the door with a sledge hammer. It was bending in the middle, and each strike left a new dent, but it simply would not open more than a couple of inches. A light came on inside. Through a window at the top of the door, we could see a large wooden cabinet that was preventing it from opening. An outside light came on, and we no longer needed our night vision. We had also lost the benefit of surprise.

I paused for a second to figure out my next move, and a woman pulled back a window curtain and waved at us frantically. With our rifles pointed at her, she motioned to the side of the house. About that time, a small boy, maybe ten or eleven years old, came walking out from around a corner and gestured for us to follow him. A man in his early forties met us at the side door and invited us in. In the main room, where Fraleigh had been kicking the door, we found a China cabinet that stood seven or eight feet high, and ran the length of the room. It was full of all sorts of stuff: silver platters, little trinkets, and lots of newly broken dishes.

I called for Sergeant Bridges to bring up his team and help secure the first floor of the home. There was an elderly man, a younger woman, and four children ranging in age from toddler to about ten or eleven. They were cooperative but not very happy with us. The old man kept shouting at us. Our interpreter said that he wanted us to know that he was not a terrorist. He wanted to know why we were searching his home again.

We secured the first floor and separated the men from the women and children. With the help of an interpreter, I asked about any weapons in the home. The younger of the two men explained that there were two AK-47 rifles in the house, and pointed to where I could find them. He said that they worked with the Sons of Iraq and that they were allowed to have the rifles and the ammo pouches. I checked their ID cards, and they were indeed on our payroll as checkpoint security guards in that area.

That figures, I thought.

"Tell them that we are still going to search their house for weapons and contraband."

Our interpreter relayed the message and told me that they understood.

"Maggot Six, this is Maggot Two. Over."

"Go ahead, Maggot Two."

"Six, first floor is secure. Moving to second floor now. Over."

"Roger that."

Lieutenant Schardt entered the house with one of Leo's fire teams and asked which rooms the occupants were in. I pointed to the room where the men were being held, and started up the stairs with Sergeant Fraleigh and his fire team.

At the top of the stairs, there was a landing and four doors. The door to our right was metal and had a window much like the door downstairs. It was access to the roof of the home. One open door revealed a room that was mostly empty except for a few large bags of dates, presumably from the palm groves that we had just walked through. The second room was used for storage. It was piled full of all sorts of junk. I could see burlap sacks, car parts, pots and pans, broken chairs, and all kinds of other things. The door to the third room was closed.

Sergeant Fraleigh gently checked the door handle and signaled that it was locked. I nodded to him, and he kicked it. Unlike the plain metal door downstairs this door was very ornately carved wood with a brass door handle. The handle and latch mechanism fell to the floor as wood splintered around it. The door was destroyed, and the latching side of the door frame came out of the wall as well. We thought we were ready for anything as we entered and cleared rooms, but we were not prepared for what happened next.

We rushed into the room, and a man rolled out of a large bed onto the floor in front of us. A woman rolled out of the other side of the bed, taking the sheets along with her. She was screaming as she pulled the sheets up to her neck in an effort to cover herself. The man, probably in his mid-thirties, was startled and confused. He got up from the floor quickly, his eyes wide with fear and surprise. He had one hand over his head and was attempting to pull his pants up with the other. When he realized that our weapons all pointed at him, he dropped his pants and raised his other hand. He still stood there awkwardly bent at the waist, as if he really wanted to pull his pants up, but he wasn't sure he could do it without getting shot.

A quick glance around the room confirmed what we had busted in on. His pants were around his ankles. His naked wife was curled up in a corner of the room holding a sheet up to her neck. There was a red light bulb glowing in a wall fixture above the bed's headboard, and there was a box of peach scented douche sitting on one of the nightstands. I looked at her and then back at him, and I started laughing.

Sergeant Fraleigh laughed too and said, "That sucks, dude! We had no idea you were gettin' some ass in here."

The man gave an uneasy smile. He didn't understand English, but he knew we were laughing at him.

I looked at the interpreter. "Tell him to pull his fuckin' pants up. I don't want to see that shit. Tell her to get dressed too."

Once the woman was dressed, she was escorted downstairs to the room with the other woman and the children. I kept lover boy in the room so that I could ask him some questions.

"Ask him if there are any weapons in the house."

"He says that there are two AKs downstairs and that those are the only weapons they have."

"Has he heard any gunshots in this area recently?"

"He says no."

"Ask him if he knows anything about a sniper firing on the Iraqi Army checkpoint out on the highway? I'm sure he can see the checkpoint from the roof of his house."

"He says he doesn't know anything about it."

"He's a fucking liar."

I walked him downstairs and handed him off to some of the 3rd squad soldiers who were now in the house. I walked over to where Lieutenant Schardt was standing and gave him a sit rep. "The house is secure. We have two women and four children in that room. Three military-age males in this room. I'm going to start searching the place upstairs first."

"Sounds good Sergeant T. Let me know what you find."

I walked back upstairs where Jimmy and Frolo already had their teams starting to search the rooms. I looked around as well, watching what the soldiers were doing, and rifling through drawers and closets that hadn't been checked yet. I knew that this house had just been searched, and I wasn't very confident that we would find anything. I didn't see any reason at that point to totally trash the place.

Then I found something. In the back of the top drawer of one of the nightstands, I found a little glass dish that held about ten bullets for a 9mm handgun. Iraqis were allowed to have an AK-47 with one 30-round magazine for home protection, but there were no handguns allowed. I grabbed the dish and walked downstairs to ask lover boy about them.

Speaking to the interpreter, I asked, "Where is your handgun?"

As our interpreter spoke, he looked at me and shook his head no.

"He says he doesn't have a handgun, only AKs."

"Why do you have ammo for a handgun if you don't have a handgun?"

"He says he doesn't have any handgun ammo either."

I showed him the dish and said, "What the fuck is this then?"

He backpedaled a bit, but still insisted that there were no other weapons in the home.

"Tell him that we will leave if he just gives up the handgun."

"He still says that he doesn't have one."

I left my lieutenant to continue asking questions, while I went back to searching. We looked in all of the usual places and found nothing out of the ordinary. By this point, we were hours into the mission, and I was tired and pissed off. Captain Veath, my company commander and our first sergeant, 1SG Angulo, were now in the house poking around and asking why we hadn't come up with anything yet. I pointed out the bullets in the dish.

Captain Veath said, "Where is the gun?"

"I don't know," I said. "It has to be here somewhere, but they won't give it up. Without flipping this whole place upside down, I'm not sure where else to look."

"Flip this place, and find it then."

"Roger that, sir."

Back upstairs, I called all of the soldiers out of the rooms onto the landing at the top of the stairs. "We have a handful of 9mm rounds that were in a nightstand drawer in that room," I said, pointing toward the busted wooden door. "You will check every nook and cranny in this mother fucker. Flip the beds. Take the drawers out of each piece of furniture. Check the bottoms of them. Check inside to make sure that there is nothing taped above or below the drawers. Turn the furniture over, and check the back and bottom of each piece. Toss everything." We broke to continue searching.

I walked into the bedroom with Private Shane Steward. He went to the night stand where I had found the 9mm bullets, and pulled out the top drawer and dumped it. He dropped the drawer on the bed, and looked into the bottom drawer. Then he got up and started to walk over to the closet. I told him that he needed to remove the bottom drawer, and check under and behind the nightstand too. He turned back, pulled the bottom drawer out of the nightstand, and dumped it.

"Umm, Sergeant Taylor? I think I found something."

I glanced over and saw the excited look on his face as he pulled the bag from the nightstand. He placed it on the bed and opened it. He shook his head as he reached in and pulled out a handful of 7.9mm rifle rounds.

"Nice job, Steward! Take that out on the landing and dump it."

When he dumped the bag, hundreds of 7.9mm rifle rounds on stripper clips, loose 7.62mm AK-47 rounds fell out onto the floor along with several loaded AK-47 magazines.

I called for my lieutenant to come up, and some of my privates started organizing our find so that we could get an accurate count. When Lieutenant Schardt came up, he smiled at me and asked if we had anything else. I told him that we still had a couple of rooms to check and that we had found yet another caliber of ammunition. I started thinking we would find more weapons.

Next was the junk room. Jimmy and I started searching this room. After finding so much ammo, we were feeling a second wind. We started pulling stuff out of the room. There were burlap sacks full of sheep's wool. It was now daylight outside, so I carried the bags out onto the rooftop. I pulled out my knife and slit the side of each bag and dumped their contents onto the cement roof.

As we moved further into the room, I found a green cylinder with white military markings on it. The cylinder was empty, but it was a shipping container for a warhead for a Brazilian surface-to-air missile. I set that aside, and continued digging. Next I found a navy-blue child's backpack with UNICEF embroidered on it. Inside the pack I found a cowboy style leather belt with bullet loops all around it. There were a few AK-47 magazines, three strands of Christmas lights with no bulbs, which are commonly used to make IEDs, and finally, wrapped in a piece of cloth, was a rifle scope. After moving all of these things out of the room, we reached several large rolls of canvas on the floor. They appeared to be large tents or something of that nature, but when I tried to lift one of the rolls, it was much heavier than plain canvas. I unrolled the first one, and inside I found a bolt-action rifle. I held it up for Jimmy to see. He unrolled the second roll and found a sniper rifle that went with the scope we had found. In another larger roll there was another green cylinder, this one filled with rifle cartridges for the sniper rifle. Two more rolls revealed two more rifles and two more shipping containers filled with ammo.

Jimmy and I carried the rifles and ammunition out onto the rooftop, and I called for Lieutenant Schardt, the commander, and the first sergeant. When they came through the door to the rooftop, I held up the sniper rifle and the scope.

"We didn't find a handgun, but here is your sniper rifle, sir."

"Damn, Sergeant Taylor, we'll have to call Charlie Company and tell them that you found what they were looking for."

"No shit, sir."

I went down to speak to the three men who had claimed that they only had two AK-47s in the house. I asked again where their handgun was. They continued to deny that anyone in the house had a handgun.

Talking to the interpreter, I said, "Okay, I believe that you don't have a handgun in the house. I have searched upstairs, and we didn't find a handgun. Are there any other weapons in the house?"

They all told the interpreter that there were no other guns in the home, and they looked relieved that I hadn't mentioned finding any weapons.

I turned to the other soldiers in the room and instructed them to put flex-cuffs on all three of the men. Once they were cuffed, I told the soldiers to bring them upstairs to the rooftop. The looks on their faces were priceless when they came through the door and saw all of the weapons and ammunition laid out across their rooftop.

In all, we discovered more than three thousand 7.62mm and 7.9mm rifle rounds, almost thirty AK-47 magazines, and seven rifles. We also had materials that were commonly used in making IEDs and evidence that these men had gotten their hands on some sort of missiles or warheads that could have potentially been used against American soldiers in a number of different ways. It was a fruitful raid. We found what we were looking for. We accomplished our mission, to conduct a raid on the target house in order to kill or capture an enemy sniper. There was not a single shot fired, and there were no casualties, aside from some dishes and a couple of doors.

All of our success aside, I felt guilty about that raid. It was approaching lunchtime by the time we had processed all of our evidence, and prepared to move our three detainees. As my soldiers escorted the three handcuffed men to our vehicles and placed blindfolds over their heads to protect the secret materials in our Stryker vehicles, the oldest boy came out of the front of the house. He watched armed American soldiers blindfold his father, uncle, and grandfather. His face was emotionless as the armored ramp closed, concealing the men in his family inside. My company commander walked over to him and patted him on the head. The boy's stare changed to anger and hatred when Captain Veath handed him a soccer ball.

I saw it right then: *we took his dad, and his uncle, and his grandpa, and gave him a shiny new soccer ball in return. What a fucked up war.*

We took weapons away from insurgents that day, and we interfered with insurgent sniper activity in that area. What else did we do that day? Did we help reinforce negative feelings toward Americans in another generation of Iraqi people? Did we create another insurgent or another terrorist that day?

Jarrod L. Taylor served as an infantryman in the U.S. Army from 2000–2009. He deployed to Uzbekistan and Afghanistan in 2001–2002, Horn of Africa in 2003, Afghanistan in 2004–2005, and Iraq from 2007–2009. He graduated with a BA in history from Eastern Illinois University and currently teaches history at Next Generation Middle School in Champaign, Illinois. His work can be found in previous volumes of *Proud to Be: Writing by American Warriors.*

The Wire

Sean Taylor

Captain A. Sean Taylor enlisted with the Iowa Army National Guard on October 24, 2002 at the age of 35. He deployed to Bagram, Afghanistan, with the Iowa Guard from August 2010–August 2011 as the Medical Operations and Plans Officer for the 334th Brigade Support Battalion. Upon returning from deployment, he transferred to the Army Reserves, where he currently serves as the Public Affairs Officer for the 649th Regional Support Group.

For the Love of One Another

I feel blessed to have been chosen as a receiver. During Jonathan's three tours in Iraq and Afghanistan, he was vocal, very vocal, about many of his actions and the things that he witnessed there. Chief among them was the camaraderie he felt at a time when it was just him and his fellow soldiers, holding each other down and having each other's backs. Missions were to be completed with the immediate purpose that everyone would get to live another day. The end purpose being that they would all go home. Home was always at the center and it was my constant plea, my prayer to him—"Do what you gotta do so that you come home." Physically, mentally, emotionally, spiritually—I just wanted him home.

Jonathan, my godson, first went to Iraq when he was 24 years old—a baby, really, considering that life or death depended on split second decision-making. He loved his fellow soldiers, his comrades, his boys, his brothers. It was a mutual affection. Even though he very possibly could have avoided going to war, he refused that as an option. With each and every tour, he would say, somewhat mystically, that the Unit had to stay together. The Unit had to get there together. The Unit had to come home together. He supposed that a chink in the chain—his not being there—might result in one of his fellow soldiers getting hurt. How, then, would he ever be able to live with himself? No doubt, each soldier who goes to war has the same mentality. It's not for the love of war that they fight; it's for the love of one another.

A few of my friends and relatives had been to previous wars. Only one has spoken about it, and that conversation began 30-plus years after the war had ended. Jonathan was different. As a nurse at Walter Reed Army Medical Center, he had seen first-hand our courageous men and women come home, battle-weary and haunted by their own thoughts, memories, and deeds. For some of the heroes of those previous wars, it seemed as though they'd wrestled with their sanity for years and then one day, simply lost their grip. It was of this that Jonathan was most afraid.

I don't know if it was a conscious decision on Jonathan's part or if he was responding to his natural instincts, his professional training, or the Holy Spirit, but he was explicitly vocal about many of the acts that he witnessed and was a part of. He would share chilling accounts and paint shocking pictures of exactly what had occurred, with an incredulousness that he himself couldn't believe. It seemed almost like an out-of-body experience for him, as if he were watching himself from the sidelines. From Iraq, sometimes he would call me at work, "just to say hello." I came to know that these were never "just hello" calls but that something had happened, and he was having difficulty trying to digest it. It was a call that, for me, would result in quiet tears, prayer, the best encouragement that I could muster, and my mantra of "come home." Once, he very calmly but almost pleadingly told me that he was a healer, not a killer. Another time he wondered aloud about his own humanity. I was afraid that a lonely, disengaged space was being created inside of him.

Jonathan bared his emotional battles and—the key—he bared them soon after they occurred. To his credit, he didn't allow those pains to sit and fester. He and I had an unspoken and unplanned routine. He would call me (and others) and share a painful, often horrific experience. A soldier shot and killed by a sniper's single bullet to the head and what it meant to go out and retrieve the otherwise pristine young body. The effects of an IED and the accompanying sights, smells, and sounds one experiences when medically treating a comrade who is actively burning alive. How one manages the situation when an enemy is shooting at you with screaming, non-consenting children serving as his shield. Figuring out how to mentally and emotionally process the experience of participating in a firefight and, when the enemy has surrendered, hooking those very same enemies up to an IV and taking them to your hospital to heal. And the silent ride back to the safety of camp.

Upon hearing each experience, I would soon after then tell three or four of my pre-selected, pre-conditioned, forewarned, and sturdy friends. Talking it out would then ease my burden. I didn't want the pain to be allowed to sit inside of me. I had to get it out. With each telling, it was a release that offered me some relief. I prayed hard that it offered the same to Jonathan when he told it to me.

This peculiar sharing experience has created an unbreakable bond between Jonathan and me. And it made my heart ache for all of the soldiers who had gone to war—in this generation, in the previous generations, and in the generations that we all know are yet to come.

Jonathan's way was the best way for him to begin to process his pain. He is doing well but still on his journey and learning to find a way to live with these experiences. They are a part of him now.

It hurt me in my heart to listen. It made me never the same again. But I felt that if Jonathan could handle experiencing it, I could handle listening to it.

As I said, I feel blessed to have been chosen as a receiver.

Ms. Garcia is a native New Yorker, currently living in Montgomery County, Maryland.

Marc Danziger

Fathers and Sons

I spent five hours with him once. We were scared parents that day, watching our sons prepare to go to war for the first time. We talked, controlling our feelings, reassuring each other, and together calming my wife, as the men who we still saw as boys did what they needed to do. He was a vet and had been here himself, so he explained things to us: the logistics of the day, where they would go from here, what the departure would be like. I took some pictures, he snapped one on his cell phone. And they were gone, and we went to our hotels and homes and on with our lives.

I'd taken a picture of him sitting next to his son, thinking I'd make a print and send it to him and his wife. When I looked at the picture, the fear on his face couldn't have been clearer, and I knew I'd never be able to send it.

And then a line of text on my screen. In my alerts. I've got a dozen of them, alerting me to anything on the web that might be about my son or the unit he is with or the place where he is, and my phone shakes as my email box slowly fills up with news, and to be honest, not much of it's been good. And then it was very bad as I saw a name that I recognized, the name on a tape on the chest of the young man in the photos who wasn't my son but who my son had talked about when we spoke on the satphone. He'd been a nerd, a comic book kid in a platoon of jocks in a valley where eight of them would die over the next eleven months. They'd bullied him, my son had said, and he tried to protect him. But reading the news, I realized how little protection that could have been.

I swore, I'll admit. And I waited a day to tell my wife, who was living in her own swamp of worry.

And I went through the FRG channels and got his father's email and sent him one, saying "I remember. . ." and didn't expect anything back and nothing came. And we got a card and waited, because if it had been me, I'd have been burning the cards for a while until the rage died down. And we waited and finally sent the card, and I just put my number on it and said "call me anytime." And he did.

I was in a meeting when my phone buzzed. I pulled it out to swipe the call away to voicemail and noted the odd area code. And it rang again, same number. I suddenly remembered that the area code was from where he lived, and I said "sorry" and walked out, turned, and went into the bathroom and said "It's me." He said his name and suddenly I couldn't breathe very well, and just listened.

To be honest, I started to cry and walked downstairs into the parking lot and the Beverly Hills sun where we could talk and swear and cry together. After half an hour, someone from the meeting came out to check on me, and I waved them away.

And we talked and made plans to talk again, and then we'd said it all and I had to go back to work. And he hung up and I leaned over the trash can and wondered if I was going to throw up.

I wish I had. I wish I'd been able to vomit up the guilt that my son was breathing today and his wasn't and my terror that tomorrow mine wouldn't be either.

I put the lid back on the fear, straightened myself up, wiped the guilt off my face with my hands, and walked to the elevator and back into my day.

And I reminded myself that when we're talking about geopolitics and theories of conflict, this is what the pieces look like: two fathers, one sad and one shattered by grief, and two sons—one in danger, and one past all risk.

We spent five hours together a year ago, and I'll be tied to him for the rest of my life.

Marc Danziger lives in Los Angeles and has three sons. His oldest enlisted in the Army after college, served for seven years and three combat deployments to Afghanistan, is leaving the Army this summer to go to grad school next year. This is his first published work.

Ryan J. Erisman

Guilty Pleasures
Spring 2007, Lake Habbaniyah Area, Iraq

I felt a little guilty about taking one. A shower, that is. As a company commander, I returned to Camp Habbaniyah weekly for our battalion's operations meeting. Like my fellow captains, my Friday routine became an early morning convoy to Habbaniyah, taking a shower, eating a hot chowhall breakfast, and attending the meeting before heading back to the field. My Marines lived in four patrol bases scattered across the Fallujah Peninsula. Two of my platoons didn't even have access to running water. They took occasional baby-wipe baths and washed their sweat-crusted clothing in a series of 5-gallon buckets. Their only hot food came from Iraqis' hospitality to invite Marine patrols into their homes for a meal. Once a month, each squad rotated back to Camp Habbaniyah for a day to receive mandatory refresher training, a hot shower, and a couple hot meals in the chowhall. A good officer never asks his Marines to do something he wouldn't do himself. On the flip side of that sentiment, I felt guilty about having a luxury not available to my men. I could have used the shower trailer at our combat outpost but restricted myself to a once a week shower in Habbaniyah.

One morning back in Habbaniyah, about halfway through the deployment, I stepped into the one shower stall of the four that didn't have a fresh-cut hair-and-soap-scum puddle floating over the drain. Somebody had left his shampoo behind. I looked at the green tube on the ledge: Paul Mitchell Tea Tree Oil. Sounded a little frilly for my tastes, but I'd run out last week so it'd have to do. After soaping and rinsing my body, I squeezed a tiny dollop of shampoo into my palm. Five seconds into lathering, an aroma hit me. I hadn't smelled anything so wonderful in months. What the hell is *in* tea tree oil? Water running down my back, I inhaled in the fragrance like a fifth grader huffing scented markers.

After drying off, I poked my head out of the stall, glanced left and right, and slipped the Paul Mitchell into my shave kit hanging on the towel hook. I strolled back to the barracks, trying to remember my chronic fatigue and conceal the spring in my step. Am I allowed to feel this good? Man, I just took a *shower.*

On the way to the chowhall, my favorite part about coming back to Camp Habbaniyah, Marines greeted me with smiles in addition to the usual, professional, "Good morning, sir." By the third greeting, I started to wonder why they were all smiling at me. Then I realized they were reacting. *I* was grinning like an idiot, from my *shower.* Could they smell me? I'd always kept my hair well within regulations but longer than most Marines. A few fellow infantry officers called me a "hippie" for actually having hair on the sides of my head. Now, my relatively long red hair trailed the scent of tea tree oil

181

across stinking Camp Habbaniyah. Hell, maybe I am a hippie—though one with an M4 carbine slung over his shoulder.

In the chowhall, I made sure not to crowd the staff sergeant ahead of me in the omelet line so he wouldn't smell the tea tree oil. When I sat down across from Dan, a fellow company commander, he asked between mouthfuls, "What's got you so chipper?"

"The usual," I bluffed. "Omelet, bacon, and these," I said, holding up a French toast stick drenched in fake syrup.

During our battalion's operations meeting, my first sergeant leaned back in his chair, wrinkled his nose a couple times, and shot me a *do-you-smell-that* look. I shrugged, grateful when somebody's silent fart wafted by a couple minutes later. I shot the look back at my first sergeant. At my turn to brief my company's progress, I mentioned upcoming operations, meetings with sheiks, and our work with Iraqi neighborhood watch. I cannot conceal my thoughts easily and I never play poker. I damn near added "and I just took *the best shower ever*," but barely kept myself in check with the standard, "Nothing else to pass."

At the end of the battalion meeting, I bee-lined out of the building, faster than my usual haste to get back out to my company. Donning my sweat-stained flak jacket and helmet with its filthy pads neutralized any remaining whiff of my fragrance trail. I went back to my combat outpost outside Fallujah and back to work, glad to be away from battalion again.

A few nights later, while digging through my shave kit for toothpaste, I felt an unfamiliar shape stuffed in the bottom of the pouch. The Paul Mitchell! I'd forgotten. I could smell the tea tree oil aroma on my fingers. I closed my eyes and inhaled again. *Best. Shower. Ever.*

Ryan J. Erisman served ten years in the Marine Corps, leaving as a Major after two deployments to Iraq, the second as the commander of a 170-man rifle company that deployed outside Fallujah during 2007. Ryan lives in Madison, Wisconsin, with his wife, Sarah, and their twin four-year-olds. He is the Midwest Regional Ambassador for the Farmer Veteran Coalition, an organization that helps recent veterans transition into agricultural careers.

Zachary Ryan

Revisiting the person of the year
a decade later—23 A Day

What have we done?

I am an Army Ranger. I served four tours in Iraq.

I am part of the problem.

A problem that is committing suicide at a rate of 23 a day.

What we have done to our sons and how they are treated every day is unforgiveable. As a leader, I stood behind America's brave warriors and told them when and who to kill. Likewise, I performed my individual duties, but that is my burden to bear. As a Ranger, I lived by a creed. In that creed I proudly proclaimed that I would never leave a fallen comrade. Tonight I was truly forced to show how dedicated I am to that cause. Tonight I was there with one of my former soldiers as he was admitted to a psychiatric ward. Craig was not the first man to fall here at home. Over the last few years, I have found myself in a tragic whirlwind of pain and trouble regarding my brothers. The men I led into battle are now at home dying for reasons that make no sense to me. These reasons all point to one clear conclusion: WE have broken large amounts of valorous heroes who gave us everything and to whom we owe nothing less than the best we have to offer.

Following the drive out of Iraq in the last days of the draw down, I found myself attending yet another memorial service. Every service like this is hard to endure, but this one was special. The young man who died in his early 20s shouldn't have. Injured, he made it home. We have the best possible facilities to treat the wounded, therefore, if we get them home and alive, we should be able to enable their recovery. Thinking on this, I remembered the incident in which he was injured. It was the last attack that produced a death in the Iraqi conflict. I was on the quick reaction force that responded to a roadside bomb that ripped through one of the 82nd Airborne's trucks. As I arrived at the scene, I found the platoon sergeant of the unit I was helping. A close friend, I could see the true effects of the bomb all over his face. There was the face of a man who lost someone entrusted to him. A true leader, he loved each of his men and couldn't help but feel the full brunt of each loss. We talked, and I urged him back to his men. Every once in a while, we all need a little push to refocus. Our loss on the ground was a part of war. That is what we do. One of the young men who took an injury that day was the one whose funeral I was now at. He made it home and was released from the hospital. His injuries to his leg were significant, but he was alive. In and out of treatment facilities, and attempts to get his pain under control, left Edward frustrated and angry.

That's nothing new. The doctors from Walter Reed and Fort Bragg were honestly trying to help. They prescribed any medication they thought could help numb the pain. It wasn't working. Edwards's wife found him in his bed nonresponsive and dying because he tried to kill the pain and took too many pills. The man just wanted the pain to stop.

Every year I make a trip to Arlington National Cemetery in February to visit the grave of my dead squad leader. He was a great and brave man who died fighting for his men. I was honored to have known him. This trip, I'm in Arlington for another reason. An old friend has passed away. Kevin was injured during the surge back in 2007. Like Edward, his leg was hit by a roadside bomb. Kevin lost his leg. The amputation was under the knee and generally is the best place to lose a limb . . . if indeed you have to lose one. All the correspondence with him after our return was that he was doing well. All of us thought everything was ok. Kevin's closest friends knew the other side. Over the course of several years, the injury never really got better; there were several more amputations as the leg suffered infection after infection. This prevented Kevin from moving on in any fashion. Every time he entered training for a new career, he was forced to stop due to more doctor visits and problems. One night Kevin went to sleep and never woke up. The official cause was attributed to a blood clot. Once again, family speculated that clot was caused by the pain killers Kevin was admittedly addicted to. This proud soldier who placed himself in harm's way for you and me died here at home because he couldn't beat his pain.

Other men who I have served with have experienced overwhelming failure here at home. Jason, a sniper and reconnaissance expert, is currently in jail for turning to credit card fraud after his country failed to pay him his proper salary for over two years. Jason worked for me in northern Iraq. He served as my number two in near constant operations in the fall of 2005. During this time, we encountered what is known as an escalation of force incident. During this incident, my team was responsible for the injury of a full family that violated the immediate security of an Infantry Company. Jason, who received extensive training and was qualified as a medic, rushed to immediately render aid and medical attention to the family as soon as the firing stopped. Not only did he face the real consequences of his actions, but, clear-headed, he and our other medic saved the lives of two children and their mother. This is a man of intense integrity and character who was backed into a corner upon his return home. The bad choice he made in stealing placed this man, who received two purple hearts, in prison for 15 years.

As I stand back and observe the men who commit suicide and suffer through severe domestic problems ranging from divorce to violent encounters with the law, I am starting to understand the extent of what we have done. These men are not weak nor unintelligent. We still find them unemployed and at times homeless. There is no call for an infantryman nor artilleryman in a civilian job market. Frustration, anger, and lack of opportunities compound issues with both physical and mental health. The organizations set into place to assist these soldiers are severely understaffed and plagued by backlog. Other charitable organizations do little to help anyone, and society is quickly turning away from its temporary love affair with military members. These men have nowhere to turn and no one to help them. There are too many for the military to handle, while civilians do not understand the honest issues prevalent with veterans. Most civilian providers are honestly scared of veterans, since they have fallen victim to the stereotypes that the media is placing on returning soldiers.

Now we are back to this evening, sitting in my living room waiting on the soft flurries of snow to begin; saddened does not begin to describe the pain I feel. Today I picked a man up from jail. On the surface this is another case of a parent striking his child. The problem is that he doesn't remember doing it. The problem is that as the wars started closing down, the Army has turned on its veterans. Any problem with a soldier and he is done, out, and gone. We don't care what you did nor how much you contributed. No one cares what you sacrificed for them. The lives we saved and the lives we took are for naught when the machine has to cut weight. Craig is struggling with poverty as he is waiting for his appeal from his court martial to come back before a judge. Military justice is not like civilian law. The presumption of innocence is not the same, and we live under the mantra that two sworn statements make a truth. Unless a defendant can prove his innocence, chances are he will find himself behind bars. Craig was no exception to this. Despite the concerns for his mental health, he was sent to prison for two months. Since then the issues that result from nonstop deployments over the course of a decade have taken hold. While mental problems have surfaced in profound ways, the effects of a traumatic brain injury are ensuring that any form of recovery will not be easy. My friend now spends hours each day not knowing where he is. Hours each day talking to people who are not there, and more and more time doing things he doesn't remember. More than most, he has nowhere to turn and no one in his life who can help. There is no VA and no chain of command to help ensure he is taken care of. There is only me.

Much like his comrades, he has settled near his childhood home and far removed from others like him. We are all scattered around the country now. In every community and every city, we sit trying to piece our lives back together. I have lost too many close friends to allow one more to be taken from me. I am now in school to become a psychologist. The only way to fix the problem is to start, one veteran at a time, and do what I can. I have much to atone for. There is a problem in America today, and this evening I pushed it, in a wheelchair, into a psychiatric ward. What have we done? We have alienated, isolated, and abandoned the best of us, the best of what we represent, and the best of our values. These men and women deserve better than this. They deserve to know that the people who asked them to go into harm's way are there to help now. They deserve to have those of us who taught them to kill, teach them how to live again. We owe them not to forget that regardless of race, creed, or political view, they volunteered to go for those who can't. Veterans are not an unnecessary burden on our economy; they are our responsibility. A responsibility we have neglected.

Zachary Ryan served 4 tours in Iraq.

Buzzbomb

This was written in June of 1945 when 50,000 American prisoners of war were suddenly freed with the German collapse and flown to an obscure tent city of 20,000 called Lucky Strike *(after the cigarette), near Rouen, France. I was shipped there from Liege, our Combat Engineer Base, as a temporary clerk helper for three weeks, then recalled to my unit, which was ready to fight the Japanese who still engaged us in WWII. Buzzbomb was a real, fuzzy mutt, a terrier.*

"Buzz-Bomb," I yelled. Soon before me stood the little creature with its wiggling long tail and those gleaming eyes. Buzz-Bomb was the cute little brown pup we had picked up during the early stages of the V-I and V-II raids on London, while we were in the Midlands near Shrewsbury, building Bailie bridges. In the heart of London, during the Buzz bomb raids, the dog had grown up, the pride of the company. He had gone with us during training, lived and slept in our tents, ate our chow, and only differed from a soldier in that he never barked back.

By the time we crossed the channel on the LST, Buzz-Bomb was considered a traveling dog. Buzz-Bomb had two exceptional qualities, one being that he would run away, but always return. The other occurred at night. He was watchful and would loudly bark at strangers coming nearby. It was during those wet, stalling days in December, near the German border, that Buzz-Bomb made a name for himself.

We had just arrived, and our company split into three platoons. Our position was near a deserted shot-up village. Since there was not much activity, we only had two guards out, the front being several miles away. The time was just before the Battle of the Bulge, when the Wermacht exerted their last effort and started their counteroffensive.

German patrols and fifth-columnists, aided by paratroopers, infiltrated into our lines, caught many units off guard, and at the time captured many men, including valuable booty. We were weary from the day's combat, and with the exception of the guards, everyone was fast asleep. All of a sudden, in the pitch dark, there was a sudden loud bark. We all awoke and, by natural instinct, reached for our guns, while some of us held our pistols already. Under orders from the lieutenant, we quietly slipped away. It was useless to fight a foe that we could not see. One of our guards was missing, and the firing seemed to be much closer.

No sooner had we taken the first step back than the dog began to bark, warning us. This must have been only a hundred yards away. Then a loud BANG! A yelp. They had brutally shot the dog. We knew where their location was and, when we reached our unit, informed the C.O. and soon came the orders for a temporary retreat. We had been saved from whatever the Gerries had planned for us. Never shall I forget the warning bark of Buzz-Bomb the hero, who never returned.

Arthur Weil came to the United States as a child in the "Kindertransport" from Germany and spent his formative years in Chicago where he received his B.A. in history from Roosevelt University. He later earned an M.A. in history at DePaul University. He served in the U.S. Army during World War II in London, France, and Belgium as a combat engineer, and later as an interpreter in the U.S. for German prisoners of war.

Inconsequential

It's easier to say that part of me had never existed.

The words *service member* and *Veteran* never felt as if they applied to me. Attending Veteran's Day programs for my son's school, I sat in the back row of the folding chairs that were reserved for those of us who had served. I don't look the military type, having a facial piercing and some visible tattoos, and I'm a lot heavier than I used to be. I assume it's because of all this that I was tapped on the shoulder by an older woman sitting behind me who softly explained that the row I was sitting in was for Veterans only. I smiled and explained that I was a Veteran, which gave way to a hurried apology and thanking me for my service. It felt unnecessary, just another moment where I questioned my own legitimacy in thinking of myself as a Veteran or even as a past service member.

Despite the short time I was a soldier, I'd been so immersed in the military my entire life that no matter how far I drifted away from the person I was then, the constant feeling of having been a soldier was hard to let go of. I have always been in some sort of limbo. I signed, I swore, I served; but I had never deployed. I'd been injured, but not in combat. I was devoid of being and ignored when I needed help, but not because of long lines and stacks of backed up paperwork at a local Veterans Administration office. Those stipulations left an ever widening gap in my identity, only worsened by my continued association with the military in a new role—the supportive wife.

I had joined the Army, a broken seventeen-year-old girl needing to escape herself. Then undiagnosed Borderline Personality Disorder, Major Depressive Disorder, and anxiety and panic disorders, left unmedicated and written off as teenage angst, devastated my psyche. I thought that the familiarity of the Army would give me a home and form me into someone suitable for society. I would be given opportunity for education and advancement, prepared for a future career as a lawyer, and be given a sense of self by belonging to something bigger. I was an Army brat, spending my formative years on Fort Bragg. I walked to school while the 82nd ran by doing PT. I rode my bike to soccer practice along Normandy, passing Iron Mike on the way. I went to the 18th Airborne Corps softball games to cheer on the JAG team. By the time we moved in my junior year to a small town just outside of St. Louis where I graduated from high school, and no one was associated with the military, I still knew little of what it meant to be a civilian. I guess I still don't.

I flourished in the rigidity of Basic Training, and my level of motivation nearly annoyed my drill sergeants. Having cropped my hair off before leaving for training, I helped another soldier cut off all of her hair when she was fed up with being yelled at daily for not being able to keep wisps of her hair tucked neatly away. I worked with platoon members on PT during down time and sang an inappropriate song to a Spanish-speaking soldier in her native tongue to make her laugh when she was crying in frustration. Although I was the youngest of the bunch, I was the mother duck of the female floor, and I took care of my ducklings. I finally felt that I had a purpose.

Sadly, things didn't stay that way for long.

The unfortunate truth of my mental health was made evident after my career plan was derailed in the worst way. The Airborne school slots for my MOS were dropped the day before my graduation from AIT, and we instead were shuttled off to the hospital to get our shots updated to fly out to Korea. I wasn't going to be attending Airborne school. I wasn't going to be heading to Bragg and following the 18th Airborne Corps on their deployments, going to school and applying for the Green to Gold program to work toward a law degree. Instead, I was headed farther away from my goals than I ever thought possible.

I jokingly blamed my mother for my duty station assignment, telling her that tuning in to *M*A*S*H* reruns every night, allowing me to fall asleep to the theme song, had jinxed me. I wound up north of Seoul in Uijeongbu. At first, I tried to make the best of it. I was still determined that I would go to Airborne school after Korea, and I decided to ignore my situation, do my job, and work on improving my run times and PT scores. That determination waned almost immediately. The air reminded me of the smell an MRE heater gives off, and blowing my nose after my first company run on a freezing February morning left black residue in the tissue. I braced myself for a year of struggles, but was not prepared for what was to come.

Less than a month into my tour, my mother was diagnosed with breast cancer at thirty-six, and I didn't have enough leave to go home. My depression worsened. The sheer amount of alcohol I consumed makes me wonder how I didn't drink myself to death, while having to hide my underage drinking from a command that knew I was drinking, but couldn't prove it. I injured my foot during a ruck march that left me dragging my foot around the barracks to get my laundry done, and no one thought I was actually hurting as badly as I seemed. The assumption that I was faking it angered me. I used my lifelong skill of covering up injuries previously dedicated to tricking a coach into allowing me to start a game when something was held together only with tape to keep pushing forward. In Basic Training, while he x-rayed me for a severe wrist injury, the doctor asked if I had known my hand had been broken just months prior, which I had suspected but did nothing about. Playing through the pain wasn't a new concept to me, but this wasn't a small fracture in my hand that I could baby. The overcompensation for my foot pain caused knee troubles that left me with almost no cartilage in my right knee and sent to another camp twice a week for physical therapy and steroid treatments. After another ruck march that I finished within the Airborne standard I strove for, I couldn't walk. Still, the docs at the TMC weren't any help. One declared me to be malingering before I even took off my boot because I didn't limp enough as I walked into the office. I held back my rage. I hadn't realized I needed to be wailing with bone protruding from my body for someone to take me seriously. Only my company commander, who saw me watching a soccer match with tears in my eyes, wishing I could participate without hurting myself further, saw the truth of the matter. Still, there wasn't much he could do.

If my physical health was becoming something of concern, my mental health was even more disturbing. My Borderline Personality Disorder and depression ruled my life completely. If I wasn't indulging in one of my vices, I strolled up and down the mile-long camp at night, my mind wandering to anywhere but there. I was a walking tragedy, with no one to save me from myself. I turned inward, spending most of my sober time scrawling poetry into a notebook as I sat in the 2nd Infantry Division Headquarters' gazebo or was holed up in my barracks room curled up under a blanket, unable to move. By the time I left Korea, I was broken both physically and mentally; I had been ignored by medical personnel, abandoned by friends, sexually assaulted, raped, and treated like nothing by the people I thought would take care of me.

I arrived in Germany looking for a new start. My unit was set to deploy, and I was excited to finally do what I had joined the Army to do. My new doctor, on the other hand, looking at the body scan my new physician requested before leaving Korea, realized that the obvious black hole on my foot was something that needed to be taken care of. After a month on crutches and a year since I first injured my foot, I finally had answers. I'd broken my foot in one place the previous spring, and I had broken it again the next bone over just months later. The breaks had encased in enough calcium deposits that my only options were a painful surgery to file down the calcified bone, or let it wear naturally. Either way required a walking cast for months and no deployment. The initial feeling of pride I had about doing all those runs and ruck marches with broken bones in my foot and wanting to throw it in the faces of those who had failed me was overshadowed by the fact that yet again, I couldn't deploy.

I was only nineteen when I married a friend from Bragg who was stationed in Italy with the 173rd. We never dated, but he'd been in love with me since we were in seventh grade. I never thought anyone could honestly love me. I was an empty shell of a girl who felt worthless, and after everything I'd been through, I thought myself to be completely undeserving of being loved. As of July 7, 2014, we've been married ten years.

The transition I made from soldier to wife was a difficult one. I'd left the Army because of our deployment rotations alternating in a way that one of us would always be deployed, or we would have overlapping deployments.

Either way, our son would have a near permanent place in my parents' home unless I got out to be Mom and keep some semblance of stability for the coming years. We decided I would separate from the Army, and after a battle of office politics and personal vendettas, I was finally on my way back stateside, no longer an active duty soldier.

I moved in with my parents who were stationed in the D.C. area, my father still in the Army. It was strange getting a dependent I.D. while still having a green Individual Ready Reserve I.D. card. I didn't know if I was still my own sponsor or if I was now solely my husband's dependent. Even the Army hospitals had my status within the military confused. One visit I would be listed as my father's dependent, the next time an Active Duty enlisted soldier, and the time after that my husband's dependent. No matter how many times we fixed it in the system, even the Army was confused as to who I was.

Being a soldier was engrained in me, but as a wife I found that respect for my own service was nonexistent. Whether it was because of my lack of deployment time or the fact that I'm a woman, I'll never know for sure. I had gone from being respected even among infantrymen who said they'd go to war with me any day to given the feeling that I had never even been a soldier. My service, however dedicated, was now inconsequential. I was simply a wife of a soldier. I stopped bringing up my experiences in group conversations, when it became apparent that my story didn't matter. Wives turned to me to ask questions about this or that since my entire life has been the Army, but I found I ultimately didn't fit in with them either. I didn't have a sticker on the back of my vehicle letting people know the other half of my heart was deployed, a purse made of ACU material, or a collection of yellow ribbons.

The isolation I felt has continued. Surrounded by people I consider real Veterans, I feel undeserving of the title, a subtle speck of no importance in the presence of people who have truly been through the shit. Not finding a place with the wives either, I don't know where to turn. My foot and knee still don't work right, and when I go down stairs my knee creaks as if something will snap any second. I never filed a VA claim for my injuries because I felt as if another file added to the stack would take time and space from someone who really needed help. My sexual assault and rape are things I talk about through advocacy in support of others, but I don't think I've ever come to terms with them myself. Even thinking about my time in the military makes my stomach turn, more often than not. I don't even recognize the person I was then and distance myself from her in part to keep my sanity. I'm not ashamed of my service, but I'm ashamed of how I was treated and left to self-destruct. My experience as a soldier was not with the Army I know and love.

Of course, not everything has been bad. I've kept in touch with a few of my Army friends over the years that knew and liked the girl I was then, but absolutely love the person I am today. I finally got help for my mental illnesses, and I've been working toward wellness for a few years now. I deal with my soldier's field time, deployments, and PTSD in all its sometimes nightmarish forms with as much ease as I can. Sometimes I quietly pat myself on the back because I manage this with an emotional regulation disorder.

My stories now don't include as many drunken nights. Instead I get to tell stories about how when we were stationed in Italy I survived a pulmonary embolism two months after having our second son while my husband was deployed to Afghanistan, and at the same time had to take care of a two year old with the flu and was breastfeeding a newborn. I baked five hundred made-from-scratch cookies at a friend's house for our company while we waited and hoped I didn't suddenly keel over dead, and gave myself four heparin shots a day into my stomach instead of going to the Italian hospital because I didn't want to leave my children. That might be my favorite story, mostly because I lived to tell that kickass tale of motherhood with an epic display of stress baking. I've moved twenty times and lived in four countries. I've driven thousands of miles with just me and my kids. I've flown across oceans and international date lines. I've done ruck marches and ranges. I've been to welcome-home ceremonies with a case of Guinness on my hip for one of our friends because my husband wasn't coming home that day, and I've driven halfway across the country to give a eulogy for another friend, who was an extra husband to me, and to hold his wife's hand. I've made Thanksgiving dinner for twenty-five joes with two turkeys, four pies and a cake, three dozen deviled eggs, and everything else that my boys wanted. I've flown in a Blackhawk. I've given Non-combatant Evacuation Operation briefings to Colonels and Generals. I've comforted my husband and mopped up the sweat when his memories get the best of him in his sleep. I've loved deeply, have more family than I ever thought possible, and have experienced heavy loss.

So no, I don't know if my service mattered. I'm not sure if I should stand with the Veterans of Iraq, Afghanistan, Vietnam, and WWII when they ask at Veteran's Day ceremonies for anyone who has served in the Armed Forces to be recognized. Instead of being recognized alongside them, I'd much rather share with them warm embraces that give a moment of peace and understanding, and listen to their stories over coffee or a few beers. I don't know how to do wives' teas and attend balls without feeling out of place.

Being a woman, a mother, a wife, and a daughter does not erase or negate my experiences as a soldier. No matter how I feel about my service and the things that happened, I did serve honorably, and no one can take that away from me. I did my job and, despite my mental and physical health, I did it well. Whether I am considered by others around me as a Veteran or just a dependent will always be a question looming in the back of my mind at ceremonies and get-togethers when a topic comes up that I can chime in on, unsure if I should even make mention of having been attached to this infantry division or that and my involvements with them. But I do know my family. I know my friends. I know who has been there and will continue to be there for me at two in the morning when I need them, and who has shared in my joy and my grief. My military family will always be my home.

It's easier to say that part of me never existed, but it did.

Ashley D. Wallis is a full-time student and writer. An Army brat, Ashley grew up surrounded by the military and was an enlisted soldier before marrying her husband, an active-duty Army infantryman. The mother of two boys, any free time Ashley can find is spent on social media providing peer support as a mental health advocate and proponent for various non-profit organizations, and working on her never-ending list of projects.

We Are American Soldiers
Guardians Of Our Nation

The American man and woman soldier are very extraordinary persons. On the surface they are no different from any other nationality. Yet inwardly they are peerless in their own way. While other nationalities in the world are not as sensitive towards life as the American, the American goes a step further. They willingly give of themselves to our country and the American way of life, of which there is no equal in their eyes.

The uniform of a soldier stands for this service, though there are a few who do not acknowledge it. They abuse it by not conceiving the full complexity of the cloak of the dress for freedom that men and women put on and become living symbols as guardians of our nation. While the uniform they proudly wear is the component of its guardianship, it is not a becoming piece of cloth overall. Yet one can visualize the men and women through all generations who have died for what that garb defends.

Freedom, just what does it mean to the American, who leaves all and goes to a strange land far from home?

The word does not mean only doing what you want, going where you want, or saying what you want. It entails being able to feel free, to know in your heart and soul that you have a choice to do anything as long as it does not infringe upon another.

The American soldier, whether male or female, are very complex persons. They will carry out any task, even going to the pits of hell during problematic missions. They convey great pride in what they can accomplish, and yes, they will shield this nation at all costs.

Francis Scott Key summed up patriotism in his rendition to the American Flag and what this symbol stands for, which has become our National Anthem. The Flag is the rallying point for the unique soldier, the material part in the immaterial force of their acceptance that will carry them forward.

They are not persons seeking dissension; on the contrary, if they think and believe in what they are doing, they will stand up and fight for freedom for all their loved ones.

They will not eschew their responsibilities when put to the ultimate test of laying down their life, even to the everyday life they must live. They know who and what they are, and what they stand for. Then they will give their utmost to carry them through any obstacle.

The American man and woman guard our nation because they have raised the value of our country within their minds and hearts. They do not desire their descendants to be raised in any other state. They want them to grow up in a world where peace prevails, and where personal rights of an individual are treated with regard, respect and tolerance of each other's beliefs.

My name is Daniel Evans, and I am 70 years of age. I am also blind. I am an Army Veteran and served from 1964 thru 1967 during the Vietnam Era. I am happily married; I have four children, eight grandchildren, and one great grandchild. I love to write on just about any category. My computer talks, and this allows me satisfaction, in that it reads all that I write.

An Unsent Letter

I'm sorry about your face. That's all I could think to write. It was an exercise, a tool for getting over traumatic things in my life. My therapist suggested I try it: write a letter to my friend who had been wounded in the war.

The letter was never going to be sent, or probably never going to be sent, but it would give me a chance to work out my fucked-up head, maybe not kill myself with Jack and Oxy, maybe feel something other than numb.

But all I could come up with was, "I'm sorry about your face."

You see, and I didn't always know this, but our faces, I mean the skin that covers them is truly like the rubbery molds of a Halloween mask. Think of the droopy masks of Nixon or Bush, shells with nothing of substance underneath. But with real skin, when something changes under the surface, say a cheek bone is shattered or part of the skull is vaporized by a high-powered rifle, then the fucking skin just won't fit right anymore. It's fucking crazy, but it's true.

It puffs in places it didn't before; it sags in others. Eyes droop and mouths are crooked, when once they were straight and strong. Maybe nobody notices, maybe some believe he always looked this way. But I know better. I sweated and laughed and cried with the old mask. Drank shots and chased women. The new face doesn't do that. The new face hides the old eyes that are now vacant, maybe so filled with something so big that the new face is unable to give words to it, so the eyes just give up and become black holes, sucking everything in, but letting nothing out.

My pickled brain and foggy eyes see his fiancée sitting on the couch across from me holding his hand, doing most of the talking. Like an attentive mother licking her fingers to right an unruly cowlick . . . here let me fix your face dear . . . it's . . . it's just a little off . . . move the nose to the right a bit . . . the check to the left a tad, and stretch . . . stRetCH the jaw line something like this. Now much better . . . almost normal . . . almost, dear one.

The day it happened, I was called by a friend whose unit brought Brady to the field hospital. He said Brady was a slab of meat on the O.R. table, unresponsive, shot in the head. At the same time, on another line, was his fiancée, and on another line was his mother. Thanks, AT&T. What in the fuck do you say at a time like this?

So I lied, "He'll be fine. He's strong, a fighter. We have great Docs." The words were hollow, I heard the echo as I said them. Nothing was going to be okay after that. Nothing ever again.

Now all I can think to write is—I'm sorry about your face brother . . . I truly am.

dutch franz served in the United States Army for twenty years. His career included assignments with the Airborne, Ranger Regiment, and Special Forces and included hazardous duty assignments in Central and South America, Asia, and the Middle East. dutch's last combat tour was in Iraq as part of Operation Iraqi Freedom. Now dutch is a freelance journalist, writer, and peace advocate.

Crater in Mosul

Kingpin told me that we had a TIC (Troops in Contact) in Mosul. Fozz and I were on the tanker already. I told the tanker to start heading north. Mosul was about 300 miles north of our current position in Iraq.

If you go fast for 300 miles, your F-16 runs out of gas before you get there. Hurrying, in a normal sense, meant we wouldn't even arrive. So we took our gas and asked the tanker to cap directly over Mosul. Fozz and I pressed on ahead. It's excruciating to travel at a middling speed when you know somebody needs your help.

The city was nestled in the brown hills to the northeast. The sun was setting over Syria and Turkey to the west. We were the only air in town except for a couple of helicopters.

We checked onto the frequency and the chopper guy fed us some coordinates. We plugged them into our jets and plotted an intersection on the southern edge of town.

We said we didn't have contact with anything unusual at those coordinates. The helicopter dude sounded a little exasperated as he tried to get our eyes onto where the action was. We just couldn't find it. I gave up looking through the targeting pod and just "looked out the window." No luck.

The chopper pilot said something like, "Dude. Do you see the huge crater?"

I looked around as the darkness increased. City lights. Car headlights. I was feeling pretty useless after coming so far. I apologized and told the choppers I'd keep searching. The helicopters begged off and said they had to go to get fuel at the FARP (Forward Air Refueling Point). We kept looking and finally, there it was, a few miles north of where we initially plotted it.

Flames flickered out of a giant gaping hole in the city. It was a crater the size of my house. It was in the middle of what used to be a street. I felt like a dumbass for not being able to see this enormous scar in the earth.

The helicopters returned from their refueling and asked us to look around the perimeter of the explosion for snipers. We scanned with our targeting pods. The chopper pilots said that our opponents liked to torch off bombs and then start shooting at the people who show up to help. It seems odd to know a pattern of behavior about something so awful.

There was a bulldozer working inside the crater. I'm not sure what it was doing. I just remember that bulldozer pushing piles of debris around in the dark, surrounded by little flaming piles of wreckage. We didn't find any snipers. As the darkness fell, I watched in infrared as the ambulances came and hauled people away.

We got word that this was a VBIED (Vehicle Borne Improvised Explosive Device) in a truck. They suspected another truck was supposed to participate, but it was leaving the scene. We needed to find it. We expanded our search and found a big truck, like a gasoline tanker, driving out of town to the west. We reported it. They said the bomb builders were based on a road near where the truck was headed. We circled over that truck and followed it to an encampment to the west, so far that we had to modify our orbit for the Syrian border. We were excited. We expected to do something about it.

And then, like so many other times in Iraq, nothing came of it. The interest in the target petered out. It wasn't a TIC anymore. We left to do other things.

I used to pick up the free copy of *Stars and Stripes* every day as I left the chow hall. I would often find details about what I did in the air a few days prior. Sure enough, I read about the explosion in Mosul. It was a deuce and a half, loaded with bags of wheat. And explosives. It drove into the market and got people to line up.

I imagine the guy on the bed of the truck saying, "Come get your wheat here! Great prices!" I picture mothers and little children walking closer to buy some food. And then I see them engulfed in flame.

Eric "Shmo" Chandler recently retired after flying the F-16 in the Minnesota Air National Guard. He flew in Operation Southern Watch three times, Operation Iraqi Freedom, and Operation Enduring Freedom in Afghanistan. Visit ericchandler.wordpress.com for his published writing. He's a husband, father of two, cross-country skier, and marathon runner who lives in Duluth, Minnesota.

Those Orange Skies of Baghdad

A lot of soldiers who have been deployed say the most memorable days of a deployment are your first day and last day. To me, my first day in Iraq stands out as one of the most memorable days of my life. I can hear it as if it was yesterday; the song "Politik" by Coldplay blared through my headphones. I felt the body numbing vibration of the AC-130 gunship beginning its descent. My knees rattled against my elbows as I sat on the floor, balanced on top of my body armor, attached to the floor of the plane by a chord and a belt harness. The lights in the cabin emitted a haunting greenish dim glow that appeared to hide everyone's facial expressions. My fingers tapped nervously against my ammo magazine, the pitter-patter blending in succinctly with the music vibrating in my head from my headphones. All of a sudden I could hear the voice of the pilot over the intercom; I quickly turned the volume down on my MP3 player. I missed the first part of the pilot's monotone announcement, but I understood his last part loud and clear. I could hear the pilot say in an enthusiastic tone, "Welcome to Iraq, fellas, speedily remove all equipment and personnel; we are wheels up in 15 minutes."

Before I could process any of the pilot's words, the mechanical hum of the rear cargo door opening begin to fill the cabin. As the rear door to the plane begin to open, everyone begin to pour out onto the landing tarmac. In a display of operational discipline, everyone quickly helped get all of the equipment out of the plane in what seemed like less than ten minutes. Despite the busy atmosphere on the tarmac, everyone moved along in complete silence in an effort to not tip anyone off about our impromptu arrival.

For the first time, I noticed the sky was filled with an opaque grey ominous cloud; the night air smelled like gunpowder and exploded munitions. The air seemed to cut at your nostrils. I can remember the piquant taste of war dancing on my taste buds. The dead silence was broken up by the arrival of our transportation; the growl of the engine broke through the silence, perfectly in unison with the other engines. I remember hearing the sound of everyone loading up their weapons, and the familiar metallic click of the safety switch rotating to the semi-automatic setting on their rifles. With no knowledge of my final destination, I locked and loaded magazines into my M9 pistol and my M16 rifle. We were on the move.

As we entered the outskirts of Baghdad along an abandoned highway, the night sky was illuminated by burning enemy military equipment and plumes of smoke. The dark hues of black and gray highlighted by vibrant orange ribbons of fire was one of the most captivating and tragic sights to behold. I was somewhere in Iraq, and I was officially in a combat zone. I learned a lot about the human condition during the two years I spent in Iraq, but the fondest memory was how innocent and untarnished my perspective was that very first night. My perspective of war was incubated that night. And for this reason, that moment will always be near and dear to me.

My name is Jameel Hakeem. I'm 31 years old and I live in Tampa, Florida with my wife and three boys. I am originally from Baton Rouge, Louisiana. I graduated high school in 2000 and immediately enlisted in the U.S. Army for eight years. While in the Army I served multiple tours in The Horn of Africa, Afghanistan, and Iraq. Currently a civilian, I've worked for the Department of Defense for the past six years.

Hansford C. Vest, SSgt. USA
Edited by Jay Hansford C. Vest

The Shredded Parachute: A Paratrooper's Account of Vision and Survival in World War II Europe

We children were rummaging in the attic where we found an old army suitcase full of letters. My sister began reading them aloud and laughing at our parents romance, but there was something else in the suitcase. There was love and an old shredded parachute. The letters had kept father focused on survival during the combat he faced when confronting Nazi occupied Europe in World War II. An original paratrooper trained in jump school class 22 at Fort Benning, Georgia, father had fought in all the campaigns of the 101st Airborne during the war in Europe. Making combat jumps in Normandy and Holland, he also jumped off a truck at Bastogne before entering Germany. Wounded six times without ever leaving combat, he won many honors, but his greatest honor was survival. Of the "D" Company, 502nd Parachute Infantry Regiment, only 6 of the initial 187 men who began the war in the night jump over Normandy survived all the way through the combat, reaching Austria in 1945. As one of them, he had beat the odds, which amounted to one in thirty chances for survival.

Having grown up with the oral tradition of our Native American heritage at Grandma's, I learned to listen when adults talked, and although Dad suffered much post traumatic stress from combat and seldom spoke of the war, I do recall many heroic tales from the battlefields in France, Holland, and Germany. Nearing his end, he began writing these war memoirs, but they are too extensive to include here; however, he did offer the following mysterious account of his adventure.

* * *

We were training near Reading, England, for the allied invasion of Nazi occupied Europe; there we took part in a great maneuver designed to simulate our coming night drop over Normandy. When our parachutes were issued for the jump, I got mine and I knew something was wrong. The chute pack was damp and musty smelling, but I didn't say anything, because you learn not to complain in the army. So I boarded the airplane with others of my stick, drop group, and when the signal to stand and hook up came, I did so without a word, like so many times before. As I leapt from the plane and my chute opened, there was a terrible tearing sound. Looking up, I could see that my chute had shredded up, and it was torn open in the middle. So I pulled my reserve chute, and as it deployed, it wrapped around my leg. Now I was falling to the ground like a stone with only my shredded up main chute creating a little drag. I hit the ground with such force that it seemed I was driven like a post into it. But I was lucky because it was a soft bog where I came down. Still it knocked me out and I lay there unconscious for a day.

It was in these hours that I was given a dream, and what a dream it was. In my dream I saw that many of my friends were going to die in the war. In the first part of my dream, I saw my home back in Virginia. There were my mother, sisters, wife, and friends praying for me, and it was an ongoing thing. Then I saw that I was going on a long trip from war and I would be in many countries. In that great trip, I was involved with a train, and it was a troop train of those times. I saw places that I had never been before. There were very large vineyards with grapes in neat rows that went on for miles and miles. The dream was in a country that I had never seen before, except there was one country in particular that seemed to me I had lived there before, and I saw many things that were to come to pass. Afterwards I woke and found my outfit had moved on and was in preparation for the coming invasion.

So on D-Day, June 6, 1944, we jumped at night behind the beachheads in a night drop. After that it was on to Holland and the battle for Best. With three airborne divisions, we jumped miles and miles behind the German lines and in front of the British 2nd Army. Too many bridges, but the airborne prevailed, and after a very long stay in combat, we were moved back to France. Lost here was 26 percent of our company, which were killed in Normandy, and again, the same amount was killed in Holland at Best and Zon. We missed our Thanksgiving, but in war, what the "heck." Our outfit was pulled back to France, but not for long. The Great Battle in the Ardennes was on, the Battle of the Bulge, and we were called into Bastogne.

The American Army had been victorious until then, but everything was about to change. Some divisions up front were not ready for what they were about to experience in battle. Their lines were rolled back on a large front, and many of the men were caught by surprise and thus were thrown back, killed, or captured. In the overall campaign, American armies sustained 77,000 causalities in just that one big battle. Things happened so fast and we were surrounded for three days during Christmas. Bastogne was a communications center with four key crossroads and a railroad crossing. It was a must that we hold it and stop the enemy in their advance. We were told to hold until relieved, but we faced several panzer or armored divisions that cut our supply lines. At Bastogne, we were the hole in the donut, and we were surrounded, cut off from the rest of the world. Again we lost another 26 percent dead. Now it goes something like this: we original soldiers who came over with the division were becoming fewer and fewer, there were only six of the original company remaining.

After Bastogne, we moved onto the Alsace-Lorraine region and then through Germany. I became a "high point" soldier, so I prepared to go back to the states. On the train ride from near Austria, I embarked on a troop train ride to Marseilles, France, in preparation for my return home. There it was, my 1943 dream alive; like in a movie, it was deja vu. The dream had shown me these very scenes those years before in England. As the train moved through Germany, it was a land where I thought that I had lived before as I passed down the Rhine Valley. I remember what a very strange feeling that came over me, as if I had been there before and knew the place well. I shall never forget the place as long as I live, and I didn't make any of this up; it was real. In France, especially the south of France, I was able to see the vineyards of my dream. In fact, the train stopped and we tasted the grapes, but they were the wine variety. So it was in Marseilles that I boarded a troop ship for America. I met new friends on the way to the states. One soldier was from the 327th Glider Regiment who had survived all the battles like me. I found that we each hated the war more than we had imagined. The terrible loss of life on all sides weighed on each of us. Then there were those silent crosses of our comrades who paid the price for our victory, which were always in my vision when I closed my eyes.

* * *

So it was that Dad had been given the rare gift of seeing the outcome before the engagement. In considering his dream-experience, I am reminded of those Plains Indians war coups and their accounts of seeing outcomes in their dreams. Again I marvel at the gift accorded my father in knowing that he would survive against the impossible odds, one chance in thirty, but fighting with purpose, courage and determination against a merciless enemy.

Hansford C. Vest (1919–1997) born at Hico (Buzzard Rock) in Amherst Country, Virginia, was a Monacan Indian and a direct descendent of Opechcancanough (Pamunkey) who arrested Captain John Smith as a murder suspect during British Colonization of Tsenacomoco (Powhatan Virginia). He volunteered for the U.S. Army Air Corp in 1941, later to transfer to initial paratrooper development in 1942. A Staff Sargent, he served with the 101st Airborne throughout all its campaigns during World War II in the Europe.

Jay Hansford C. Vest, Ph.D. is an enrolled member of the Monacan Indian Nation, a tribe recognized by the state of Virginia. He is a direct descendent of the seventeenth century chief Opechancanough who took John Smith captive as a murder suspect during British Colonization of Tsenacomoco (Powhatan Virginia), and he is an honorary Pikuni (Blackfeet) in ceremonial adoption (June 1989). Dr. Vest is a full professor in the Department of American Indian Studies at the University of North Carolina at Pembroke. He is author of *Will-of-the-Land: A Philosophy of Wilderness Praxis* (2010), *Native American Oralcy: Interpretations of Indigenous Thought* (2014), and *The Bobtail Stories: Growing Up Monacan* (forthcoming), as well as more than 150 scholarly journal articles, chapters in books, and other published writings. For more information see http://www.uncp.edu/home/vestj/

Kathleen Palmer

The Lady in the Gray Suit

She stood on the stage, stoic and proud. A flash of gray linen in a sea of green polyester. Her tired eyes briefly found mine and immediately pulled me out of my jet-lagged stupor. I was in an audience of other supporters drunk on the same proud punch, as we sat in the inner courtyard of the Pentagon waiting to watch our soldiers receive a leadership award. At first I was confused, wondered if she was a civilian receiving the award, and my first thought was, "What's on her resume?"

But as my curiosity led me to read deeper into the printed program, I realized that she was the widow of a soldier being posthumously awarded for his actions and leadership. My blood froze because I immediately thought (as many of my sisters in service do when we meet a widow), there but for the grace of God go I.

The ceremony finally began and I was lost in the pomp and circumstance. Music played, awardees marched in, VIPS were introduced, and the chaplain led us in prayer. We had flown all the way from Germany for this ceremony, and I could not be prouder of my husband of 10 years. I wanted to focus on him, but I could not take my eyes off the slight woman standing shoulder to shoulder with the uniformed mass. Her small frame, short cap of dark hair, and gray suit made her look like a small rock embedded into a mossy field.

As General Schoomaker was introduced, I was jolted out of my fog by the snapping of cameras and the shifting of seats. I remembered why I was here, and I smiled down the row to my in-laws and friends who came to support us. As the General began reading the names and biographies that accompanied each of the soldiers, I caught the loving gaze of my own warrior. I was feeling a myriad of emotions, but at that moment, pride was replaced with relief as I realized how lucky he was to be on that stage.

When it came time for the lady in the gray suit to step up to the podium to receive her husband's award, most of the crowd had stopped moving. The air seemed to hold out all sound as a collective audience of 200 held their breath. As her late husband's achievements were read, she stood fast and firm with her eyes transfixed above the crowd. Not a muscle moved on her face as she held herself erect and dignified. When she turned to receive the award (which weighed almost as much as she did), the crowd quietly rose to their feet to honor her the way that military families innately know how to do. She nodded slightly to the crowd and sat, while trying to balance the huge bust of General MacArthur on her lap. She slipped back into her stoic shell and kept her eyes straight ahead for the rest of the program.

After the ceremony was over, there was cake and punch followed by big smiles, fierce handshaking, and more pictures than were necessary. After playing the proud wife for about 20 minutes, I finally garnered enough courage to go over where the lady in the gray suit was standing, flanked by her support system. I waited patiently to shake her hand, not sure of what I was going to say and even more unsure of my emotional state. When she turned to me, I was greeted by tired but kind green eyes. She firmly took my hand as I told her how amazing she was. She smiled politely and simply told me to "enjoy the day." I felt as if I should say more, but I had no idea what else to say.

At that moment I realized that in our experience as military wives, we try not to let ourselves go to that place. That place where stories become reality and the plot changes mid chapter. We are taught early on not to play the "Who has it worse" game. We know that it is dangerous and futile because someone's story is always worse. At any time we could all become the lady in the gray suit. As I turned back to see her greet the next person with the same handshake, the same smile, and the same response. I felt a strong hand press into the small of my back. I realized with relief that no matter how much I ached for her loss, it wasn't my story today, and God willing, it never will be.

Kathleen Palmer is a proud spouse of an Army Warrior of 26 years and 7 deployments, a mother of 2 Army brats. She has served with some of the most amazing people as a wife, teacher, counselor, and battle buddy. She believes that we have a divine duty to never forget those who survived the war, were widowed by the war, and the children who now bear the weight of the sacrifice.

Michele A. Boyle

Reading of the Names

We are heading to Washington D.C. for the 30th Anniversary of the Vietnam Veterans Wall Memorial for "Reading of the Names" during the week of Veterans Day 2012. This would be the fifth time those who lost their lives in Vietnam had their names read. Previous years are 1982, 1992, 2002, and 2007.

Gray skies and blustering winds show threatening signs of rain, and it's so cold, you can see your breath when you talk. As we pass Arlington Cemetery, many are walking among this vast land of graves that are lined up with precision, like soldiers marching on. We are dropped off on Constitution Avenue, where I check in at the Registration Tent and begin the long journey towards the Wall. Lincoln's Memorial looks daunting as I feel like his eyes are following us. I shiver, pulling my scarf tighter, and worry that Michael's coat is warm enough. We continue walking past the Reflecting Pool, such a beautiful park, and finally see "The Wall" ahead of us.

I haven't been here for years and forgotten how emotional it makes you feel. It's beautiful, peaceful, and sad at the same time. We see all ages looking to find that special name, some wearing their worn, torn uniforms, staring in disbelief like it happened yesterday; an elderly man shaking his head, asking why. As we continue further down the path, my heart breaks when an aging mother strains to see "her boy." "I just want to hold my hand on his name and feel his life again." A tear drips from her eye as she brushes it off, "I can't let him see me this way." What do you say to someone who lost her child so many years ago? A young boy is tracing a name. I smile and wonder does he really know what all of this means. I feel grateful his family brings him to experience the site and keep the torch burning.

I'm freezing, needing a very hot cup of coffee or tea before I am scheduled to read, but the nearest vendor is closed and the next place is across the Reflecting Pool. They are getting ready to start the opening ceremony shortly, and I can't miss that. Michael offers to go, but I feel it's too long a walk for him. He departs without waiting for my objection. I don't think any of us were expecting it to be so cold this early in November, but once you are here, you are overwhelmed and feel the warmth of those who made your life possible. While waiting for his return, I walk around looking at the memorial displays; the Vietnam Women's Memorial was dedicated in 1993, honoring close to 12,000 women veterans who served in Vietnam, very impressive. A few people walking through the arena stop and chat with us, most very somber. One man told us he drove all the way from California for one reason, to read his brother's name. He said it's the least he can do for his brother and those who died for us. He comes here every Veterans Day to honor his brother and this will be the fifth time he has read the names.

The speakers gather on the podium, holding onto their hats. As I wait with the other volunteers, a woman sits next to me. She told me she walked here from the University where she works, and has done the readings since they started them. She lives nearby and will stay to the end if they need her to fill in for someone who couldn't make it, so that all names would be honored.

Michael comes back empty handed, no coffee, no tea. The other vendor was also closed. So I keep my complaints about the miserable weather to myself; after all, this was my decision to be here, a very, very honored decision.

Jan Scruggs, founder of the Vietnam Memorial Association starts the Opening Ceremony and introduces his guest speakers: The Honorable Chuck Hagel; Brigadier General George Brice, U.S.A. Retired; Robert Patrick Colonel, U.S.A. Retired and Director of the Veterans History Project. As each of them speaks, the winds are kicking up, and they decide to shorten their speeches, if you can imagine a Politician doing that! However, as I wait in line for my turn, suddenly, for some reason, I didn't feel the cold anymore. The skies were still gray, but the winds had died down.

After the Opening Ceremony, the readings began promptly at 4:00 P.M. Over 2,000 volunteers began to read names for approximately eight hours from 4 P.M. on November 7 to midnight, and then again for 19 hours daily from 5 A.M. until midnight, November 8 through 10. These volunteers were parents, sisters, brothers, other family members, friends, and military brothers, speaking each name slowly, clearly with reverence.

The first readers are the son and grandson of one the first casualties in Vietnam. My reading began at 4:52 P.M. Everyone was synchronized with the timing of their list. For days I practiced my 30 names, how to pronounce them, timing myself, how loud I was. I wanted this to be perfect to show no disrespect by botching a name. It was the least I could do for the person I was honoring and the family. The only problem I had was standing in front of others and being that person who is focused on. I usually take a back seat and watch, but I wanted to do this for every veteran who never made it home, every veteran still fighting the war, the families who still ache for the loss of their loved ones, my husband Michael, and those he fought alongside.

I can do this, I say to myself. I have my list of names. I actually increased the size of the print so that I could read them without glasses! I also looked up each name to see where they were from, and came across two names who were from towns near me. I was about the tenth reader and the nervousness started again in my knee caps. As the readers spoke each name, despite the darkened afternoon, the black granite behind the podium seemed to shine brightly. Each reader honored their list with dedication.

As I slowly walked across the podium, I no longer felt the cold. My knees were no longer shaking, and suddenly I was not afraid of speaking in front of all those who were in attendance. I stood as proudly as I could and clearly read each of my names. As I left the podium, I felt something come over me that I can't explain: a feeling of warmth, satisfaction, something good. I also had a nice surprise, my niece Genine and her husband Sean drove over from Maryland to the memorial in honor of Michael and Veterans. This will always remain in our hearts. Michael stood and hugged me and said thank you, making it complete.

Michele A. Boyle is married over forty years to Michael Boyle, a United States Marine Vietnam Combat Veteran, has three sons, and their first grandchild. Michele is originally from Pittsburgh, Pennsylvania, but has lived in the warmer climate of South Carolina for several years. This is her third submission to *Proud to Be: Writing by American Warriors*. Michele enjoys writing in personal journals to help get her through the tough times.

Richard Kirshen

My Night On The River

I've got to keep quiet. The boat's gone. It's probably somewhere on the bottom of the river now, with the current dragging it. Did anyone else make it? Was anyone captured? I have to swim, but which way? To which shore? Too dark, I can't see. Ok, calm down, what do I remember? We were cruising on the river, just finishing some C-rations, heading back to Nha Be, and a quiet, restful night in a barracks. Nha Be, home of the Mobile Riverine Forces, and my present home away from home. Then a bright light, loud noises, screaming, and now I'm wet and treading water. I have a headache. I'm dizzy. My body aches. No more river patrol boat beneath my feet. There is nothing beneath my feet. Damn, which way? Have to pick a way and get out of the water. Snakes, crocodiles, giant catfish so large that a grown man could stand upright in its open mouth, Khorat (giant fanged frogs), it's all coming back to me now: the orientation class about the rivers here in the Mekong Delta, just before they made me a boat captain. What to look out for, what, besides the enemy, was dangerous. Have to get out of the water and have to stay quiet. I don't know what side the enemy is on.

Oh, geez, mangroves. We have those at home, in South Florida. They're great for the environment, but a real bitch to climb out of. They don't really need any ground under them. They grow right in the water. These things are so damned slimy and slippery. I can't seem to grasp anything. I have to get out of the water. I need to pull myself up onto something hard. This is scary. I don't want to be here. I seriously don't want to be here. Can't see much, so dark. My leg is stuck in a mangrove root. I can't move. I'll be here forever. There, free, but now what?

The darkness is punctuated only by the light of the tracer rounds, and now I hear the bullets. How come I couldn't hear them before? Different sounds now. Return fire. Some of our boats are still fighting. I recognize the sounds of the .50, and the M-60. My boat is gone, with all my stuff on it. I have to get out of here. Crawling now, on slimy, stinking mud with things cutting my fingertips and my knees, away from the river. Have to find dry land.

Ok, tired now, have to rest, can't crawl anymore. Fear encompasses my very being. I shake. How am I going to get out of this? Who the hell knows where I am . . . or even, if I am? I hear noises in the jungle. Tell me it's not a freaking tiger. They have tigers here. I could get eaten by a tiger and no one would ever know. Wait, maybe it's just a Saola, one of the local deer type animals, or an Ibis or Crane walking around looking for food. I'm hoping for a deer.

Have to take stock of what I have with me. Not much, just my knife, my wallet, a belt, my jungle boots. No food, no drinks, no survival stuff. No gun or ammo. What did survival school teach me? Find protective shelter and hide from the enemy, if you think they may be close. Close??? They just sunk my god-damned boat. Of course, they're close. Should I seek higher ground? Hide in a tree, maybe? No, I could fall out. There could be snakes in the trees. Have to find some dry land and hide myself.

I walk, crouched over, eyes searching the darkness for anything recognizable. Moving slowly now, almost sloth like, listening to every noise. I am totally aware of my surroundings. The jungle teems with noises at night. I categorize them as either friendly or harmful. The ground is harder now, my boots squish, I have mud everywhere.

This is very disconcerting. This never happened to me back in Miami. Nothing there ever scared me. Thinking now, I can't remember ever being scared before I came here. Maybe just that one time I wrecked my dad's car while he was watching. But then again, I've never been in a jungle before, surrounded by things that either wanted to eat me or kill me. I sit under a tree and listen. The gunfire is dying down now. Did we win? How many of our boats were sunk? Did anyone die? What the hell am I going to do?

I hear voices and strain to make them out. Let it be English. Let it be a platoon of Army guys. Shit, the sing-song sounds of Vietnamese. I lie down and pull palm fronds over me. The voices get closer as they walk through the jungle. No sounds of machetes cutting anything. They must be on a path. I lie still. Insects devour me. There's buzzing in my ears: gnats or flies or who knows what else lives out here. The footsteps come closer now. Sandals break small branches and crack the dead fronds. The path must be only feet from where I am. Like a marble statue, I lie there motionless, barely breathing . . . on the verge of screaming.

They pass by whispering, walking one behind the other only feet from where I am frozen in this humid, wretched place. I don't move. Motionless for hours, becoming a home to unseen mites and insects. I feel small stings, bites like the fire ants back in Florida. I still don't move. Night encompasses all. Pitch black with only a minimum of twinkling stars visible through the canopy of trees. I look through a break in the vegetation covering me and then sleep.

Daylight, birds chirp, and something large bellows off in the distance. I inch the fronds from my face and move my head back and forth. I see nothing, only streams of sunlight filtering down through the tree tops. I slide the vegetation away and stand up. The mud has dried and caked on me, protecting me somewhat from the insects as I slept. Brushing myself off, I head back toward the river. I want to douse everything off of me, but think about the camouflage that the dried mud offers, and reconsider. I sit on the bank of the river.

I am thirsty, and hungry, and I itch everywhere. My body is ravaged and abused. I think about what I am going to do now. I need food, but most importantly, water. A man can survive about 3 days without water, but that it is very uncomfortable. I can't drink the river water, but as a last resort, that will have to be it. The locals drink it and bathe in it and wash their clothes in it and use it as a toilet. Would I drink it as a last resort? Yes.

Engines, I hear engines and hide behind a tree. The roar gets closer and I see small brown/green boats. PBR's (Patrol Boat River) heading right for the ox-bow in the river where I have secreted myself. As they unknowingly close in on my position, I wade out to waist deep water, put my hands above my head, and begin waving and yelling. They see me, and go to general quarters, manning all of their weapons, and aiming them at me. I yell in English, and they close in. I know the boat captain. We got here about two weeks apart. I exhale loudly as he comes in to pick me up. He barely recognizes me, covered in mud, disheveled, arms and face covered with insect bites.

Heading back to Nha Be now, sated with water and some more C-rations, I learn that the other three on my boat were picked up. Two were wounded, but no one died. I was presumed captured, dead, or lost, and a search party was sent. On the way back, I went over my ordeal in my head. Of the gamut of emotions I ran through in such a relatively short time, the overriding emotion was fear. It was a fear of what nature has to offer in its basest form. Beyond nature, it was the fear of being alone that dominated my being. The fear of not being found.

Richard Kirshen has spent his entire life, with the exception of his time in the US Navy, and some extensive traveling time, living in South Florida. He owned and operated a business in Miami Beach for 37 years, before selling it and retiring this past October. His Navy days included one year of sea duty out of Yokosuka, Japan, on the USS Banner, AGER-1, a small spy ship. He graduated from Navy Dive School in Subic Bay, Philippines, then off to the IUWG (Inshore Undersea Warfare Group) in Cam Ranh Bay, Vietnam, where he was the base diver, and finally down to the Mekong Delta region on river boats, attached to the Mobile Riverine Forces. He now spends his time playing golf, tending to grandchildren, and taking road trips with Mary, his wife of 41 years.

Order of the Spur

I was assigned to the 11th Armored Calvary Regiment at the National Training Center, in Fort Irwin, California, one of the few posts where you will find Calvary traditions and Calvary troops. The Spur Ride is the only means of being initiated into the Order of the Spur (aside from a wartime induction). The organization of a Spur Ride varies, but it is generally an event held over multiple days during which a trooper must pass a series of physical and mental tests relevant to the Cavalry. Some of the tests evaluate leadership, technical and tactical proficiency, physical fitness, the ability to operate as part of a team under high levels of stress and fatigue under both day and night conditions, though the specific tests vary by unit. A written test is often also administered, with questions that cover United States Cavalry and unit history.

During ceremonies I saw soldiers and officers walking around wearing spurs, black Stetsons, and Cavalry belt buckles. They were the elite, they were distinguished and proud. I decided I was going to be one of them and I was going to earn my spurs. I spent the next three months preparing for the two-day event. I had all the required gear and even a few accessories that I thought might bring me some additional luck.

The morning of the ride, I received a call letting me know that the uniform for the ride had changed and I needed to show up wearing the green battle dress uniform (BDU) and the classic black combat boots. I hadn't worn my BDU's in over two years; my black boots were folded over in the bottom of a duffle bag below my musky smelling uniforms. The military often tests your ability to be flexible under unexpected circumstances; this inconvenience was nothing more than the first of countless tests of my patience. I dug my uniform and boots from a cold duffle bag and rushed to formation. I arrived flustered, anxious, and ill prepared. I immediately noticed that everyone else was having the same reaction. We were broken down into teams—each team was given a shortwave manpack radio, a first aid kit, a list of grid coordinates. It was nearing mid day and it was blistering beneath the desert sun. As I completed the lengthy written test I noticed that my feet were sweating and rubbing on both sides of my ankles. I closed my eyes in frustration when I realized that due to them being folded and improperly stored in my duffle bag, they were going to rub blisters and the Spur Ride was going to suck. I completed the written test with confidence, and I sat on the ground, preparing for the land navigation portion. I took advantage of the extra time to wrap my feet and ankles; I had no idea how long the course was or how my feet were going to look after wards.

During the land navigation portion, I volunteered to carry the manpak radio that weighed nearly fifteen pounds, in addition to the rest of my gear, including my M16/203 (grenade launcher). I had to prove that I could do it, that even though I was the only girl on my team I would be able to pull my load. At each grid coordinates on the course was a skills task station where we had to perform tasks that were designed to be physically demanding, technically challenging, and a few team building exercises just to keep it interesting. The physical tasks include dragging a CPR training dummy up and over a hill, only to turn around and pull him back down the hill. We had to carry full water containers between trucks parked on inclines, fill enough sand bags to construct a fighting position, change a flat tire and recover another vehicle that was stuck in the sand, and finally there was an obstacle course with a wall that we had to scale including barb wire to crawl under and multiple logs to cross. Then came the technically proficient tasks, such as perform first aid measures, break down my rifle and reassemble it in the dark—thankfully there was a full moon which illuminated the desert basin—and plot multiple grid coordinates using night vision goggles and a red light.

Before the sun went down, I could tell that my feet had began to swell, and I knew that if I took them off even to change my socks, I would not be able to get them back on, and I would not be able to complete the Spur Ride. I took all the Ranger Candy (ibuprofen) I had in my first aid kit and repeated "you are one step closer, you are one step closer" over and over to myself. By midnight I was seriously regretting my decision to carry the radio, but I was way too proud to ask for help. I thought the night was never going to end; I began doubting my ability to finish. Thankfully my spirits were lifted when we came to the team building station where we were to spin round and around, bent over, with our helmets on plastic swords while we sang the Army song. I don't know what was funnier, the fact that we screwed up on the song or the fact that we looked like a bunch of dizzy kids spinning around jubilantly. They had us spinning until we nearly vomited (I heard later that many people did in fact puke), then we had to mount a barrel disguised as a horse and pretend like we were riding off into the sunset.

We stopped to rest, and the lieutenant on our team sat next to me and proceeded to whine and complain about how hard the obstacles were and how he wished he would've trained harder for the course. I sat in shock because he seemed to be doing fine; he didn't even look tired. I chuckled to myself as I leaned against the radio for support and tried go get a bit of shut eye before we started the next leg of the course. I woke to the sound of the radio letting us know it was our turn to begin the last span of the nearly twelve-mile course. We finished the Spur Ride a little after 11 A.M. the following day. I was so excited I nearly forgot how bad my back hurt due to the radio and how bad my feet hurt due to my stupid boots.

We had to wait for all the teams to finish before we began the ceremony, several teams got lost, and some teams actually quit—I was shocked by how small the formation for the ceremony was in comparison to the formation at the starting point the day before. I was ecstatic because I am pretty sure I was delirious during the obstacles and during the hike across the desert. I looked around the ranks and I couldn't find any other females; I was the only woman to complete the Spur Ride.

Yes, I was the only woman to complete the Spur Ride.

My feet were so damaged, I had to have help peeling the leather from around my swollen legs. Blisters covered my ankles, toes, and the soles of my feet. Thankfully I had the weekend to celebrate and recover. Completing the Spur Ride and being awarded my spurs was one of the toughest and most rewarding adventures during my Army career.

Starlyn Lara served nearly twelve years on active duty in the US Army from 1995-2007. During her service she achieved the rank of Staff Sergeant (SSG-E6) and was assigned to multiple duty stations as well as deployments that included Bosnia during Operation Joint Forge and Iraq during Operation Iraqi Freedom. She was awarded the two Meritorious Service Medals and a Combat Action Badge for her service.

HQ10

I received an Army ROTC commission as a second lieutenant from a state university in the Midwest. I immediately went on active duty, attending Signal Officer Basic Course, then serving as a platoon leader stateside. I received promotions to first lieutenant, then captain, and after completing Signal Officer Advanced Course, I transferred overseas to Germany where I served as an adjutant and then assumed command of a company.

I became commanding officer of over 200 soldiers a few months after the fall of the Berlin Wall. Later that year, Desert Shield began, and on Christmas Eve Day, half of my company deployed to Kuwait. The soldiers in my company provided maintenance, electronic security, and logistics support to the line companies in the battalion that provided communications to the battlefield. The remainder of my battalion stayed in Germany awaiting orders to deploy.

So the day the air raid commenced over the country of Iraq, starting Desert Storm, those soldiers of mine deployed to Kuwait weighed heavily on my mind. Significant changes had taken place in Germany as well. In the months during Desert Shield, building up to Desert Storm, all of the military installations in the Frankfurt area had been heavily fortified with concrete barricades and concertina wire. I had been given a mission that had taken me from my kaserne in Hoechst, Germany, to the Creighton W. Abrams complex in Frankfurt.

Being a company commander, I was assigned a humvee and a soldier to drive the vehicle. Each military vehicle, for reasons of identification, was assigned letters and numbers painted on the vehicle. The letters HQ stood for headquarters—the name of the company I commanded, then the number 10—HQ10. My humvee was new, painted in a green, black, and brown camoflouge design and clean inside. I and the young soldier driving found ourselves in heavy bumper-to-bumper traffic as soon as we reached the autobahn. We progressed toward our destination, amidst signs saying "Kein krieg fur ol" in the windows of the cars around us and hanging from buildings of businesses and apartment buildings.

Upon approach of our destination—a compound that took an entire city block—we found all gates closed and locked, with no gate guards or anyone else in sight within its confines. This compound housed the V Corps Headquarters. My battalion commander had mentioned being unable to reach anyone by phone, one of the reasons why someone needed to be physically sent. Only a serious threat would have caused such drastic measures. No wonder! Thousands of protesters on foot lined the streets carrying banners that too read "Kein krieg fur ol." When translated "No war for oil" is what the signs read.

Back then we did not have cell phones. The Army still used stationary black telephones with the rotary dial. Word had not gotten out to the smaller outlying Army posts. Had my superiors known there was no way to access the Abrams complex, we most likely would not have been sent.

Due to traffic and one-way streets, our return route took us by the U.S. Consulate a few blocks away. The world had seemed to stop its daily routine to protest the Persian Gulf War. The mob of people at the main gate spilled onto the street. German police in full riot gear stood atop large green water trucks with long, powerful hoses used for crowd control. Being in a U.S. Army vehicle and uniform amidst a dense crowd of war protesters and riot police with high-pressure hoses put us in a precarious situation.

My legs shook uncontrollably. I flexed my muscles to steady them, but they continued to tremble. I used my arms, placing my fists just below each hip, in an attempt to brace them, hoping my driver didn't notice. I glanced over to him. He focused only on the crowd before us—wondering how we were going to get through.

"Keep going," I told him. "Just look straight ahead. Don't let your foot off the gas."

I prayed then. I prayed hard. My driver adhered to my directive not to stop, and we kept moving. Our vehicle seemed to become like a boat in a body of water and we floated. Despite being amidst what seemed like a sea of protesters where no distinction could be made between the road, sidewalk, or lawn, we were out of there.

We made our way back to the relative safety of our unit. My driver took the bragging rights, lauding his driving skills and my ability to stay cool under intense pressure. I never did discuss much about happened with anyone.

My battalion did not deploy to join our comrades. My soldiers along with the soldiers in the line company returned to Germany from the desert in Southwest Asia when Desert Storm ended.

Over the years, whenever I recalled the event, the memory seemed to terrify me more than the actual incident itself, though I know I experienced plenty of fear at the time. I remember the helplessness I felt amidst the crowd of hundreds of thousands of protesters. I hated having no control over a situation I had not intended to be part of in the first place.

Occasionally, I think about the soldier who so skillfully drove HQ10— the vehicle assigned to the commanding officer: me. And I think about the vehicle itself, a humvee—and how God allowed it to provide the protection and escape I needed in Germany on the day the Persian Gulf War began.

Susan is a native of Chicago, Illinois, and received her Army ROTC commission from Western Illinois University. She served as a platoon leader, company executive officer, supply officer, adjutant, company commander, division staff officer, and readiness group while on active duty. She is the 2010 recipient of the Ann Darr Scholarship for Female Veterans and Active Duty Military Personnel awarded by the Writer's Center in Bethesda, Maryland. She lives and works in suburban Chicago.

F-16 Pilot, Major Ian 'SHOUT' Billington preparing to step from the jet to greet his family after a 6 month deployment overseas.

Kimberly Billington is an expectant mother & wife of an Air Force F-16 Fighter Pilot. She resides in Phoenix, Arizona, with her husband and their two silver labrador puppies. Although considered a 'jack of all trades' in the media world, she most recently worked as a television producer and journalist in tv news before switching hats to work in the freelance world as a media specialist. Kim was born and raised in Detroit, MI, where she attended Eastern Michigan University for her undergraduate degree and Specs Howard School of Media Arts where she specialized in Broadcast Journalism/ TV/Radio and Film. A former collegiate athlete, she loves to stay healthy & active in the Phoenix mountains, her family is her inspiration.

Life on the ODA

The only way in or out of the camp was by air: either helicopter or the fixed wing, twin engine DHC-4 Caribou aircraft. Just outside the camp lay a helipad and a 1000-foot runway, both paved with PSP (Perforated Steel Planking). The camp sat in the middle of a free-fire zone. A free-fire zone is an area where anyone passing through not cleared by the ODA was considered the enemy and could be engaged at will. Old deserted rice paddies dotted with tree squares ruled the horizon. A tree square is just what it sounds like: a group of trees growing in a square on built-up ground. In the middle of the square, the rice farmer built a little house for himself and his family. These houses had long since passed into history. These dry oases were the only places where we (or the bad guys) could hole up during the day or night and expect to be somewhat dry. Many a fire fight occurred around these tree squares. When we moved into one, we could often see old Napalm hanging like blackened candle wax in the trees. A monument to more dangerous times.

We conducted interdiction operations along the Ho Chí Minh Trail, a logistical system running from North Vietnam to South Vietnam through the neighboring countries of Laos and Cambodia. The system provided support, in the form of manpower and material, to the Viet Cong (VC) as well as to the regular North Vietnamese Army units operating in the northern part of South Vietnam. It served as a critical strategic supply route for the North Vietnamese forces.

The Civilian Irregular Defense Force (CIDG) with Vietnamese Special Forces teams or Luc Luong Dac Biet (LLDB) and US Army Special Forces A Teams manned camps like ODA 325 at Duc Hue. The CIDG were basically mercenaries who lived with their families in the camp. The US Special Forces trained, equipped, and fed them and their families. Having their families there proved to be a good thing in that it basically ensured that when the VC or North Vietnamese Army (NVA) attacked a camp, the CIDG would stay and fight.

The UH-1H chopper I rode in settled down on the helipad, blowing fine sand and bending grass in all directions. The Team Commander, CPT Robert Romero, stood holding his beret on his head, leaning into the rotowash. Romero, a half-blooded American Indian from somewhere out West, wanted to return to the States and marry the Chief's daughter. And I later heard he did.

Romero welcomed me, and I walked with him through the gate and into the camp, which was only a few meters from where I landed. Here I met the rest of the motley crew of ODA 325. All were wearing Tiger Fatigues, the uniform that SF issued to the CIDG for field operations.

At the time, the ODA had three slots for officers: Commander, XO, and CA/PO (Civil Affairs/Physical Operations Officer). I had been slotted as the CA/PO, pending departure of the XO. It didn't matter what our titles were: we all did the same job when it came to field work.

Life in the camp was similar to life in a small village. We had a mess hall; a medical clinic manned by our senior medic, SSG Jungling, a sharp faced blond guy; a parade field (not that we ever used it); and "homes" in the form of sandbagged bunkers topped with corrugated tin. These bunkers helped define the defensive walls of our star-shaped camp. Fifty-five gallon drums lay aimlessly around, acting as cook stoves, water containers, and support for squares of wood on which rice dried. Coils of concertina wire held in place by engineer stakes and laced with claymore mines lay row upon row to form the camp's outer perimeter.

The CIDG and their families cooked over open fires and ate on tables set up outside their sandbagged homes. The US Special Forces paid the CIDG and also brought in baskets of fish, vegetables, squash, and gallon plastic jugs filled with Nuoc Man, a spicy dipping sauce (extract) made from raw fish. Of course, we enjoyed local delicacies like seven-foot cobras, which were caught, killed, then eaten.

Doc Jungling, the senior medic on the Team, was the most knowledgeable in his field and not only provided medical support to the Team, but he also supervised Vietnamese medical personnel he had trained to take care of the CIDG and their families.

The young wife of one of the CIDG was going to have a baby. It wasn't supposed to be a big deal, since Jungling and his trained Vietnamese medics delivered babies all the time. As luck would have it, the birth wasn't going as well as it should have, and we called for a medevac.

Several of us helped Jungling get the girl to the helipad. It would rain, then clear up as a thunderhead passed over. As she screamed and Jungling worked on her, I held the corner of a poncho that seemed to weigh fifty pounds. I closed my eyes as the blood drained from my head and my knees quivered. I prayed for her, and I prayed that I wouldn't pass out. I would've never lived that one down.

It was a breached birth, on a helipad, in the rain, under a poncho, and Jungling pulled it off, or maybe I should say "pulled it out," just as the chopper touched down. He, the new mother, and her husband, who was holding a corner of the poncho and trying, like me, to stay conscious, climbed into the chopper, and it lifted off. Mother and baby would be just fine. Then and there

I realized that there was just about nothing that an SF soldier couldn't and wouldn't do.

Our teamhouse was constructed mostly underground, with walls of sandbags protecting it from incoming indirect fire. I moved into a room recently vacated by another soldier who had DEROSed (Date Estimated to Return from Overseas). It was fully furnished with an iron cot topped with a thin four-inch mattress, a metal chair, a desk made of old crates that had housed 105MM howitzer rounds, a fan, a small lamp, and, last but not least, a wall decorated with rare art from old issues of *Playboy*.

Since most of the teamhouse was underground or behind layers of sandbags, it was humid and filled with bugs. On my first night, I lay awake in my boxer shorts, enduring the oppressive heat and humidity, trying to get to sleep when something ran across my back. I jumped out of bed and grabbed my flashlight just in time to see a three-inch cockroach scuttle into the shadows. Eventually, I got used to sharing my bed with these and other creatures. It worked fine as long as they didn't stop when they crossed my back or legs.

I enjoyed the use of our three-hole outhouse and even mastered the conservative use of toilet paper, which was always in short supply.

A few months before I arrived at the camp, President Nixon had authorized a major push into Cambodia. Units all along the border captured scores of weapon caches and killed many VC. Prior to that very successful invasion, the VC shelled and probed Duc Hue regularly.

We had our own indirect fire weapons: a 4.2 inch mortar with the range of about 4Ks (4000 meters) and a towed 105mm howitzer that could reach out and touch folks up to 11Ks away. These weapons, along with 30 cal and M60 machine guns at each of the five points of our star-shaped camp, provided us with adequate protection. However, since the big push across the border, the camp had not received a single shell or probe. I wrote Dad that whatever else Nixon did, he did a good thing for me when he authorized the invasion of Cambodia.

In addition to ground forces pushing into Cambodia, B52 Stratofortress conducted Arc Light operations, bombing the hell out of the area. The bombings left huge craters which pocked the countryside and made great swimming holes. At night when the Air Force conducted an Arc Light operation, we could hear the rumble in the distance that sounded like thunder (ergo the name Operation Rolling Thunder), except it went on for several minutes. God help anyone anywhere near one of those bombing raids.

Combat operations consisted of patrols with two US and around 80 or so CIDG. We conducted interdiction operations, seeking out and destroying any enemy personnel found within our free-fire zone. Often I thought that we were doing more seeking and avoiding than anything else.

On my first operation, Romero handed me several cans of mackerel packed in tomato sauce, telling me how great they were. I had packed my ruck sack with Principal Indigenous Rations (PIRs), the green tinfoil bags of dried food that we provided the CIDG for field operations. For that operation I had packed fish, squid, and pork packages. When we stopped at noon for "pok time" (a rest period during the day which lasted sometimes up to three hours), I opened a can of mackerel and took a bite. God, it tasted like slimy raw fish. About the only thing I could eat was rice from the PIRs. It was a hungry five days for me.

As I said, the camp sat in the middle of rice paddies. Whenever I stepped off the compound to conduct combat operations, I waded through water thick with long-bladed, brownish-green grass that reached from knees to chest. I've walked through some very tough terrain in my day, but this was the worst. Between the water and grass tangling my legs, and the oppressive heat and humidity, I was ready to stop at a tree square, hang my hammock, and rest. The only problem with that plan was the ants that usually covered the tree square since it was the only dry ground around. No amount of bug juice would keep them from crawling from the trees into the hammock.

We would RON (Rest Over Night) in the tree squares; I would set up a poncho, blow up my air mattress, and hang my body mosquito net under the poncho and over the air mattress. Then I would dig a body trench about a foot deep. Of course, the trench filled with water, but should we receive incoming, I could roll over into it, finding some protection. As daylight gave way to twilight, the ants left the scene to be replaced by mosquitoes. I have never seen anything like it. I could lie on my air mattress and watch the outside of my mosquito net turn darker as the infuriating little insects blocked out the twilight. I would tap the net with my finger and a hole of light would appear, then close up again as the mosquitoes returned.

As I have written, contact with the enemy was, at this point in time, hard to come by. In order to be awarded a Combat Infantryman's Badge (CIB) in the 5th Group, you had to receive fire by a 51 caliber round or smaller. Being shelled or setting off a booby trap didn't cut it. It looked like I might finish out a one year tour in Vietnam and never see any action. Fortunately or unfortunately, depending on your perspective, this didn't happen.

I was accompanied by SSG Jungling on the operation which would earn me a CIB. Jungling and I, along with about 60 CIDG, approached (what else) a tree square to take pok time when all hell broke loose. We fanned out on line and began returning fire. I grabbed the radio and called back to the camp to see if we had any tac air on station and to inform them that we had made contact. I don't recall actually seeing any bad guys that day. There probably weren't more than four or five holed up in the tree square, but I did hear rounds flying overhead, or thought I did. The whole affair only lasted maybe five minutes, then the VC cut and ran, keeping the tree square between us and them. Later on in the day, one of the CIDG tripped a homemade booby-trap made from a mackerel can and was wounded, proving that those cans of mackerel could mean the death of you.

As luck would have it, I stumbled onto a copy of the situation report in the B-Team's Tactical Operations Center (TOC) of that operation. I kept the yellow flimsy copy just in case anyone ever questioned my orders dated 27 October 1970, awarding me the CIB. Below is how the first paragraph of the sitrep read:

FM: CO, B-32 TAY NINH
TO CO, CO A BIEN HOA

C O N F I D E N T I A L / CITE NR 271- //

SUBJECT: SITREP NR 271, 280001H - 282400H SEP 70

PARA I. OPERATIONS SUMMARY:
A. CONTACTS AND INCIDENTS:
(1) FM A-325 AT 280920 SEP 70 OPN P-69A MADE CONTACT AT XT277036 WITH AN EST VC SQUAD ARMED WITH AK-47'S UNIFORM UNK. FRDLYS WERE MOVING TO SECURE LZ. ENEMY WAS IN STATIONARY POSITION. FRDLY INITIATED CONTACT AT 500 METERS. VC BROKE CONTACT AT 280925H DUE TO FRDLY FIRE SUPERIORITY AND WITHDREW TO THE SOUTH WEST. NEG FRDLY CAS, VC CAS UNK.
(2) FM A-325 AT 281430H SEP 70 AT XT256036 1 CIDG ON OPN P70C TRIPPED A BOOBY TRAP CAUSING FRAG WOUNDS IN HIS LEGS AND FACE. BOOBY TRAP WAS HOMEMADE MACKEREL CAN TYPE. CIDG WAS MOVED BACK TO VIC XT275035 FOR MEDEVAC. MEDEVAC COMPLETED 281630H SEP 70.

The word came down that we would be turning over the camp to Vietnamese Rangers and that the CIDG would be converted to regular soldiers. There would be two U.S. advisors from the U.S. Military Assistance Command, Vietnam (MACV), assigned to the camp. This was really going to suck for them. All U.S. Special Forces would be assigned elsewhere in country. With these orders in effect, we began sling-loading equipment under the belly of CH-47s and a large Sky Crane (a huge helicopter that looked like a dragonfly). It wasn't long before I received orders sending me to B36, the old 3rd Mobile Strike Force headquartered in Long Hai. The 5th Group was pulling out of Vietnam, leaving behind forces that would train Cambodian soldiers to fight the Khmer Rouge, followers of the Communist Part of Kampuchea in Cambodia. We would retrain our green berets, but with a different flash. Most importantly, we would still draw jump pay. As a member of the 5th Group in Vietnam, I'd been awarded honorary Vietnamese jump wings. I never made a jump with them. Similarly, I would be awarded honorary Cambodian jump wings.

Thus ended my tour with ODA 325. None the worse for wear, I was eager to face my next challenge. Especially, since the next challenge would find me located along one of the most beautiful stretches of beach in Vietnam.

Tom Davis's publishing credits include *Poets Forum, The Carolina Runner, Triathlon Today, Georgia Athlete, The Fayetteville Observer's Saturday Extra, A Loving Voice Vol. I* and *II, Special Warfare,* and Winston-Salem Writers' POETRY IN PLAIN SIGHT program for May 2013 (poetry month). He's authored the following books: *The Life and Times of Rip Jackson*; a children's coloring book, *Pickaberry Pig, The Patrol Order*; and an action adventure novel, *The R-complex.* Tom lives in Webster, North Carolina.

Edmund Pieper

My Trip to the Wall

I am a Vietnam vet; I live in south St. Louis County. I am debating in my mind if I should go to the Wall. The infamous traveling Vietnam Wall will be set up very close to my house.

Should I go to the wall? I feel it would be very emotional and tears would flow. I hate to cry in public. Avoidance has been my "go-to" status when things are uncomfortable. Paranoia dances in my brain with all kinds of negative scenarios.

I decided I must go, because I will never go to Washington D.C. to see the real Wall. My wife agrees to go with me to help me with this high anxiety.

It was a pleasant sunny Saturday morning. It is not very crowded, which is very important to me. There are lots of flags flying and people milling about. I notice most of all, there was a solemn aura of a church that lies over the wall area.

I see items left by the names of buddies or family. It is sad to see these items there. The items must have great meaning and emotion. The 58,195 mothers and 58,195 fathers, and countless friends and family, are impacted by the war. All these years, all these heartaches don't ease the pain. I stopped in an area they had set up showing the statistics of the Vietnam War. Soldiers are not numbers or body count. The soldiers' names represented on the wall are human beings. Heartless, bare numbers cannot tell the story of the lives of truly great people. The misadventure statistic of 3,000-plus soldiers. I truly hate the word. Richard was a victim of misadventure.

I finally decided to get the rubbing I came for. I went to the tent where the computers gave me the panel and line numbers. I feel nauseous, a splitting headache hits me. My breathing is rapid. Fight or flight. I should leave. My wife grabs my hand. She knows I would pick flight. We head for the panel and line number, one of the best soldiers to ever hump the boonies. Above his panel was the date he died. The date he died. I relive that date very often. As I etched his name, I started crying. This is where the living and the dead meet. The visible and the invisible wounds request peace. Guilt as a survivor hurts more at this moment. It is time to get with the program.

This will be a moment that I will never forget. To honor, respect, remember these GIs forever.

Ed Pieper is a Vietnam Veteran. His branch of service was the United States Army Infantry, Vietnam 1968. He resides in St. Louis, Missouri, with his wife, two kids, and two grandkids.

Going, Going, Gone!

On May 29, 2004, almost 59 years after the end of World War II, the memorial to its veterans was dedicated in Washington, DC. Both The History Channel and C-Span carried the two-hour ceremony live.

The World War II Memorial is the first national memorial dedicated to all who served during the Second World War. Established by the American Battle Monuments Commission, the memorial honors all military veterans of the war, the citizens on the home front, the nation at large, and the high moral purpose and idealism that motivated the nation's call to arms.

A month before the formal dedication, the memorial opened for public viewing for the very first time. I got a good look at it on a TV special shortly afterwards. It was beautiful—long overdue, but beautiful; as fitting as any monument could possibly be.

I watched it all and fantasized about seeing it someday, knowing deep down that for various reasons, it was not likely.

When Brookshire's Grocery Company, a 150-store supermarket chain, headquartered in Tyler, Texas, announced their first *Heroes Flight* for World War II veterans, it got my attention.

The purpose of the flight was to allow World War II veterans in Brookshire's Texas-Louisiana-Arkansas service area the opportunity to see their monument in Washington, DC. May 11-12, 2010. I was one of the first in line to fill out the required form. I was disappointed when I wasn't chosen, but was told there would be a second flight October 5-6 and was confident I'd be on it. I was wrong.

In checking with Brookshire's I learned that one of the major criteria in selecting vets was age, the older vets being chosen first. I had gone into the military at such a young age, there were just too many ahead of me. I was crushed. My dream of seeing the memorial, it seemed, would remain just that—a dream.

One afternoon in April 2011, my wife answered the telephone and, after a brief conversation, came into the study where I was watching TV. She could hardly contain herself.

"That was Brookshire's corporate office calling," she said. "They asked if you'd be interested in flying to Washington May 10 with a group of veterans to see the World War II Memorial."

Interested? I was ecstatic. Finally, I had made the cut.

On May 10, along with 31 other World War II veterans from the Tyler-Shreveport area and 22 volunteer caregivers, the three-day odyssey began. It was everything I had imagined— and more. For the first time in years, I was with a group of senior citizens in which I was the youngest one in the bunch. That was a novelty in itself.

The trip included an American Airlines flight from both Shreveport and Tyler to DFW, then to Washington, D.C., and back home. Ground transportation was provided at the destination to our hotel and tours to the World War II Memorial and other significant sites.

The experience was an emotional rollercoaster for everyone, as was evidenced by the solemn expressions and the shedding of tears various memorials provoked. This was interspersed with instances of laughing and joking as we re-lived an important part of our past.

Although there are vantage points in Washington from which you can see the Capitol and most of the best-known monuments in a way that make them appear to be in close proximity, it's an illusion.

It wouldn't have been possible to do what we did without the aid of a bus to get us from one location to the next. Once this newfound knowledge soaked in, veterans (even those who vowed they'd never use a wheelchair) were quick to accept one, with a volunteer to push it.

Upon arrival at Reagan National Airport, we boarded our bus for Arlington National Cemetery for the changing of the guard at the tomb of the unknowns, a solemn ceremony showing high respect to those who have fallen in America's wars. The tradition began on March 4, 1921, when Congress approved burial of an unidentified American soldier from World War I in the plaza of the Memorial Amphitheatre. The around-the-clock ceremony continues to this day. It will continue always.

The next day included what for most of us was the main attraction, the World War II Memorial. I sought out the section dedicated to the North Pacific Theatre, which included Okinawa, where I served in the last months of the war. Others in the group did the same, visiting the sections most significant to them.

The Memorial is an elegant expanse of light gray granite. Its elements are arranged in a circle 100 yards in diameter, located in a place of honor between the Washington Monument and Lincoln Memorial. Soaring bronze eagles flank victory arches marked "Atlantic" and "Pacific."

Tall pillars with wreaths representing states and territories are connected by a sculpted bronze rope signifying the nation's unity in war.

To the West, a wall of gold stars honors the more than 405,000 Americans who gave their lives in the war; another 671,000 were wounded.

"HERE," the inscription reads, "WE MARK THE PRICE OF FREEDOM."

The other sites we visited were the Capitol, the Lincoln Memorial, the Korean, Vietnam and Iwo Jima War Memorials, and the Women's Hall of Fame.

Our final day included a tour of the Dulles Air and Space Museum, after which we boarded our plane at Dulles International. To set the tone for our return flight home, a wise-cracking veteran brought down the house when he shouted, "Don't worry, guys. What happens in D.C. stays in D.C."

227

There are other groups and entities besides Brookshire's that take WWII veterans to Washington, D.C. The largest and oldest is Honor Flight, founded in 2005 by Earl Morse, a physician assistant at the Department of Veterans Affairs and a retired USAF captain. Honor Flight has chapters, called hubs, in all but nine states. These are local non-profit entities that raise money to take the veterans to D.C.

Brookshire's learned about these programs in early 2010 and decided to take a group that spring. Since that time, they have continued the flights every May with no cut-off date yet announced.

Brookshire's is not affiliated with either Honor Flight or similar organizations. Their effort is unique in that it is 100% company-funded. No outside fund raising was done.

There were many things that this trip did for everyone. For me it did three things:

In my mind it elevated my service on a small Navy repair ship at Okinawa to something significant, of great importance, and something for which deep appreciation was shown. The displays of gratitude shown us at airports, restaurants, and other public places was overwhelming

By underwriting the cost and overseeing these *Heroes Flights,* Brookshire's Grocery Company laid to rest my long-held belief that *Big Business* is only interested in the bottom line.

It proved that sometimes dreams do come true.

Of all the wars in recent memory, it was World War II that truly threatened our very existence as a nation. With over 1,000 World War II veterans dying each day, the time to express thanks to these brave men and women is going, going, and soon gone.

Hugh Neeld is a native Texan, born in Fort Worth in 1929. Educated in public school and Texas Christian University, he served in the U.S. Navy from 1945 to 1948 and retired from a forty-five year career in radio and TV in 1994. Today, he and his wife, Cris, live on a golf course in Jacksonville, Texas. Interests for both are writing and gardening.

Robert A. Cunningham

Saipan Invasion,
June 15–July 10, 1944

On June the 15, we hit the beach. We had come from Camp Tarawa on the Big Island of Hawaii on L.S.T.'s via Honolulu, where, due to an accident, we had to get a replacement L.S.T. because the first one we were on blew up while tied up at a pier in Honolulu loading on extra final supplies for the invasion. We were inland on trucks picking up the supplies when this happened. Several of our L.S.T.'s were lost in this mishap.

We had an early breakfast on D-Day; they advised us not to load up too much because we would spend several hours in our landing crafts getting into position and forming waves. We were in the first wave to hit the beach, which consisted of three lines. The first line was landing craft tanks, then two lines of us. The tanks were supposed to go in and clear out everything for the first hundred yards with our two waves 75 yards behind them.

Each of our landing craft held a squad. When we arrived at the beach, we found that most of the tanks had not made much penetration, so, chaos. On top of this, we were about a hundred yards out of position, which we soon corrected by moving to our right until we found members of our company. The beach was only about 50 feet wide from water's edge, and at the end of the 50 feet rose up a berm of sand about 6 feet high and about 10 feet above water's edge. A pretty good slope. There were Marines that had inched their way up the berm to see what they could, only to be picked off by snipers. Tough scene. When we did reach our company, we were ordered to move inward. More of our troops were arriving on the beach, so it was getting stacked up. We moved over the top, running and jumping into shell craters left from the bombardment from our ships, who had been shelling the beach days and nights before the invasion. We finally made a beachhead line, in about a hundred yards, and stayed there trying to catch our breath. It was plenty scary. Guys getting shot up all around us. Shell bursts all over coming from the enemy and 12- and 16-inchers coming overhead from our battle wagons bombing the Japs positions. Wow! What a day. Finally dusk came.

During all this, supplies were arriving at the beachhead. I think we were able to advance another hundred yards before it got dark. One would think with the darkness the enemy would let up, but they did not. Our command ordered flares to light up the approaching enemy as they were trying to break through our lines. The flares came from our supporting ships off shore. It worked until about 3:00 A.M. when all hell broke loose down on our right flank. A huge number of tanks tried to break through our lines, with foot soldiers following in support. A real battle took place. Thanks to our bazooka squads, they knocked out every tank. When daylight finally came, we saw what had happened. The Japs didn't make it. The tanks were still smoking. Hundreds of dead Japs lay around, and our fellow Marines were hit hard, too, but the line didn't budge. They hung in there and did an outstanding job. It was a great victory for us because the Japs lost most of their fire power. We advanced another couple hundred yards and dug in for the night. My assistant bar man and I took turns on our watch during the night.

For the first couple weeks, there was some activity during the night when our beaches were being bombed by enemy aircraft. The whole sky would be lit up with tracer bullets being fired from our anti-aircraft guns and our ships offshore. Quite a spectacle.

I think it was D+4, when we started moving up into the hills, that our line came to a halt because of some major resistance. Our command called for air support to knock out the enemy positions that were holding us up. It was our practice on the front line to place white square markers (2' x 2') on the ground in front of us, about 10 feet apart to mark our positions so the dive bombers would know where we were. But something went wrong when one of the dive bombers wiped out our company command post, killing six Marines, including our commander. What a mess it was. However, thanks to our leadership, they were replaced immediately, and we didn't miss a beat, as I can remember. This bomb was only about 70 yards right behind us.

The next couple of weeks consisted of moving ahead during the day and digging in before night. All sorts of activities were happening when we made contact with the enemy. Some days our forward movement would not amount to much because of enemy resistance at our front or on one of our flanks. We tried to keep our front line as straight as possible to fit the terrain. The jungle is a hard place to keep a functional straight line. It is very hard to see any distance in dense foliage. It is like squirrel hunting with the squirrels having guns.

I remember one particular day, some replacements came up to fill in some of our positions. We were getting short of man power. These fellows had not yet had any experience of what it was like, and lo and behold, two of them were shot before they had been with us for two hours. One was really a nice person who came over with us with our original squad. On D-Day, he developed a sickness or something that prevented him being with us on the invasion. He stood up when he shouldn't have and got it right in the head. The other fellow was shot in the leg. They called that "happy wounds." Right after this happened, our command called for some mortar fire to knock out the resistance. In doing so, one of the mortar shells dropped into one of the Jap ammunition dumps. Wow! What a close call. The dump was only a hundred yards in front of us. We really had to duck.

Another incident was a couple days later. We came up on a ridge and were immediately pinned down. After a half hour of no movement, our sergeant had crawled up behind me and asked me to swap weapons. He is my boss. I gave him my B.A.R. and took his carbine. What could I say? What this brave guy did earned him a Silver Star for his heroism. He felt he knew where the resistance was coming from, so he asked for fire power support to cover him and then ran to the top of the ridge and started shooting. Soon there was quiet. He had wiped out a machine gun nest. Killed them all. Saved many of us. This guy really had some guts.

Our other enemies were the flies in the daytime, mosquitoes at night, wasps, spiders, centipedes, and especially the weather: hot in the daytime and cold breezes at night right after it rained. One of the hardest physical duties was carrying the wounded and dead back from the front line. Four men to a stretcher walking over rocks and vines at times was rough duty, especially when crossing creeks and up and down embankments. We were pretty exhausted to begin with, but it was work that needed to be done. One of the sadder experiences was when, as we were advancing our line, we came across an area where one of our forward scouting patrols of 12 men had been ambushed 3 or 4 days before. They were dead and all swollen up. A really bad sight for us, but not uncommon. We had seen many dead swollen up Japs but never a Marine.

We were finally relieved from our front-line duty after almost three weeks to go back and rest up for a bit. So we marched back several miles during the morning, set up our camp site, and were preparing to rest up when we got orders to move out on the double because a Banzie attack was approaching our front lines. It was a last ditch stand for the Japs, who had been pushed back so far they said "let's go for it" rather than surrender. So we high-tailed back up to the front line and set up to meet them. We arrived at our positions right before dark. It wasn't long before they came, by the hundreds. By now it was dark, but with the aid of flares, we could see plenty of movement. The heart of their thrust was about a hundred yards down on our left flank, but we had plenty of action. We seemed to be shooting half the night at anything that moved up front. They never got to our line for hand-to-hand combat, but they pushed back our line on the left maybe a hundred yards or so. When daylight finally came, we saw hundreds of the enemy lying all over the place. On returning to our rest area again, we saw plenty of the dead, including many Marines.

It was all over for the enemy now because their majority was either killed or taken prisoner. This huge mass of the enemy had been hiding in the caves on the north end of the island. In the next couple days, the island was declared secure. At our rest area we prepared for the invasion of Tinian—three miles south of Saipan.

To my knowledge, only one in our company did not receive the Purple Heart. My wounds were not serious at all. The medic just treated them and wrapped them up.

—Cpl. Robert A. Cunningham L-3-6 2nd Division

Robert A. Cunningham served in WWII with the U.S. Marine Corps, Love Company, 3rd Battalion, 6th Regiment, 2nd Marine Division.